Letters to Lori

The Family History and
Stories of Opal Corn Myers

BARBARA LEAGUE

Acknowledgments

I will be eternally grateful to my Lord and Savior for bringing Opal Myers into my life and giving me the opportunity to share her story of dedication and service with each of you. Thank you, Manly, for always being supportive. You have truly shown me unconditional love. You are the love of my life. I am also indebted to my editor, Pam Guerrieri; my graphic designer, Steve Plummer; and my proofreader and friend, Marilyn Mitchem.

In Loving Memory of Jenna Wilson
August 1, 1978 to April 23, 2007
I will always love you.

Letters to Lori
The Family History and
Stories of Opal Corn Myers
By Barbara League

Barbara League
3779 Harvest Way
Elsmere, KY
41018

lmci@fuse.net

Printed in the United States of America
Cover design and layout by Steven Plummer, Bethany Press International

ISBN 978-0-615-15761-0

Table of Contents

Opal's Grandparents:

Toliver Joshua "TJ" Corn
Suzanne Angeline ("Toby) Corn

Thomas Andrew Hall
Charity (Clark) Hall

Ben's Grandparents:

Columbus Washington Myers
Saphronia "Fronie" (Burrell) Myers

Ben Perry Bruce
Polly (Pruitt) Bruce

Opal's Parents:

Arthur Jackson "AJ" Corn
Flora Louise (Hall) Corn

Ben's Parents:

Marcas Samson "Sam" Myers
Rosa "Rosie" (Bruce) Myers

Ben and Opal Myers Children and Grandchildren

Corene Eugenia (Myers) Wahler
(m) Raymond Wahler
├────────●
Kenneth Robert "Bobby" Wahler
Susan Francis "Suzie" Whaler

Cary Alvin Myers
(m) Cathy Webb – divorced
├────────●
Barry Alvin Myers
Benjamin "Benji" Anthony Myers
(m) Pam (Rice) Myers
divorced
Heather Shelle Rice

Seldon Perry Myers
(m) Stella (Sipe) Myers
├────●
Penny Nicole Callihan
Lori Denise Myers-Hammonds

Larry Conn Myers
├──────────●
(m) Margret (Williams) Myers
divorced
(m) Regina Myers
divorced
(m) Karen Myers

5

Prologue

I guess you could say I have a passion for history, and a passion for people. Perhaps that's why I felt so connected when I stepped into the world of real-life missionary Opal Myers. My fascination began years ago with a story. It was in late summer of 1971 when I first read *Christy*, the 1968 national bestseller by Catherine Marshall. The book was based on the life of Catherine's mother, Leonora Whitaker Wood, who, according to the book, in 1912[1], at the age of nineteen, left the comfortable home of her parents in Asheville, North Carolina, to become a teacher at a mission in Cutter Gap, an impoverished back mountain area of eastern Tennessee. In the book, Christy (Leonora) struggles with the harsh realities of the poverty-stricken community but is determined to improve the lives and education of the children. She is encouraged and challenged through the mentoring of Miss Alice, while caught in a love triangle with John Wood, the mission preacher, and Dr. Neil MacNeill.

Once I started the book, it was almost impossible to put it down. I was absolutely magnetized by the story, the proud mountain people, the way of life with its everyday human struggles, and the courageous mission workers. Catherine Marshall painted a vivid picture of the cove with all of its poverty and smells! I was in awe of Christy, young and pretty, innocent and naive, confused by her romantic feelings for

---

1   Leonora was listed in the 1910 census as a resident at the mission. Her sister Essie, age 17, was also listed. It is important to remember that the book *Christy* is a fictional book based on the life of Leonora and the families she grew to love and desperately wanted to help. However, a character in the book may be an actual person, two individuals combined to make one personality, or totally fictitious.

the preacher and the doctor, but all the while tenaciously dedicated to the well-being and education of her students and their families.

At the time I read *Christy*, I was living in Greenville, South Carolina, not all that far from where the story took place. I couldn't help but wonder if maybe, even after sixty years had passed, there might be some evidence left of the mission's existence.

The real names of the towns had not been used in the book, but there were enough clues to narrow down the location, especially with the map in the front of my copy of *Christy*. If the general layout of the towns were the same in conjunction with the French Broad River, I felt we could certainly get close to where the mission had been and then we could ask the locals for more specific directions. I compared the map in the book with a road map of that area. The French Broad River and the railroad tracks coming from Asheville seemed to match up, and there was a small town with a Spanish name next to the railroad tracks no more than ten or fifteen miles into Tennessee. Could Del Rio possibly be the same town as *Christy's* El Pano?

It would be an adventure to solve the mystery of its location and I was fairly certain that we could find this Cutter Gap no matter how remote it was. I was determined to at least give it a good try.

Manly, my husband, Matthew, my son (four at the time), and I twisted around most of the winding Cocke County back mountain roads outside of Del Rio. On our second day of exploring, we stopped at a little country store, a slightly modern version of the stores of the late 1800s. Several men idly sat around a cold, potbellied stove, chewing large tobacco cuds while spinning their yarns, frequently spitting into a box of sand, usually hitting their target.

The lady behind the cash register said she could give us the exact directions to the mission location. "Ya go down yonder a spell and turn back thataway 'n cross back o'er the crick. After ya go quite a spell, take the rat fork. Ya can't miss hit, budhit ain't thar no more."

Well, after we "turned back thataway" and had "gone a spell," we bumped along one of the roughest, if not *the* roughest, roads in all of Tennessee. It was like driving on a washboard. In some places, four to six-inch-deep gullies of running water streamed across the road, and where there were bridges, they were rickety and scary to cross. In other places, big chunks of dirt and gravel had broken out of the edge of the road and fallen down the mountainside, leaving large semicircle gaps in the already narrow road. In fact, the road was so narrow in many places that it was not wide enough for two cars to pass each other. When we took the right fork, the road immediately narrowed down to one lane. That single lane soon became two ruts with grass growing in the middle.

At a big curve, the road ended and became what looked like an overgrown trail. Hidden within that curve, back off the road a few hundred feet, a little white house was guarded by an overgrowth of vegetation. Animals scampered off the footpaths as we walked toward the house. The modest home itself seemed to be encircled by barnyard animals: a mule, a few pigs, and several dogs, while the roosters, hens, and baby chicks were everywhere. A sun-kissed lady came out to greet us and it was obvious she was thrilled to have company. I'm quite sure she didn't have many people dropping in on her, and she was eager to do everything possible to encourage us to stay around a little longer.

She enthusiastically told us all we wanted to know about the old Ebenezer Mission. "Opal Myers owns all that mission land up thar." She extended a weathered hand. "Lived in the old mission house too 'till hit burned down in '62. Burned down to the ground, hit did. Nutt'n left now but some ol' foundation stones. Miss Opal's livin' out, down thar in Slab Town now. Thar's still a few cabins a standin' 'n maybe a barn or two."

She then offered to take us the rest of the way to the mission on foot. "Hit's a mighty grown up up thar, but I reckon we can find some of them foundation stones. That young'un of your'n thar can ride on my mule." Of course, Matt loved that!

We walked through knee to hip high grass all the way up to where the mission had once stood. There was still a crumbling rock wall and a foundation of stone peeking through the weeds. Looking around, I wondered what it would have been like to be standing in that exact spot half a century earlier.

In 1972, we moved from Greenville, South Carolina, to Savannah, Georgia, where we added two new members to our family: Jonathan, our son, who was born in 1975, and an Alaskan malamute named Tosha. Our work, activities, and the distance did not make it possible for us to return to the mission for some time.

In 1976, Manly, who then worked for General Electric, was transferred to Atlanta. We purchased an old Victorian house in Jefferson, Georgia, about an hour north of Atlanta. We were much closer, but restoring the house and our involvement as senior high youth counselors at the United Methodist Church consumed all of our free time.

It wasn't until '77 or '78 that we went back to the mission. As we turned off Hwy 107 onto the Old Fifteenth, it was as if time never touched the place. Everything looked just as I had remembered it: washboard roads, rivulets of water trickling from one side of the road to the other, places where the edge of the road had fallen down the mountainside. Going down the road by Sand Hill were the huge washed-out gullies which crisscrossed the road a couple times at the bottom.

The only noticeable change was in that last fourth of a mile to the mission property—the road was now scraped and covered with a dusting of gravel. However, it was still only one lane, narrow and rough with washouts and ruts. In one place, a spring produced a trail of water flowing from one side of the road to the other. As we passed the mission's foundation, there were two places where large rocks protruded from the middle of the road, giving us the option of carefully navigating around them or scraping the bottom of our car and possibly removing our exhaust system.

As we pulled up to the old log cabin at the end of the road, Opal came out to greet us and immediately made us feel welcome. Opal spoke quickly, moving without hesitation from one subject to another, from the past to the future, and then back again to the past, many times answering our questions before we had even asked them. It was as though she had been waiting years for our arrival and now here we were. All the things she had been saving up to tell us couldn't wait to spill out. Opal was like this with all who visited her. She loved people—loved being around them—and in return everyone who met Opal loved her. Since our last visit, there had been many others who had fallen in love with *Christy* and found their way to the mission.

Opal told us how her parents had moved to the mission community in 1915, living on a portion of property owned by her grandparents. Her sister Maggie started attending the mission school with Opal's Aunt Flora. Opal started school at the mission in 1919 at the age of eight. In 1944, she had purchased the mission property and later acquired some adjoining parcels of land which gave her a total of one hundred and eighty acres, including all of the mission land plus the home sites of many of those who had lived around the mission.

We continued coming back two or three times every year. Being the hardy crew we were, "roughing it" at Opal's was always a great adventure. Our tents were comfortable enough for a good night's sleep. Even as late as the 80s and 90s, indoor plumbing and running water were considered a luxury back in the cove where Opal lived, so we bathed and washed our hair in the "swimming hole" of a close-by mountain stream. That stream was always frigid, even on the hottest days in July and August, but Matt and Tosha never seemed to mind that. To this day I chuckle when I remember the time Manly carried Jonathan across that stream, carefully moving from one rock to the next. A slippery rock caught him off-guard, sending them both into the icy water.

Opal's grandsons, Barry and Benja, lived with her and Matt enjoyed playing with them while Tosha preferred sniffing out the pigs. Benja would take the go-cart he had made up the side of the huge hill behind the house and heedlessly fly down that mountainside, nearly scaring me to death; when Matt decided to drive it I nearly had a coronary.

Opal's house was much like those described in *Christy*. The holes in the screens were an invitation to every fly that hovered over the chicken yard, and that chicken yard came right up to the entrance to her cabin. In fact, it was not uncommon for the chickens and roosters to perch on the porch just outside the door, sometimes finding their way right into the cabin.

We would always bring food to cook over a campfire or on our camp stove, but most of our meals we ate with Opal; she always insisted. Opal had two stoves in her kitchen—a wood burning stove by the door as you came into the cabin, and an electric stove at the other end of the kitchen where she cooked. In all those years, I only saw Opal cook on one temperature: HIGH. Her handmade biscuits and mud pudding will always be a part of our memories, as will the curly strips of flypaper that hung suspended over the table, only slightly above eye level, as we sat there eating. The strips were usually already well covered with flies, half of them still buzzing, with maybe enough room left on the sticky surface for the flies that we had just shooed off our food.

After dinner we would wash the dishes in water that had been carried up from the spring and heated in big pans on the wood burning stove. Oh, and visiting the outhouse was ALWAYS a thrill!

Yes, it was like going back in time to the days of Christy. But I can tell you for a fact that I would not trade a moment of my time with Opal to be the guest of honor in the palace of a king. Being in Opal's presence and hearing the stories of the past was purely fascinating.

We spent hours talking with Opal about the "old days," sometimes relaxing around her kitchen table, other times walking, exploring the long deserted home sites of the early 1900s in what is now the Cherokee National Forest. Opal wore her customary hat when we went walking and was never without a walking stick. Sometimes it was a favorite stick that she grabbed as we left her cabin or, as we entered the forest, she might select one from the fallen tree limbs along the path.

In the national forest, she pointed out the Christmas fern and explained how it got its name. She talked about arbutus and other plants and their uses. On one memorable hike, we walked down across the field towards where her grandparents had lived and she instructed me in the art of naturally repelling insects as she carefully selected plants and stuck the ends of them under her hat. This, she explained, would keep the pestering gnats and other insects away, and it did.

Opal talked of the past and history breathed life as we walked about together in the cove. She recounted how Morgan Branch and Morgan Gap got their name from Morgan's Raiders during the Civil War.

Back in the 30s and 40s, many of the young men in the community traveled to surrounding states, especially North and South Carolina, to work in the mills while others went north to work in the factories or in coal mines. Many of them sent their paychecks back home to help support the family they left behind. We found evidence of this as we explored deserted old cabins. In one we found boxes of clothes, some of which had been torn open and flung about the floor along with other old papers and letters. Among the papers were pay stubs from cotton mills in the Carolinas.

Sometimes we went exploring on our own, taking long walks over to the next ridge or taking the steep trail down through Morgan Gap to where the railroad tracks followed the twists and turns of the French Broad River. It was there, years before, that Opal's father had caught the train at the West Myers whistle stop to ride into Newport with crops to barter for needed supplies. The three miles down to the river were always much easier than the same three-mile climb on the way back.

As Matt and Jonathan got older, Matt didn't come with us as often, but Jonathan still enjoyed our "trips back in time." He loved to swing out over the banks on rope swings and vines and to start our campfires while Heather (born in 1981) preferred helping Opal make biscuits and mud pudding. She even made sure her handprint and initials were permanently placed in the wet cement on the backside of the new log outhouse. We all loved going to church with Opal. Sometimes Opal would let Jonathan or Heather help ring the church bell. It was understood in the small congregation that nobody rang the church bell except Opal. Even after she became very ill and no longer had the strength, even then they would always ask her permission before letting someone else ring the bell. We could tell that she was well loved and respected by everyone in the community.

Opal had always dreamed of writing stories about the mountains and her people, but it didn't quite happen as she imagined. Instead, the Lord sent Catherine Marshall to write the story of her mother Leonora and the mission school. Catherine started researching and writing *Christy* probably around 1957. In 1959, she came with her mother and father to visit the mission. All the old church and school records Opal had saved fascinated Catherine. Some of these records included bartering transactions between the families and the mission to pay the mission school's tuition. These were only some of the treasures that were lost when the mission house burned. Miss Mary Ruble, Mrs. Wilford Metcalf, and others in the community also furnished Catherine with information about the area. Opal later met and became friends with Catherine's sister and they corresponded. Opal let me read some of her letters.

Opal treasured the book *Christy*, but far more than the fiction of *Christy*, she loved the true story of the mission. In her own copy of the book, on the pages listing the characters, Opal had written the name of each local person that character was based upon.[2] She had made additional comments on other pages of her book, which I also copied.

It was one of her greatest hopes that one day the book *Christy* would be made into a movie. That hope was most likely sparked, over the years, by visits from movie producers, photographers, and location managers who came to look over the area where the story had taken place. Some spent hours talking with Opal and the photographers took numerous pictures of the area, Opal, and her grandsons.

Each year, as Opal got older, she talked more and more about having her family history written. She was concerned that the past would be forgotten and the family and local history would become distorted. It was very important to Opal that her granddaughter Lori

---

2 Opal's Copy of *Christy* – See Appendix A

have an accurate copy of this history, and that she in turn would pass on to her children the stories and strong heritage of their ancestors.

Even though I knew she wanted me to write her family history, I didn't volunteer to do so. I felt much too inadequate to take on such a task. I was convinced that someone better qualified than I, a "real" writer, a genuine published author would come along and be absolutely thrilled to embrace such an opportunity. After all, there were hundreds of people who had searched for and found the mission, as we had. There were doctors, lawyers, teachers, and even that movie producer, so surely a writer would come to record and tell the incredible story of this extraordinary mountain woman and her family. But, no one came and when Opal's health started to fail, she became more insistent.

In 1989, she asked me to listen to a tape she had made for Lori two years earlier. After listening to it, I agreed to write her family history and we started by making several tapes with her and some with her sons as well.

It was wonderful seeing her excitement as she relived event after event. The more I learned about Opal, the more I realized what a treasure God had given to me and to the people of this back mountain area. I diligently transcribed the tapes and put the information in chronological order. That in itself was a huge task, but simple enough. When it came to writing the story, the rough draft was easy, but putting it into its final form seemed impossible. From time to time, after Opal died in 1991, I would dig out the old files and try, but I just could not finish. How could I retell this amazing story? The story of a woman who deeply loved Ebenezer Mission and the school she attended. The story of a courageous woman, who from the time the mission formally closed up until the day she died *was* the mission, giving hope and encouragement to all those around her. Her life was powerful in the most simplistic way. Her life to this day shines as bright as any mission worker who ever set foot at the Ebenezer Mission. Opal deserved a Catherine Marshall to tell her story, but all she got was me. I can only hope that somehow my love for her and her family will make the difference.

Opal Corn Myers
February 1, 1911 - May 8, 1991

Lori Myers-Hammonds with her husband Seth
and daughter Isabella Opal Hammonds.

Lori graduated from Lee University with her Masters of Arts in Teaching and is now teaching the 5th grade at Waterville Community Elementary School in Cleveland, TN. Seth graduated from Mercer University in Atlanta with a Doctor of Pharmacy degree and is the Pharmacist in Charge at Moore & King Pharmacy also in Chattanooga. They attend the Mt. Olive Church of God.

For years, every time I saw Opal, she talked about having someone write the history of her ancestors and the events of her life. Confident that someone else would come along and jump at this opportunity to tell the story of this great mountain woman, I said nothing. Knowing that her years on earth were numbered, Opal started taping and jotting down the things she would one day want Lori, her five-year-old granddaughter, to know. These tapes, along with a collection of handwritten letters, were all she had to pass on. Late in 1989, as her health was failing, I was inspired to take on the task of putting Opal's story on paper. With the project underway, we discussed the details of life as it was in her growing up years, attending the Ebenezer Mission School and Highland Institute, and life as it was later—the life of a woman dedicated to her family and the community, and most of all committed to God. Here is her story through letters that share more than a history, but a legacy...

1
Letter to Lori
1986

If I should die before you're grown,
I pray my love for you is known.

Dear Lori,

*Y*ou are my youngest grandchild, and so very special to me. I've always wished you lived closer to me so that I could see you more often and spend time with you while you're growing up. You know, just to be able to sit down and talk. I used to sit on the porch and snap beans with my Grandma Corn and we would talk for hours. I loved being around her and I knew that she loved me. I hope you know how much I love you.

Your father left this community early in life to go off to where he could get a good job. Don't misunderstand me—I'm glad he has a good business, but I am sad that I never get to see you except at homecoming or Decorations Day or on other special occasions. Even then, it's just for a meal and there are always so many people around that I can't talk to you about all the things that I want you to know about your family—your ancestors.

Your ancestors have lived up in these mountains for many generations. They were hard working, good people with a strong sense of right and wrong. And, as children, if you knew what was good for you, you had sure better be doing what was right.

Your ancestors were very poor by today's standards. But when everyone around you is poor, you don't pay that much attention to it. You just live your life every day and share what you have. You certainly don't have to have money to contribute to your community and help your neighbors. And that's exactly what we were brought up to do. People helped each other and did what had to be done. You didn't stop to think about it; you just did it because it was the right thing to do.

My Grandma Corn was like that. If you just could have known her! She was one of my favorite people. She was short and fat and had thirteen children and I wanted to be just like her. Well, I'm not quite as big as she was, and I can't say that I ever really wanted to have thirteen children either, but I still wish to this very day that I had been able to be around her more. I loved to listen to her stories of the old days. I'm so sorry she died before we ever got to do more things like that. I always wondered what she would have told me. I don't want it to be that way with you. I want you to know about your family's past and I want you to be able to know me. But you are so young, too young to understand, even if we had the time now. All you know is that I love you and you love me. I'm seventy-six now, and by the time you are old enough to grasp the tales and legends that make up our past, I may not be here anymore. And I don't want you to feel that you've missed out by not hearing the old stories of days gone by.

There are so many things that I would like to teach you. I want you to know how we did things when we were young—how we fixed our foods, how we made medicine from the plants around here, how we carried out our work and chores, and I want you to know about the games we played.

I'd like you to know about the values that were so vital in the old days. Nowadays nobody seems to give those things much thought, but I'd like you to know how to recognize the things that are really important in life, like respect for others, keeping your promises, and caring for those in need. I'd like you to know and truly believe that you can be anything you want to be if you're just willing to work for it. Never give up on your dreams. I would like to be there as you're growing up to remind you of that—to encourage you.

So many, many things to tell! And it's hard to remember them all at one time, so I'll just write you little notes now and then or talk into this tape recorder like I am now—whenever I feel like it and have time. There's no use trying to keep this in any special order. Later someone will come along who will put it all together and then you will be able to know your heritage and find out about the things we used to do.

I wish I could write or tape more at night when everything is quiet and there are no interruptions, but when I try, I get so sleepy that I just can't seem to stay awake. I imagine that's because I usually don't go to bed until eleven or twelve o'clock, and then I have to get up at 4:30 in the morning to heat water for your cousins Barry and Benja's bath so they can be ready to leave for school at 6:00. Barry and Benja have lived with me since they were just young'uns, younger than you are right now as I share this.

Heating bath water on the stove must seem strange to you, I know. You don't have to carry your water in from the spring and heat it. All you have to do is turn a spigot and you have hot water, but I have to go down and dip the water out of the tub at Morgan Branch. I have a little spout, a pipe I pushed into the spring, so that the gentle flow of water pours out of the spring right into the tub. That way I don't have to climb up and down the bank; but I still have to tote the water from the branch. Totin', that's what my parents used to call carrying water—totin' water.

Of course, usually Barry and Benja bring a big bucket of water up every night so I don't always have to carry it in, but sometimes I do.

Before the schools consolidated in the mid-fifties, there were many small one-room community schools, and the children would walk to school. After the consolidation, all those schools were closed and the children had to ride the bus into town.

Before Barry and Benja were old enough to drive to school, I'd have to take my big ol' lantern and walk down to the end of the Cliff Spring and wait there with them for the bus. In the wintertime we'd nearly freeze to death waiting for that bus. When it finally came, I'd watch them get on and then I'd walk back to the house by myself. The bus carried them all the way around through Punkton and Piney Grove, all around up in that section, and then back into Del Rio where they changed buses to go on to the high school in Newport.

As soon as they were old enough, their uncle and their daddy got them a truck and gave them gas so they wouldn't have to stand out in the cold and spend all that time riding the bus.

Well, you can tell from this tape, by the time I get all my chores done and Barry and Benja are asleep and I'm able to sit down to write or talk into this recorder, I am so tired that it seems like I start to ramble from one thing to the next until I just can't stay awake any longer.

I don't know if you will ever hear this tape; if you do, you'll hear the chickens and that ol' rooster of mine a-crowin'. That's part of this life up here too. You don't know much about chickens, but they're actually a lot of fun to have around. And that ol' rooster—that ol' rooster starts crowing every time he sees me sitting up here on the porch. Guess he thinks it's his job to wake people up and keep them awake. I like to hear him crow.

Sometimes I prefer to sit out here on my porch, like I am now, and look at the trees and flowers and animals while I talk into this tape recorder and remember. I have a very good memory, especially for an old person. In fact, sometimes the past seems to come to life for me and it's like it was only yesterday when I ran barefooted right through here playing tag with the other children.

I like to think about the days of *Christy* and the mission people who came up into this impoverished—that's how Catherine Marshall described us—back mountain community. Our lives would have been so different if they had not been willing to come here to educate us. They taught the people, all of us, so much about health and about life. They taught us how to read and they taught about God—how He loves us and cares for each of us. How He created us and has a purpose for our lives. They taught us that even though we were poor and lived way back up here in the mountains, we could still be anything we wanted to be and accomplish anything we were willing to work hard enough for. And I believed them. I still believe them. I want you to know all about the mission and the mission people who gave us hope.

I guess, Lori, that one of the most important things that I have learned in my life is that it's really not how much you accumulate that makes you important or a "somebody." It's what you do with your life and what you do with what you have that causes you to be a special person and to have purpose. That's something people seem to forget when life is easy.

Well, since I tend to ramble a good bit, I'll at least try to start at the beginning. The beginning, the birthing of Ebenezer Mission, was probably the most significant thing that's ever happened in these parts.

There are many versions to the story of Ebenezer's beginning[3]. Most of them are fairly close, but I guess after all this time no one knows for sure exactly what happened. This is another version, and though there is no way to know how accurate it may be, it depicts the events and general order.

Back just before the turn of the century, probably in the late winter or maybe the early spring of 1895, there was a young preacher, a circuit preacher ...

---

3   The "birthing of Ebenezer" has become a legend with many versions. Through meticulous research, Marilyn Mitchem has documented the authentic dates and events in the history of Ebenezer Mission. See *Important Dates in Ebenezer Mission's History* by Marilyn Dean Mitchem, Appendix B

2
Ebenezer Mission
1895–1902

The Circuit Preacher

The circuit preacher was an important part of life back in these secluded mountains. He not only carried the "Good News of the Lord," but I reckon he was just about the only source of any news from the surrounding communities. I also imagine he was practically the only connection to the outside world, even though that world was merely a trip to the other side of the mountain, or at best barely a few miles away.

Most circuit preachers traveled a hundred miles or so on a regular route from one community to another. Some traveled on the back of a horse or a mule, but most traveled on foot carrying their treasured Bible, a bedroll, and maybe a rifle. They would conduct meetings in houses along the way, but more than likely in a special building that doubled as a school and church and housed other such community gatherings. They'd preach at funerals, baptisms, marriages—anywhere they got half a chance.

In our back mountain area, the people were extremely poor, and there was no money to pay for the services of a circuit preacher. A place to sleep and food to take back to his family was probably his only earthly reward.

I don't know a lot about who the circuit preacher was at that time or his exact route, but I do know that his circuit included the communities of Fair View, Edwina, Pig Trot, and several more.

Whoever he was, he was the preacher who'd heard about someone wanting to start a mission church and boarding school, or orphanage for boys in a mountain area where there was great need. After talking with people in the various congregations he served, the preacher contacted the Moravian Church in Watertown, Wisconsin. Touched by the deep concern he expressed for his people and the poverty and sickness that plagued them, the Moravians sent a representative to further explore the possibility of establishing a mission in this section of Tennessee.

Every congregation was excited about the news. A mission here in this area would mean a great deal to the people. Why, there'd be someone to take in the young'uns that had no one to properly care for them. There would be clothes for those with none and a real school taught by workers who'd not only care for the children but also for their entire families. There would even be classes so that the older ones could learn to read the *Good Book* for themselves. A mission would mean help and hope for a better life.

Of course, the church-going people would welcome a mission, but no one was so naïve as to think that everyone in the community would accept outsiders. Many would be too proud to listen to anyone. And most of them wouldn't be willing to change just because someone suggested they might need to do so.

Grandma Corn and Family

My grandparents on Papa's side were God-fearing people. Toliver Joshua, known as TJ, and Suzanne Angeline Corn were a part of the Edwina congregation.

Papa's family attended church every time the doors opened. Yes, Sir. Grandpa Corn made sure of that! He didn't have to ask them, "Are ya gonna get ready ta go ta church?" or "Are ya goin'?" They had to go and they knew it, so everybody just automatically got up and got ready. There were no other choices about the matter.

TJ Corn and Suzanne Angeline Tobey were married at the home of Will McMahan probably sometime in 1873, but the exact date is not known. Suzanne was one of three children born to Mary Ann Tobey.

Suzanne's family has always been a mystery. Whenever she spoke of her ma, she always called her Polly Ann, never Mary Ann or Mama. She was not called "Grandma" by the grandchildren either. No one knows why. Nor is it known who her father was, or anything about him, for that matter, except that he was a scout during the Civil War. Those days left many scars and great devastation even in the hidden corners of these secluded back mountains.

By 1895, Papa—Arthur Jackson—was the fourth of eleven children. First, there was Mary, who was 20; then Nathan, who had only lived fourteen days; Frank, 17; Papa, 16; Jonah, 14; Christopher, 12; Amanda, 10; Dora, 9; Howard, 6; Winnie, 4; and Martha, 2. Suzanne had quite a brood, but that was not at all uncommon in those days. Her last child, Flora, was born about one-and-a-half years later in 1896, giving her an even dozen. She was also caring for TJ's father, Nathan Corn, who lived with them for several years before his death in 1902.

Suzanne was truly an amazing woman; it's no wonder that I admire her so. Not only did she give birth to twelve children of her own and care for her father-in-law, but she also took in four of Grandpa's strays. No one knows, but he may have had a lot more than that.

Jessie Corn, who was born July 30, 1897, was the son of TJ and Nan James. Grandpa also had two other children by her. And then there was a boy named Curtis by a different woman.

Suzanne took them all in. Jessie and his two sisters were so poorly taken care of that they weren't much more than skin and bones when Suzanne took them into her home. The two girls died young—one was about four and the other died at about age six. Curtis died young too— he was only about five. Uncle Jesse was there until he went off and got married. Nathan Corn, who used to come to all the homecomings and died not long back, was one of Uncle Jesse's boys.

Grandma was a good-hearted woman. She always felt that the child couldn't help what its ma and pa had done. Even when the child's own mother didn't want them or couldn't keep them, Grandma was there and she would take them in.

We were never aware of any problem between them, or even if there was one caused by Grandpa's messin' around. If my own pa had ever had children outside of marriage, that would have been a different story. Mama would have shot him dead! She never would have taken them in, I can tell you that right now. She would have taken in other's young'uns, but not children of my pa. But the culture was different back here in the mountains. It was not all that uncommon for a man to have children by more than one woman, and his wife had little choice but to accept it as the way life was. There was also a lot of intermarrying within families.

Whatever the situation was with Grandma and Grandpa, it never hindered their family's involvement in church or their excitement about the coming of the mission.

Building the Mission

In the fall of 1895, Miss Katherine Plantz of Watertown, Wisconsin, stepped off the train in Bridgeport. I can just imagine how she must have felt. She had never before seen the likes of back mountain people. And here she was, all of about twenty-two or twenty-three years old, all by herself, looking around for someone who was supposed to meet her at the station—but no one showed up.

Alone and confused, Katherine picked up her bags and walked over to the Bridgeport store. When she entered the store, she saw a half-dozen or so men sitting around a pot-bellied stove, telling their tall tales. Some of them planted themselves in rocking chairs, while others leaned into straight-back chairs tilted backward on two legs. Each face held a respectable-sized plug of chewing tobacco.

Why, those men probably thought they were dreaming when they looked over and saw this tall, attractive young lady with deep-set brown eyes. Her black hair was loosely drawn up into a soft mound on top of her head, and she was all gussied up in her fine store-bought clothes and fancy shoes. I reckon those men were just a spittin' all over each other trying not to swallow that tobacco juice. The faces of the older men were stern with deep lines and creases. The younger ones just stared, not believing the wonders their eyes were seeing.

"Excuse me, gentlemen, but I'm not sure that I got off at the right station."

The sound of her northern brogue and the need to maintain their cuds brought them back from their fantasies. One healthy spit of tobacco juice, then another, and another landed in the sandbox around the base of the stove. Some missed and landed on the already stained floor.

Marion Fish spoke up first. "Well, where ye headin fer, young lady?"

"A place back in the mountains, somewhere outside of Del Rio. Someone was to meet me at the station there." She went on to tell him how earlier that year a preacher from the area had gotten in touch with her about starting a Sunday school and an orphans' mission home and school for boys.

"Del Rio's the next stop down yonder, 'bout six or seven miles. Reckon that's where ya shudda got off. Thar be a lot of talk 'bout a mission out at Fair View not fer from my place. That bein' so, reckon ya shudda got off at the whistle stop. Mor'n likely thar be sumun a-waitin' fer ya thar. Tell ya what," he continued, "ya can come stay with me'n the missus fer a spell. Ya can ride my mule. She's old 'n not much fer comfort, but those shoes of your'n ain't gonna get ya far in these here mountains."

Marion helped Miss Plantz up on his old white mule and threw his turn of meal onto his shoulder. They started back over Yellow Mountain to his home near Fair View.

One can only imagine the reactions of Marion's wife and other family members! Pure disbelief would be my guess. "Miz Plantz, this here be my wife Laura."

"I'm so pleased to meet you, Laura. Please, call me Katie." Katie found Laura to be as friendly and accepting as her husband. They took her in and treated her just like family. She remained with them through the winter, and in the spring Katie moved into a vacant log cabin and busied herself fixing it up. Fred O'Dell now owns the cabin where Katie lived.

Katie taught Sunday school at Fair View and helped out in the community. She would visit and nurse the sick, help with the young 'uns—whatever she could do. All the people in the community took an instant liking to Miss Katie, especially Marion's daughters and their families. Three of his daughters had married three of the Click brothers—Jack, France, and Hoss—and all of them lived just up a piece from Marion. It was the Click brothers who donated the three acres of land used for building the mission. Years later, more land would be purchased for the church.

The building of Ebenezer Mission and its school was a community project—a huge task for these mountain people. Although everyone wanted to help, none of them had ever built anything other than log cabins and outbuildings, except maybe a barn or shed with wood planks.

The mission was to be a large three-story board structure with a basement. Trees would have to be cut and hauled or dragged to the mill a mile away, and then the boards brought back to the building site and dried out. None of the people there had ever heard tell of curing wood before building with it. Rocks would have to be selected and gathered for the foundation and basement walls.

Another challenge would be finding the time to build. The fields had to be prepared to plant crops and gardens. Because of the abundance of steep hills and the lack of flat land, much of this work had to be done by hand with a hoe. Entire families were involved from sunrise to sunset in planting, weeding, and harvesting. Building the mission was going to take a while, but the people were excited and willing to work hard when time permitted.

Katie had been corresponding all these months with a young Moravian preacher and former schoolmate, William H. Nowack, telling him about how accepting and appreciative the people were and keeping him informed of the progress she was making teaching Sunday school and helping in the community. William would soon be arriving to supervise the actual building of the mission. He also planned to establish new Sunday schools in the surrounding communities, like Pig Trot, during the times when the community people were too busy to help with the building.

As the preparation started, Katie became more anxious—excited about more than the building of Ebenezer Mission. You see, William and Katie had been very close friends in school and their separation had convinced them both that they were in love. When William finally arrived, it was a bit more than obvious that the two were indeed very good friends, not only sharing a love and concern for the wellbeing of the community people, but also sharing a love for each other.

Papa, who was already as big or bigger than most grown men, spent most of his spare time helping to build the mission house, often working side-by-side with William. He would laugh and tell us about how Katie and William would talk to each other in Latin when they were courting so no one could understand what they were saying. But, of course, everyone pretty well knew what kind of talking they were doing and enjoyed teasing them. "We're gonna get us a teacher up here ta teach us all that fancy talk!" The people may not have understood the words, but they knew by the way those two talked and the way he treated her that they were in love. I guess you could say that was one time when Latin wasn't considered a dead language.

In the book *Christy*, the students wanted to learn Latin because of their heritage, but it was really because of the Nowacks. Of course, the other mission workers who came later had no way of knowing that. They just never would have thought that it was all because the people wanted to know what a fancy preacher man would be saying to the lady he loved. The young people had a great deal of respect for Miss Katie and William. By learning Latin, they could be more like them.

It wasn't long before Katie and William slipped off to get married. They built a cabin close to the mission. It burned sometime later after the big mission house was built.

While the construction was under way, months before the building was scheduled to be completed, Katie and William made several contacts to churches and individuals for help in furnishing the mission. When the final work was being done to the house, shipments of furniture and supplies began arriving in Del Rio. Wagonload after wagonload for maybe two weeks or more made their way seven miles back up in the mountains over nearly nonexistent roads to Ebenezer Mission. Papa said it was the most exciting part—helping the Click brothers, Jack, France, and Hoss, unload and move crates and furniture around as the women did the fancying up and planned who was going to make what for the gathering. The entire community had been invited to come see the mission.

Marion Fish and his sons-in-law made tables out of planks laid across the empty moving crates and barrels for the food to sit on. That's how picnic tables were made back then. Nothing fancy to it.

When the people started turning up, Marion and Laura helped Katie and William welcome everyone. One of Marion and Laura's daughters saw to it that the food was placed in the right spot while the other two gave tours of the mission house.

I have no idea how many showed up that hot summer afternoon, or what they thought when they stepped into the front room. I can imagine it—the sun casting long shadows as they opened the front door; the eager whispers and clicking footsteps on the wooden floor as they poured in. Everyone called it the "big room." It was spacious, probably as large as 20x30 feet—about the size of some of the cabins up here.

The dwelling house, as it was often called when I went to school at the mission, was heated by several potbelly stoves, all fired by logs. I would guess that's how it was always heated, because it had no fireplaces. The big room was used both as a meeting room and as a classroom. It was modestly furnished, with long, functional benches against the walls that could be pulled out for the school classes, which consisted of Bible, catechism, reading, writing, and some math.

From the big room you passed into a large hall which was about ten feet wide. The kitchen with a large pantry and the dining room were on the other side of this hallway. Each of these two rooms was close to 14x16 feet in size. There was another outside entrance into the big hallway, as well as one into the kitchen. The cooking, however, was done in the basement of the mission house and the food was sent to the main floor by way of a pulley-operated dumbwaiter located just off the kitchen by the pantry. The dirty dishes were returned to the basement in the dumbwaiter to be washed.

The basement kitchen entrance was under the kitchen porch and could only be entered from the outside. There was a window in this kitchen through which food could be passed to people outside the house. The basement only had two big rooms: the kitchen, which had a wooden platform floor, and a storage room with a hard packed dirt floor.

There was a large staircase in the big hallway on the main floor which had thirteen steps, a landing, then six more steps leading to the second floor hallway. The layout of the second story was identical to the main floor. The big room there was used as the dormitory. One of the other rooms housed two of the mission workers and the other room was used sometimes as an office and at other times for an additional staff bedroom.

Sewing classes were offered for the community girls, while the boys helped William around the house and garden. Girls, however, were not admitted to the school until the church schoolhouse was built some years later.

The third floor had only two rooms, both of which were large with slanted ceilings and used mainly for storage.

The Nowacks also started the Sunshine (Sonshine) Band, a rough combination of daily vacation Bible school and Boy Scouts or 4-H. They would meet once a week to work on different projects, like helping the mission people raise garden crops. If one of the men in the community was sick, they might go over and hoe out his corn. They also took Bible courses, memorized Scripture, and read books. They really learned a lot from the experience.

The Sunshine Band ended shortly after the Nowacks left. I would guess their successors offered something different.

Some of the first boys to live in the mission home were Cleland and Uranus Rector, brothers from Madison County, North Carolina, and Mallie and Frank Rigsby, whom I recollect were from Ohio. There were also Dallas and Cecil Giles, Wilbur Hall, Clarence Nelson, Hubert Henderson, and Charlie Hall, who was from the Edwina Community of Cocke County, Tennessee. Nobody knows the details of why or the story behind it anymore, but Charlie Hall had been found with his mother, Mourning Hall, who had run away from home with him. The bloodhounds that the authorities called in from Morristown found them up there on Hall Mountain. Charlie was taken to Ebenezer Mission, and Mourning was sent to East Tennessee State Hospital in Knoxville suffering from a nervous breakdown.

There were probably at least ten to twelve boys living at Ebenezer. Most of them were from the local and surrounding communities, but there were others from the Tennessee Valley area, as well as the Carolinas, Kentucky, and Ohio.

Along with the increasing number of residents, the mission staff grew as well. In addition to Katie and William Nowack, there was Miss McWilliams, Mary Elkins, and Mary E. Godden.

The boys were quite disciplined and unusually well-behaved. The boarding school was structured so that the boys were kept busy all the time, leaving little room for mischief. Each boy had certain chores, some working in the kitchen while others replenished the firewood supply for the night and the next day. When they finished their work, they had freedom to meander through the countryside, talk to neighbors and friends, or play around the mission, but they were always supervised.

Their daily routine was fairly strict. William established a Sunday school that met at the Pig Trot schoolhouse on the other side of Yellow

Spring Mountain. Being a well-liked man, the people there considered it a great honor when he and "his boys" spent Sunday dinner with them.

The Harper home was one of his favorites. He felt that because of their rich family life, strong work ethics, and good manners that the Harper boys were a positive influence for the boys from the orphanage. He even invited them to visit the mission, and I'm sure they took him up on the offer.

The Nowacks didn't stay as long as everyone would have liked. It was sad how it came to happen, but they had an infant son who died, leaving them childless. They buried his tiny boxed coffin by the mission house. The grave is still marked by a wall of stones. Not long after his death, they felt the Lord was calling them into foreign mission work. But not before their purpose was fulfilled here at Ebenezer.

Before leaving to become missionaries to China, the Nowacks placed each of the boys in other schools. The mission property was turned over to Dr. Edward O. Guerrant,[4] founder and president of the American Inland Mission, also referred to as the Soul Winner's Society, and editor of *The Soul Winner*.

Guerrant, a teacher, was an officer in the Confederate Army attached to the headquarters of Confederate generals Humphrey Marshall, William Preston, George Cosby, and John Hunt Morgan. During this time he became aware of the spiritual and health needs of the mountain people. After the war in 1865, he entered medical college. He practiced medicine in Mt. Sterling, Kentucky, until 1873, when he decided to enter the ministry. Dr. Guerrant served as pastor to several Presbyterian congregations and as an evangelist for the Synod of Kentucky.

The Nowacks were pleased with what had been accomplished through the Ebenezer Mission, but there was no way that they could

---

4 Dr. E. O. Guerrant (1856-1916). Bachelor of Arts degree from Center College in Danville, Kentucky (1860); school teacher (1860-1862); Confederate Army officer (1862-1865); Jefferson Medical College in Philadelphia and Bellevue Medical College in New York City (1865-1867); practiced medicine (1867-1873); Union Theological Seminary in Richmond, Virginia(1873-1875); pastor and crusading evangelist (1875-1901); and served as founder and president of American Inland Mission from 1897 until 1911 when he transferred control of his home mission work to the Executive Committee of Home Missions of the Southern Presbyterian Church.

have possibly known the long-term effects of the work they started. Generation after generation, their work continued to strengthen, encourage, and bring hope to our mountain cove and the communities that surrounded it.

Most of the boys who stayed at the mission home while the Nowacks were there became prominent leaders and businessmen. Charlie, the little boy whose mother was institutionalized, grew up and became an attorney in Ohio. The Rector Brothers, who owned several boats and operated a fruit boat company on the Great Lakes, came back here several times to visit during their first years of retirement.

After leaving Ebenezer to go to the international mission field, Mr. Nowack continued to correspond with Neil, the youngest son of the Harper family, until around 1960. Mr. Nowack died four years later at the ripe age of ninety.

The Nowacks only made four trips back to the United States. Mrs. Nowack died and was buried in China. Mr. Nowack remarried some years after his wife's death. As late as 1975, his second wife was still living in a nursing home in Chicago.

I don't know of anyone who has any recollections of what happened at Ebenezer Mission from the time the Presbyterian Soul Winners took over until around 1908. Right before they came in, sometime between 1902 and 1904, Papa's thoughts moved on to more than helping at the mission and his work at home. He was a young man at the time, and it was amidst all this change that his parents moved to a farm not more than a mile from Ebenezer.

3
My Beginnings
1904–1911

The Halls—Mama's Family

*P*apa had taken notice of a girl who occasionally visited his church there in Edwina. Now, when it came to church, Papa was just like his family—there every time the doors opened. She, on the other hand, had parents who were not church-going folks.

That young lady, who was to become my mama, was Flora Louise, the older child of Charity Clark Hall and Thomas Andrew Hall. She was born October 14, 1882, in Teague, North Carolina. I have tried many times to find where Teague was located, but I have found no record of such a town or community ever existing. All I know is that it was somewhere around or just beyond Waynesville.

Thomas was probably born in 1862 or '63, about one year before the Civil War was over. He had some sisters, but I don't know who they were or their birth order. I do know that one of his sisters married one of the Vanes boys, securing herself a respectable family name.

His mother was Harriet Elizabeth Simons; his father, Big John Hall, was from Edwina over in the Hall Top area. John was supposedly taken prisoner by the Yankees, but no record of him was ever found. We have always believed that he was the unknown Rebel scout, killed by the Yankees and then buried by some of the community people in an unmarked grave in the cemetery on Persimmon Hill.

After John's death, his wife moved to North Carolina with her children, where she married an Ellison. We don't know when my Grandpa Hall moved back to this area or when he bought his big farm. But we do know it was before he fought in the Spanish American War, which took place between April and August of 1898.

Mama told me stories about when she was a girl, probably close to sixteen years old, when her papa was away during that war. She and her mama and younger brother John were left there all by themselves and they would get so scared, especially at night, because they thought some wild animal might get into the house. Back then, there were many more wild animals in these parts than there are now. Since there may have been good reason to be afraid without a man around, Grandpa had asked the nearest neighbor, who was still not very close, to watch out for them. He would have never heard their cries in the night through the acres of dense forest, should they have been attacked.

So, the door of their little cabin was fastened with buttons and latches, but they were pretty sure those would not be stout enough to keep the animals out. Every evening their neighbor would come over to secure their cabin as best he could. He would latch the door from the inside and roll a big log up next to it. Then he would wedge a large pole up against the door. This would keep the bears and panthers out, but it also trapped him inside the cabin. In order to go home, he had to climb out the narrow window, not any bigger than two logs tall. The window was also about four-and-a-half to five feet off the ground. In the morning, Mama and her mother, with the help of John, were able to remove the pole and roll the log away from the door.

Grandpa had some peculiar ways about him. He was very strict with his family. He was one to believe that boys should get the educations so that as men-folks they could get some kind of big important job like teaching, owning a store, or something like that. The woman's place was to work at home and serve her man—no need at all for her to have an education. She had no time to be lollygaggin' around reading or writing. And when my grandpa thought that's the way it should be, that's the way it was! Mama wanted to attend school, but Grandpa never even thought it worth discussing. So, Mama never did get to go to school and, of course, Grandpa always made sure no boys got too close to his daughter. She had to stay home and plow, doing her work and part of John's. And when John got home from school, he still had chores to do as well as his studying.

Both Mama and her brother were very unhappy. One night when John was fifteen, he slipped off and joined the army. In order to enlist, he had to lie about his age, and this caused him much regret later in life.

Living with Grandpa's hurt and disappointment in John made everyone's life harder, especially Mama's. She had more chores than ever to do and very little freedom. I guess he thought she might run off too. However, despite her upbringing with parents who never stepped foot in a church, Mama was allowed to go to services if she had all of her many chores done.

Papa had taken notice of Mama on her occasional visits to his church there in Edwina. Every time Mama came to church, Papa tried to sit by her and talk to her, but she shied away from his advances. Their families had lived fairly close together for a time when they were younger, and she had known who Papa was most of her life, but she was timid around boys and rarely offered more than a "howdy" to him.

Yes sir, Papa had for certain noticed what a fine job of growing up she had done. She was just about the prettiest thing he had ever seen. My papa was not one to give up easily, and once he applied his charm and sense of humor to the task, why, he could charm the hide right off a bear. Wasn't long at all until that girl's attendance improved considerably. She had fallen in love.

My Parents' Marriage and First Home

Even though Mama was twenty-two years old, she was not allowed to date. Since her folks never darkened the church's door, they never knew she was seeing Papa. Papa, who was nearly twenty-five, made plans to slip off and marry Mama at the home of a friend who was a justice of the peace.

On the cold morning of January 22nd in 1904, Mama dressed in layers, using all the clothes she owned, and put her coat on over them. She went out as usual to do her chores. When she had finished, she just up and left and walked all the way to Edwina from this side of Hall Top with all she had on her back. With these meager possessions she'd start housekeeping.

Back then, in the early 1900s, most of the couples from around here would slip off to a justice of the peace to get married, but almost always their families knew of their plans and when it was going to happen. Aunt Martha was the only one in Papa's family to have her own real wedding, but I don't know if she was married at the mission house or at Grandma's house. Not much is known about what took place at the mission during that time.

I don't know where Mama and Papa stayed until they got their house built. I don't recollect ever hearing anyone say. Papa may have already built their cabin, for all I know, but I had always thought that they probably lived with his parents until spring. Winters were very cold back then; not a good time for building. That spring was also probably about the time that his parents moved over to Fair View.

One thing I do know for sure—they didn't go back around her parents for weeks, maybe even months. It took Grandpa Hall a long time to get over Mama leaving home.

My mama and papa got a land lease from the government at a dollar a year for a section of land. The wooded government land had to be cleared for building sites and fields, and the logs were used for building the cabin and outbuildings. The remaining timber was hauled to the mill and cut into floor joist, flooring, and maybe lumber to line the house.

All the neighbors and family members would get together and have what they called "a working." Working together, it didn't take long to clear a site for a cabin and build it. Sometimes they could put up a house in just a day or two. It would depend on how much help you could get.

Papa certainly had a big enough family and many friends, so I'm sure it didn't take them long to build the cabin. I don't know if it was at the same time or not, but they also helped Papa build a barn for the animals, a crib for grain, and storage buildings.

For the "working," the women would bring food and cook while the children would run through the woods and play. It was free labor, good fellowship, and fun for everyone. People took turns helping each other that way. It was a nice way to live.

The other day this lady was telling me about how her daddy had a "working" just after World War II when he built his big log house. It's that first house down at the end of the lane, and it's still in good shape.

Her daddy and two younger brothers, along with another man and his two sons, built that house in no time at all. Her daddy taught those young men how to notch logs along with other skills his grandfather had taught him years before. Those same young men used the knowledge they had learned from her father, who could neither read nor write, and started a log home builder's business over at Hartford.

Today when a couple purchases a home, most likely it's equipped with a heating furnace, electricity, running water, and indoor plumbing. When Mama and Papa first started housekeeping, and even for years after, things were completely different, especially back here in the mountains. All a cabin had was a fireplace. They had to make their own furniture. They may have had to buy pots to cook in, their eating utensils, and muslin for their mattress and pillows. It would not be uncommon for the young bride and groom to each bring the plate, cup, fork, and knife they used at home before marrying. Grandma Corn and Papa's sisters helped Mama set up housekeeping. They were just like that, always helping someone.

To make their bed mattress, Mama sewed the muslin, which they called "domestic," together on three sides, like making a giant pillowcase. They didn't have a sewing machine, so she had to do all that stitching by hand. On the fourth side she left an opening of about three feet right in the middle. Papa and Mama took the casing to the straw stack. It took two people to cram it just as full as they could make it, stuffing it like a huge pillow. Then they put it on the sled and brought it home.

To make the bed frame, Papa went out to the woods and cut four posts, all close to the same size. He boxed in planks around them to make the frame. The slats went across the frame and the straw tick mattress was placed on the slats.

Mama was so proud of their little cabin. She was accustomed to hard work and it didn't take her long to have everything just like she wanted it, with plenty of flowers and a big vegetable garden.

They raised crops of corn, beans, potatoes, and a little tobacco, just enough to chew. They raised all kinds of animals too, like cows, pigs, chickens, and mules.

Mama found some beautiful honeysuckle vines growing in the woods and set them out at the cabin. She let them grow up on the porch and around the door. Nowadays most people don't like honeysuckle because it can be so difficult to control, but Mama kept hers clean and neat as long as she lived there.

Mama had a lot of flowers that you just don't find much anymore. One was trailing arbutus, which comes up real early in the spring and lays close to the ground. It has a single leaf shaped like an ironwood leaf and small pink flowers with the most wonderful fragrance all over it. There used to be a lot of it around here. The road bank from Clark's to Philip's was once covered in it—solid arbutus. Oh, it's the best smelling stuff.

At one time there was a grave at the cemetery covered with arbutus. I tried to talk them out of mowing over it because I had planned to bring some of it up here to set out. Arbutus is so pretty and doesn't get tall. It wouldn't hurt a thing growing there, but to them men it was just trash and before I could get any, they had mowed it down. If I ever catch any more, I'm just going to dig it up and set it out.

The Plant that Ate the South

I remember hearing Mama talk about how Aunt Martha came and they planted all those cedar trees. Everyone knew of Mama's love for plants and pretty flowers and there were many people who would give her a start of this or a start of that.

Louis Clark, supposedly a direct descendent of William Clark of the Lewis and Clark expeditions, was one of those people. Even though Louis was one of Mama's cousins, she always called him Uncle Louis.

He was respected by everyone and well known as a dedicated Baptist called to spread the gospel as our circuit preacher. Without a horse or mule to his name, Uncle Louis probably traveled hundreds of miles a month, all on foot. That's how he got his nickname, Traveling Toe. It was said that he knew all the paths on his circuit so well that he could actually walk and read his Bible, even at night while holding his lantern, without so much as stubbing his toe.

Uncle Louis told Mama that there was this wonderful plant that he had seen. He had met some people who were using it as pasture food for their animals. Mama asked him to bring her some and that's how kudzu was introduced to this area. No one realized at that time what an impact it would have, how it would take over the land. That plant later became known as the plant that ate the South.

Mama thought it was so pretty that she planted one stalk of it on each side of the porch. Its large leaves provided some shade and the blossoms were pretty and fragrant. She kept it trimmed and apparently had no problem controlling it.

Now that kudzu grows everywhere, there is no way you can stop it. You can't even get to where that little cabin was for all the honeysuckle and kudzu vines. I guess her vines were the start of it all.

I got so tickled a few years back. See, this man that once lived here wrote and asked me what I would charge to dig a hundred kudzu plants for him.

I wrote back and told him he could have two or three hundred, or as many as he wanted free if he came and dug them up himself. Why,

I wouldn't dig them for anybody. Those kudzu roots go down in the ground a couple feet deep. I'd be glad to give that stuff away to anybody. I don't reckon that man ever came down to take that kudzu, probably for that very reason.

One of the people that I let stay up at the Click House one time told me how you could cook kudzu and eat it, so I tried it. You cook it just like you cook greens using the young tender leaves at the top of the plant. I put a mess of it in a kettle and cooked it with a good deal of hog lard and a little salt until it was real tender. It wasn't bad.

Once I had a gang of little pups and didn't know what I could feed all those dogs. I had heard people say they bought dog food at the store, but I had always fed our dogs table scraps. So I cooked a kettle of kudzu and fed it to the dogs to see if they would eat it and they certainly did. I also fed freshly cut kudzu to my two hogs. Every morning and every afternoon I'd cut a big wheelbarrow full of kudzu and haul it down to the hog pen. It's funny how different things are out here in the back woods; we always learned to improvise and make do with what we had.

The Corn Family

Only Winnie, Martha, Flora, and Jessie were still living at home in 1904 or 1905 when Grandma and Grandpa Corn moved into a big, long four-room log house just below Fair View. The others had married and moved to places of their own, but most of them stayed around fairly close.

If you stand up there at Roy Dan's house and look across the branch, you'll see a white house with one main barn and two older barns on the outskirts. Grandma's house was once right there between those two old barns. I don't know if they intentionally moved there to be closer to the mission or not, but their house was less than a mile below the Ebenezer Mission. It was so sad to see them tear down Grandma's house. They burned all those pretty logs—just burned everything. But that place is still known as the Ol' Toll Corn Place to this day.

Grandma had been awfully strict on her girls when it came to dating. Grandpa, on the other hand, didn't pay much attention to what any of them did—except when it came to work time. Work time was Grandpa's time. He told them what to do, and, believe me, that's what they did! There was no foolishness about him when it came to that. You had to work and you had to keep up with your work. Whatever you were supposed to do had better get done.

Not too long after Grandma and Grandpa Corn moved down here, Aunt Winnie decided she was going to slip off and marry Johnny James, a boy she had met when they lived up around Edwina. She and Johnny continued to see each other after she moved, but not as often. It was just too far. Guess they thought getting married would solve all their problems. That's how people think when they're young. And they were both very young—she was only about fourteen or so.

Of course, when Grandma found out, she quickly put a stop to their plans. Grandpa just didn't like the boy much at all after that. So Johnny, believing there was not a chance for him and Winnie, married someone else. He and his wife had seven or eight children.

Winnie later married Hugh Turner when she was seventeen or eighteen. They had a set of twins and one other child. One of her twins died at birth.

Funny how many years later, after Hugh had died and her kids were almost grown, Winnie and Johnny, whose wife had also died, met again and this time they married. Johnny's two younger children, who were probably around seven and nine years old, could not accept the idea of their father being married to another woman. They caused as many problems as two young'uns could think up. There was a picture of Johnny and his first wife hanging over their bed. Winnie took it down, and thinking that the girls would like the pictures of their mother and father, she hung it in their room. They didn't do a thing but bring it back and hang it over their bed directly above Winnie's side. They did a lot of little things like that.

Whenever Winnie put some of her things out around the house, like dresser scarves or doilies, the children would take them and hide them outside. Some of them she never found.

They lived together for several years, and if it had been up to Johnny and Winnie, they would have stayed together. But the children never accepted her, and I guess Winnie took just as much as she could. Then finally when Aunt Florie got sick, Johnny and Winnie separated and she went to take care of her sister. Winnie didn't live too long after that. They never did divorce.

Birth of Mama and Papa's Children

Mama and Papa had two other children before I was born. Margaret May, or "Maggie," was born January 9, 1907, about three years after my parents were married. She was named after an old girlfriend of Papa's. How Papa ever got away with that, I simply don't know!

Burl Bernard Corn was born December 4, 1909, almost three years after Maggie. He was named Burl after the preacher Burl Wilkes, and Bernard after the new warehouse in Greeneville. Being so far from civilization, my folks had such a time getting the things they needed to run the farm. At last, they finally got this business in Greeneville, Tennessee, called Bernard Warehouse. It must have been a very important event to name their first son after a warehouse.

On February 1, 1911, I was born way back in the mountains of Cocke County in an area just under Hall Top. Much of that area had been owned by the Halls for many years and it remained in the family for as long as the older people were still living. If my mama could have populated all of Cocke County, she would have. My parents liked children and wanted a lot of them. I was the third of six, born just one year and two months after Burl.

Mama named me Othy Opal after Opal O'Dell, who was a first cousin to Lawton Turner and a little younger than Mama. She may still be living, but I really don't know. Mama would always talk about how Opal was the prettiest person she had ever seen. Even after I was grown, she'd tell me about how pretty Opal was and how she wanted to name me after her.

Having babies was different back then. After a woman had a baby, someone from the community would come in and stay with her, that is, unless she had a family to help. The women in the family and neighbors would come in to help bathe the baby and cook meals for the family. The people were awfully good about helping like that.

I don't think anyone stayed with Mama when I was born, other than the midwives that helped with the delivery. One was named Cassy Ball and the other was Aunt Jane. Since it was winter, Papa would have been in the house most of the time. And Maggie was six years old, so she was old enough to get a drink of water for Mama or to fetch whatever she might need when Papa went out to feed the animals.

I don't know much about my birth other than the date, like if I was born in the morning or in the night. I don't remember hearing anyone say. I never got my real birth certificate, so I probably will never know. When I needed a copy of my birth certificate to show the Social Security Commission, I discovered there had been a real big mix-up of recording my birth.

My certificate said I was a boy named Audy born on the 15th of February. Now, I had been told all my life that I had been born on the 1st of February and I certainly knew for a fact, especially after all this time, that I was not a boy.

All the other information, like my Mama and Papa's names, was correct and it had been signed by one of the midwives. I don't know how it happened, but there appeared to be no record of my ever being born. By the time the mistake was discovered, both the midwives and Mama had died and there was no one to ask.

I took my birth certificate to the county clerk of court who said, "You better just burn that certificate! You go down to the Social Security office and hand them that birth certificate with an entirely different name on it, sayin' you're a male child, no less, they're gonna think there's somethin' kinda phony' bout it. It'll confuse them somethin' awful and you'll never get it straightened out."

So all I could do to prove that I had been born was write to the Census Bureau and ask them for the listing of children born to Arthur Jackson

Corn and Flora Louise Hall Corn. When it came back, they showed me listed in the 1920 census as the third child born to Arthur and Flora Corn the 1st of February. That was the only way I could prove who I was.

A lot was going on around the time my Mama was due with me. My parents had found out in January, about a month before my birth, that they had lost their lease on the cabin and land. Mama and Papa said that a man decided he wanted their place and went to the government office in Greeneville and offered them $5.00 an acre. He was given the lease. That's what they did in a government area—if someone was willing to pay more, they could take your land lease. My parents received the eviction papers in January, but because Mama was pregnant, they were allowed to stay until two weeks after my birth.

My parents were not the type to be bitter and hold grudges. I'm sure they were hurt and upset, but they never said anything against that man. You would never hear them say anything like that. I knew who the man was that got our home, but my parents never would let us talk against him. They said that talking about the bad things that people did was wrong and could cause trouble along the way. Mama never would let us talk like that. She always said that a person's sin would find them out, but her family was not going to be the ones doing the talking. And we didn't.

On February 14th, Papa loaded up the wagon. They didn't have much to move. People didn't have much back then. There wasn't room for a lot in the small one or two-room cabins, especially when the average family had six to ten children. There were no heating stoves to move; the fireplace was their only source of heat. They didn't have dressers or any other furniture except beds, chairs, and a table to eat on. The biggest thing they had was their cook stove. Just one wagon full would move it all.

Papa hooked the two oxen up to the wagon. There had been a big deep snow the night before, but the oxen were strong and should have had no problem pulling the wagon. He put Maggie and Burl in the wagon. Mama wasn't able to ride in the bumpy wagon with a two week old baby, so she had to carry me in her arms as she walked the five or six miles with her long dress and petticoats dragging through the deep snow. Of course, back then nobody ever heard tell of women wearing pants.

Several people knew what that man had done to our family, and since he was not from the community, he really had two strikes against him to start with. He wasn't much welcomed. He stayed here for a while, then started going back and forth to work other places. His family stayed, even though they weren't accepted by the people either, and yet they still kept that land for some time.

The last time I saw that old man was after I had begun teaching. I was getting on the train to go visit the teacher I had stayed with when I was going to school in Kentucky. It was her niece that had helped me get my teeth fixed. There were several people on the train that I knew. One of them was my cousin Harrison Pack, who was going back to his work. Another one was a lady from Del Rio married to a government man who had something to do with the railroad. And there about halfway back in the car was THAT man.

He was a sickening man. I tried to ignore him, but he kept saying something to me, something about my boyfriend. He was talking about his first cousin and it just sort of irked me! No, it really irked me for him to say that about his first cousin, calling him my boyfriend. I couldn't have been less interested!

He just had the one child born here. I don't know where the other children were born. One of his boys married and had two children here. When his wife died, he moved back to North Carolina where the family was from.

It's a shame I never did get to see the cabin where my parents lived when I was born, except for the times we walked back up there when I was a child. By the time I started going back to Hall Top, the government had taken back the leased land and all the houses had been torn down. The land had become part of the Cherokee National Forest, and there was nothing there to show where Mama's pretty little cabin had been except for the thick growth of honeysuckle and kudzu.

It never seemed right to me how the government did their business. There had been houses all up in this hollow too, pretty log houses where people had lived for years rearing their children and raising their crops. When the government stopped leasing the land, the people were given the opportunity to buy their houses and buildings and haul them off to a new location. If they couldn't afford to buy land and move their house, it was burned to the ground. If the houses remained, squatters might come, and with them came the danger of forest fires. So most were forced to leave their homes and start over, but that's just how it was and families dealt with it.

4
Early Childhood
1911–1915

*B*y the time you read this, Lori, I'm sure it will sound like I grew up in a third world country. But some things haven't changed too much since my day. Like families today, back then it wasn't at all uncommon for people to move from one place to another. Especially if they lived on leased land. A family might build a little cabin on government land, decide they didn't like that one, get a new lease, and build another cabin. Usually a place became known by the builder's name. Everybody still calls the cabin up from my house the Hoss Click House, and the place Papa lived was called the Arter (Au-der) Place. Later, there were some families who bought land and built cabins, but then decided to rent them out so they could move to South Carolina where people were getting good paying jobs.

We moved from Hall Top to an empty cabin that had been built on some government land by George Jones. We leased the George Jones Place for about one year and then moved to the Davis Place, which belonged to some of the Click heirs, before moving up to Grandpa Hall's. We didn't live at either the George Jones Place or the Davis Place long enough to prepare the ground to plant much of a crop, but we always had a vegetable garden and, of course, everywhere Mama lived she planted flowers. That's one thing you could be sure of. She loved her flowers.

Before long, Mama and Papa were tired of moving. They wanted to have a home of their own, one that would always be theirs so that they would never have to move again. Grandpa Corn was trying to get things straightened out so he and Papa could buy a large piece of land bordering his property. They had started saving some of the calves they were raising and planned to sell a portion of their crops to use towards a down payment on the land.

Living at Grandpa Hall's —1913

Grandpa Hall offered to let us stay in one of the tenant houses on his nice, big farm by the creek until we could afford to buy our own place. The tenant houses weren't really all that close to the main house. Why, I guess our cabin was about as far away from Grandpa's as we are from here to Clark's.

Even though Mama didn't like having to stay at Grandpa's place, she knew it was the best thing for us to do. It was also good for Grandpa. He was getting older and working the farm was getting more difficult for him. Mama didn't go around her pa much at first, but I think, during the almost two-and-a-half years we stayed there, the relationship with Mama and her family improved considerably.

Grandpa's place had at one time evidently been some kind of big working farm. It had several different outbuildings, including a barn, cribs, chicken houses, hog houses with pens, a smoke house, well house, and a couple storage buildings. There was even a building that was once used as a commissary when the original owners had the farm in full operation. A commissary would be like a small general store where workers would take the due bill they received for their work and cash it in for food and sometimes other things they needed.

Back then houses were tiny—only one, two, or sometimes three rooms, counting the lean-to kitchen. Sometimes the finer cabins would have an upstairs sleeping loft. Families with six to twelve children were not at all uncommon. So, you know, a loft where the children could sleep and outside storage buildings could make all the difference in the world.

Our little tenant house had one room with a lean-to. The five of us used the bigger room for a bedroom and put the cooking stove in the lean-to.

My grandfather's house, on the other hand, was most unusual. It was actually two houses, one in front of the other, joined together by a catwalk or a dogtrot, as we called it. The dogtrot was like a big hall about six to eight feet wide with no walls or ceiling. It was just like a big walkway between the two parts of the house. If it had been covered, this walkway would have made a fine place to sit and swing in the summertime.

The front house with its porch extending all the way across the front had two rooms used as bedrooms. In the back house were the kitchen and dining room. Houses didn't have living rooms, but with four rooms their house would have been considered large.

I don't remember for sure if there was an outhouse. Most people didn't have them at that time; they would just go to the bathroom outside anywhere they wanted to. But if anyone back then had an outhouse, it would have been my grandpa. He just did not seem to be the type to be going to the woods to do his business. Our tenant house for sure didn't have an outhouse. People probably got the idea of outhouses from the mission people.

There were plenty of animals around and there was always a garden and crops to tend. Grandpa raised four or five cows at a time, calves, hogs, and chickens for food and money, and mules to help with the work. He never did raise goats. I guess he never saw much use in them.

At that time, not many of the adults had much education and many of them couldn't read more than basic words. I don't know if Grandpa Hall could read or write, but he certainly was pretty uppity. Both his family and the Clarks were kind of snooty.

Charity Clark, like Uncle Louis, was said to have been one of the descendants of the same family as William Clark of the Lewis and Clark expedition. The Clark family first settled in Virginia, then in North Carolina, and on into Tennessee. I guess being kin to someone famous might have made them feel like they were somebody special. But when you really got to know them, they were as common as could be. They didn't act a bit like they thought of themselves as better than other folks. They just did things differently. Grandpa Hall, in a unique sort of way, was a real sweet old guy. But it makes you wonder how he got to be so peculiar.

My grandparents were the only people I ever knew of to have linen tablecloths, except for the chapel women.

"Chapel women"—that's what most of the community people were now calling the mission workers. They also referred to the new church as the chapel and the mission house was often referred to as the dwelling house.

The chapel women were fancy eaters like Grandpa Hall. They used linen tablecloths and silverware while the rest of us ate off of bare tables on simple plates with old knives and forks with black wooded handles. But more and more, little by little, the community women and the girls who attended the mission school started making things nicer in their homes too. They might spread a piece of cloth over the table and put some cut flowers in an old jar and place it in the center of it. The men folk usually didn't care much about such frivolous things. But if the women folk wanted to pretty things up, they wouldn't say anything just as long as the food was on time. That's all they cared about.

But not Grandpa! He was exactly that "linen napkin type." There had to be a linen tablecloth on his table. And there had to be a big ol' white linen napkin folded and put on his plate for every meal. The silverware all had to match and it had better be laid out just right. The knife had to be in its place, the fork had to be in its place, and the spoon had to be in its place. Everything had to be precisely right! In the middle of the table was a big blue dish of honey. Everything had to be perfect, just exactly so.

Grandpa was quite an elegant sight with that big white linen napkin stuck down in his collar. Reckon he had to make sure he wouldn't get any crumbs on him. I don't know if he was raised that way or what. I really don't know anything about his family or where he got his unusual ways. The only things I ever heard about his family were rumors. Like people said that his daddy, John Hall, was killed by a band of Yankee raiders during the Civil War and was buried in an unmarked grave in the cemetery.

Grandpa Hall was always kind of a mystery, both because of the rumors and because of his peculiar habits and actions. In all my years, I've never met anyone who even came close to being like my Grandpa Hall.

After my mother ran away to get married, my grandparents always had a full-time live-in maid who slept in one of the front rooms. Of course, everyone in the community thought the maid was his mistress, but I didn't believe that. They were always older women who didn't look like they'd take much to being anyone's mistress. Grandpa kept the maid working hard, and with his strange eating habits and rituals, he kept her especially busy washing dishes. Grandpa always said his Charity "wasn't gonna wash no dishes!" And she didn't touch a dish. Grandma Hall was a quiet and beautiful woman, rather regal and elegant in her ways, and Grandpa pampered her.

Yep, my grandpa had some funny ways about him for sure. He ate six meals a day. The table was always set the night before with the plates upside down. When he got up in the morning, he would dress, come to the table, turn his plate over, and eat his breakfast.

Then the maid would do the dishes and place them back on the table, plate upside down.

At 10:00 a.m., he would have a snack of biscuits with jelly or honey, which he would eat on the bottom of the plate. If the plate had not gotten dirty, he would take his napkin, wipe it off, and place it back on the table always upside down. If it was dirty, he would have the maid wash the plate. The maid had been instructed to never put his dishes away in the cupboard, but instead each time she washed them she was to put them back on the table, always upside down.

At dinnertime, which was their main meal, he would sit down at the table, turn his plate right side up, and eat a full meal. The maid would wash all the dishes after that meal.

In the afternoon, he would again have a snack out of the bottom of his plate. The same routine over and over. If his plate was not dirty, he would wipe it off with his big linen napkin and leave it there, upside down, ready for supper.

At supper he would do the same as dinnertime and the maid would wash the dishes.

So that was five of his six meals. Before going to bed he would eat another snack out of the bottom of his plate. After wiping the bottom off with the napkin, he would leave it on the table ready for tomorrow's breakfast. Grandpa sure could eat, and it was a job keeping up with it.

Grandma would help with the milking, but the maid took care of fixing the milk and butter. The maid did most of the work around there; that's another reason why I couldn't understand why people thought he was mixed up with some of those old ladies. Maybe it was because no one else around here had a maid.

Visiting Grandma Corn

Almost every Sunday, Mama and Papa would get us up early and we would go down to visit Grandma and Grandpa Corn. All of Papa's people who lived around here attended the mission church, and of course, we always went to church with them. Aunt Flora and Martha liked to dress up in their fancy clothes that the chapel women had given them. I even have pictures of them taken with their Sunday school class, all gussied up in their white, broad-brimmed hats that had been made out of cloth and then starched stiff as a board.

The Ebenezer Mission and its workers were an important part of my family's life, at least on the Corn side. Now, I don't know about the Halls. They were hardly ever around the mission and I don't think they cared much one way or the other about it or the mission workers. As Grandpa Hall would say, "I just don't pay it no mind." That was his creed. I think Uncle Louis was the only one from Mama's side of the family who cared much at all about God and the Bible and doing what it said.

Birth—Bertha Beatrice Corn on August 7, 1914

My parents were getting to know the chapel women quite well. Miss Bertha Abernathy, who Mama especially liked, gave her a lot of clothes for the new baby Mama was expecting. They were always helping people out like that. It was no wonder that when my sister was born on August 7, 1914, they named her Bertha Beatrice. They called my sister by her middle name and pronounced it Bee-a (short a) -tris.

Miss Abernathy had come from North Carolina in 1912 or 1913 and was the mission school's principal. In addition to Miss Abernathy, the school[5] had two teachers for the sixty-five students attending during the school year of 1913–1914. Of course, there were several other chapel women also.

As soon as Mama could ride the mule, we started going back to Grandma's about every week. Mama would ride holding Beatrice while Maggie, Burl, Papa, and I would walk the five or six miles down here. I could have ridden on the mule behind Mama and the baby, but I was afraid to ride him. I liked the animal all right, but I wasn't about to ride on him.

When we got to the creek, Papa would always make me get up on that mule and ride across with Mama. He would help Maggie and Burl walk across on the foot log, which was high above the creek and sometimes very slippery. Leading a small child across a foot log like that could be about the most dangerous thing in the world. They could put you off that log just as easy as anything. Everybody was scared of it.

Well, I didn't like riding that animal on solid ground and I sure didn't cotton to riding him across a fast mountain stream. I'd make the biggest fuss until Papa would have to take a switch and whip the fire out of me to get me up on that mule. Finally, we would all get to the other side and he would let me off. I walked the rest of the way to Grandma's rubbing my switch marks.

As it moved into the spring of 1915, Mama and Papa grew anxious about having a place of their own again. Maggie, at that time, was eight years old, and it was time to be thinking about her starting school. Both Mama and Papa wanted her to go to the mission school down by Grandma Corn's.

---

5   *The Soul Winner* also stated that the mission had two buildings (church and mission house) valued at $1,000.

Mama would sometimes let Maggie spend the whole week at Grandma's and go to school with Grandma's youngest daughter, Aunt Florie, just so she could get used to the mission school. The chapel women would let her visit in the class for the younger grades too, so she could be with some of the children her own age. They let anyone visit the classes as long as they didn't disrupt the lessons or disturb anyone.

Visiting School with Auda

One time Mama let me stay with Maggie down at Grandma Corn's. I knew a lot of the younger children around there and I loved to play with them. On this particular day, I was playing with Auda Turner, a girl about my age. After we had eaten a big lunch at Grandma's, we decided to run up to the mission school and play with the other children during their lunchtime and then maybe we would go watch Charlie McGaha teach. Auda had watched him before and she said he was funny the way he would swing his arms around and make faces when he taught.

Charlie McGaha was one of the men who had lived back up there by the Moraine Mission. I don't know if he had hardly any education at all, but he was allowed to teach. Back then you could teach to the eighth grade without teaching credentials. He only taught a couple subjects.

By the time we got up to the mission, they were already playing a game called "good night." It looked like a fun game, but we had never played it before, so we just watched. To play the game, the girls got in one line and the boys were in another line facing them. The girls were each given a boy's name, and the object of the game was for the boy to find the girl who had his name and take her back across the boy's line to the base.

The boy had no idea who his girl was, so he had to make guesses. He would walk up to the girl he thought might be the one, bow, and escort her by the arm toward the base. The girl would tease the boy by going part way with him, pretending that she really was the one. Then she would yell "good night" as she broke away from him and ran back to her line to avoid capture. The boy then tried again by choosing another girl.

It was the funniest sight ever watching them play that game. They were running into each other and laughing. Most of the older children were helping their folks plant crops, so the only older students playing with them were Aunt Florie and the ol' Turner boy. He was short and as skinny as a sapling tree, whereas Aunt Florie was a great big ol' thing, round and tall, like Papa. Well, those two got their feet all tangled up with each other and down they came with Aunt Florie landing on top of him. It was a real miracle he wasn't hurt, as big as Aunt Florie was. But he got up, a little slowly, and as he brushed himself off, the bell for class rang. That bell probably saved his life, because another fall with Aunt Florie certainly would have killed him.

We waited a little while and then Auda and I slipped into Charlie McGaha's class practically unnoticed and sat at the very back of the room on one of the long church-like benches. Charlie was already busy teaching a class in physiology. That's a branch of biology; now they just call it health class. There were only two students in the class: Aunt Florie and Frank Turner, the one she had just flattened out on the playground. They were the oldest students in the school.

Frank actually lived at the mission. He ate in the dwelling house, but everyone thought it would be inappropriate for him to have his bedroom inside the house where the women slept.

The log bunkhouse where John Wood had slept before he and Leonora were married was now being used for storage, so they built a new bunkhouse directly between the mission house and the church. This bunkhouse was a frame one. It had only one room, but it was plenty big for him to sleep in and it was a place where he could relax in solitude. It was called the Franklin House. Cary[6] played in that bunkhouse when he was a boy. It was still standing, until sometime in the 60s when they tore it down. The old, log bunkhouse was torn down sometime in the late 20s. It was in the other direction down by the rock in the road where the mission outhouse used to be. You know, down there by the spruce pine. It was still there when I started school.

---

6 Cary Alvin Myers born May 14, 1947—Opal's son

So my Aunt Florie and Frank sat at the front of the classroom intently listening to Charlie McGaha talk about this kind of bone and that kind of bone. He was just a-wavin' that big red textbook back and forth while he ranted on. Auda and I kept still in our seats in the back, sometimes trying to listen and understand what he was talking about, but we soon decided that bones weren't very interesting. We thought the way he talked and waved that book up and down at his side was kind of like a one-winged goose attempting to get off the ground. We would whisper quietly and snicker to ourselves about Aunt Florie falling on Frank. We knew better than to let anyone hear us.

Well, we were sitting on that bench with our arms around each other just a-huggin' when suddenly he slapped that book on his leg making a big crack. The noise startled us so that we fell off the bench and onto the floor, making a big commotion. Why, I think we might have scared Aunt Florie more with our commotion than the book-slappin' did!

That man yelled, "You! Come up here!!" His booming command nearly sent us into tears. I can still see that big ol' red book and him a-wavin' it up and down at us like he was going to hit us.

Well, we made our way up to the front and stood there hanging onto each other, looking wide-eyed up at him. He put one hand on his hip and with the other hand he pointed that book right in our faces and said, "What was you'uns doin'?"

I wasn't answering. I was scared so bad I was speechless. But, you see, Auda had family going to school there, so she knew him. So she replied, "We's was just a-wovin' each other."

"Well, don't be doin' that no more! You get back there to that seat and I don't wanna catch any more of that lovin' goin' on." Well, we sure didn't. We got back there and we didn't do it no more. Of course, I didn't come back to visit anymore either.

That was Frank and Aunt Flora's last year at the mission school. What made me happy was finding out that it was Charlie McGaha's last year too.

Aunt Florie was nineteen years old and had gone through the eighth grade two or three times. She wanted to go to school and learn, but neither the mission school nor the public school at Sand Hill went beyond the eighth grade. So she went to the public school one year and took the seventh grade, then she'd go to Ebenezer the next year and take the seventh grade again. She did the same thing for the eighth grade. Then she'd pretend to fail and go back to Sand Hill and take the eighth grade again. She did the last two or three years like that just to be able to go to school. Since Florie enjoyed school so much, the mission made arrangements for her to teach school over at Moraine Mission, but she got homesick and didn't stay there too long.

Aunt Florie never married; I'm not exactly sure why. I think there was a time or two when she had found somebody, and one for sure that she was crazy as a bat about. He was a Click boy who lived down there on the other side of the Old Fifteenth. Don't know if he ever asked her to marry him, but she sure was infatuated with him.

He had been married before and that was probably the main reason her folks didn't approve. See, the way we were brought up, you just didn't marry someone who had been married before unless their wife or husband was dead, and at that time, his wife was living. So, it could have been that Grandma and Grandpa wouldn't let her marry him. Mama speculated that he moved to New York because Grandma and Grandpa wouldn't let them get married.

Aunt Florie was Grandma's baby girl, and she never let her do much courting. Guess she just didn't think nobody was good enough for her, so that's who she ended up with—nobody.

Don't reckon there are many mamas who totally approve of who their children want to marry, and it is true that a good many couples would have been better off never marrying at all. But if one says too much or objects to their young'un's choice, it's just cause for fighting. My mama would always say, "They made their blister; let them sit on it." About the time she first noticed us girls looking cow-eyed at some boy, she told all of us, "Now, you just remember this: if you get married, you're married! You won't be comin' back to stay with me! When you get married, your business is between you and your man and you're not comin' back cryin' to me." None of us did, either.

A lot of the people in the community still didn't think schooling was all that important, and after my first visit, I soon became of the same mind. But it certainly was important to Mama and Papa, especially Mama, for all their children, the girls as well as Burl, to have a good education. And the best education was found at the mission school.

If they didn't move soon, or at least by the time school started in September, they would have to send Maggie down to live with Grandma. They didn't want to do that because they wanted her to be with the family and needed her to help with the chores.

It was in July when Grandpa Corn purchased a hundred and some acres of land that expanded from his place all the way up to where that gravel path goes through the woods. The land, which had one little cabin on it, was purchased in Grandpa's name, but it was understood that Papa would be half owner and make every other payment. Unfortunately, this agreement was never written down or made legal, and that caused problems later on when Grandpa died.

I never did know how much the whole piece of land cost. They never talked about things like that to us. All I knew was that my grandpa bought the place and that Papa was buying half of it from him and that they took turns making the payments. The payments were not a set amount with specific payment dates. They paid whatever amount they were able to make from selling a calf, hog, rhubarb, chestnuts, or anything else they could.

From the time I was little, I walked with Grandpa and Papa across the hill here to West Myers where they caught the train into Newport. Maggie, Burl, Aunt Flora, and I would each carry a little bunch of rhubarb in a sack, maybe fifteen to twenty pounds each. Papa and Grandpa would lug a big sack of rhubarb. Then when we'd all get to the train, they'd put ours into their sacks, get on the train, and go on into town. We'd return home.

I tell you, Lori, things sure have changed since I was a girl. I wish I could tell you about all our adventures as kids, and later as adults, but it would take a lot more than this measly amount of paper to tell you all the details of your family history. But I'll try to squeeze in as much as I can.

Opal and I enjoyed our time together, me learning so much about her past, and her sharing it. There would have never been enough time to find out all the delightful details that she took to the grave, forever remaining hidden in her heart. But I dove in as deep as I could get, absorbing every ounce of memory that I could fit on my pad of paper as I wrote down her letters to her grand-daughter. In some way, her experiences soon became my own, and it opened my eyes to a whole new world in this back mountain cove of eastern Tennessee where a family and a mission once made history.

5
Cabin by the Mission
1915—1917

Dear Lori,

*W*hen I last left off, I was telling you about our new home. I'm sure it was nothing like what you're used to, but it was indeed a gift when we finally had a place of our own. The cabin by the mission was right below the spring by the gravel path. It was a cozy chinked and daubed log cabin with only one room and a loft. With no windows, it stayed fairly warm. There was a hole cut out in the wall next to the fireplace the height of one log and about twenty inches wide. The smaller children could climb up the logs and crawl in and out of the house through the hole, but at night Mama or Papa would slide a board across the opening to keep outdoor wild critters out and their wild little critters in.

Mama was overjoyed to have her own home again. She busied herself planting flowers, and it didn't take her long at all to make it the prettiest place around. I don't know where Mama got the sapling fruit trees that she planted a ways out from the cabin. She had always wanted to have fruit trees, but since she knew they wouldn't stay long in each place, she never planted any.

Mama made flowerbeds all around the cabin, as well as up and down the branch that ran behind our home. All along that branch were big bushy yellow dahlias, and there was some other plant that was kind of yellow, and we used the roots of it just like potatoes. I think it had a flower kind of like a daisy or black-eyed Susan—yellow with a black center to it.

Mama must have planned it so that her gardens flowered nearly all year round. We had a flowering almond; we called them peach roses. It's exactly like the fall aster, except it's a dark blue and blooms later in the year. Even after the first freeze when the asters die back, the peach rose is still there. She had roses all over on one side of the cabin and zinnias, which she called old maids, everywhere you looked. There were cosmos (she called them free silvers) and polecat weed, which is now known as the electric light plant. Why, I'd give anything if I could find some of those old flowers called gentlemen's walking sticks that she had planted on the other side of the cabin. They get about as high as my head and the ends have red tassels hanging down.

We weren't allowed to dig around in Mama's flowerbeds, but the chickens, for certain, gave her a fit for a while. They scratched around in all that freshly dug dirt. But my mama was a clever woman and she soon thought of a way to keep those chickens out. First, she got big ol' planks and rocks and placed them around the perimeter of the beds. Then she planted the flowers and laid blackberry briars crisscrossed over the planks. To work in the beds, she would take a stick and gently lift the blackberry briars, then put them back down when she was done. Well, every one of our chickens soon lost interest in those beds. They for sure didn't want to scratch for bugs through the briar net. Kept the dogs out too.

My Aunt Flora was always looking for advertisements for free seed catalogs in magazines that the chapel women gave her. When the catalogs showed up in her mailbox, she'd have the best time looking at all those flowers. Then she'd order something new and different every time. She could buy a lot of seeds for just ten cents. I remember when she ordered brass pinks and something she called funny bugs, but I believe they were really called "love in a mist." She was the first one in the community to have gladiolus and yellow tea roses.

No one around here could grow flowers like Aunt Flora. Why, between her and Mama, I guess they had enough flowers to decorate the whole county, and maybe in a way, they did just that. Aunt Flora would save the seeds from her flowers and give them away to everyone. Mama was the same way.

People used to trade flowers a lot, and we still do that. When someone would give us flowers, we would name our flower after that person. Maribell Hall gave us some columbine one time, and we called them Maribell flowers. Mama planted a little twig of an apple tree that someone brought her from the Fugate community just out from Del Rio. I don't know what variety of apple it was. We always called them fugets.

Years later, after Mama moved from here, why, they just started plowing up all the plants that were left. So every time I saw one of her flowers there and got a chance, I'd steal a piece. Course, I didn't feel like it was stealing, because they were going to be destroyed anyway. I was saving them. I managed to save some of the flowering almonds and took them to Mama's when she lived in Long Creek. As for the other flowers I saved, I planted them down in the cemetery. And then later, when they started cleaning up the cemetery, it seemed as though they thought that cleaning up meant mowing down everything in sight. When I saw them doing that, I brought what was left home.

We've had several of those flowers that Mama started in our family all these years. We would keep those cuttings and pass them around to whoever wanted them. They were important to us, I guess, because Mama or someone we cared about had started them. That's the reason I still have those yuccas. You know, those plants with the big white flower stems. I wouldn't fool with those things myself, but they were flowers that she had raised and they were important to her.

Maggie Starts School

After we moved in, it was time to start planning what we were going to do with the land. Papa was especially pleased because now he had enough level land to raise wheat. Well, Papa soon had crops growing and accumulated several animals. Whenever he sold a calf or some crops, he would make his payment on the land. Everything seemed to be going well. Everyone was content.

Maggie was eight years old when she started school that fall. Now, to you, that might seem kind of old for starting school, but there were not many children who started school before age eight. In fact, there really was no age limit; it didn't matter if you were twenty-five years old or just five. If you wanted to go to school, you could go. Burl and I were each eight years old when we started school too.

Neither Mama nor Papa had much education. I know that Papa could both read and write, but not well enough to read the Bible to us at home. Papa may have gone to the public school for a while when his folks lived over by Edwina. I don't ever remember hearing for sure where Mama had learned to read.

The classes at the mission were open to the parents as well as the children, but there was always too much work to do for my parents to afford such a luxury. To them the school was there to provide a better life for their children when they were grown. But even though my parents didn't go, the mission workers were more than willing to teach or help anyone and did their best to inspire even the elderly.

For about a month or two during the winter, depending on the weather, there were not nearly so many chores to do. When it was not too cold, needed repairs to the out buildings could be made. The biggest chore that always had to be done, no matter how bad the weather, was feeding the animals. It was then that I can remember how Mama and Papa would borrow books from the mission and teach themselves. Mama would sit for hours at a time just a-practicing her writing. I can remember how neatly Mama could write—a lot better than I can.

The mission people would stop by and help them learn during their visits. It's no wonder my parents thought so much of the chapel women and the mission, or that the church was one of the most important parts of their lives. My, the changes they made in all our lives! By the time I went away to high school in 1927, my papa, who could not read the Bible well enough to even read to his own family when I was little, was teaching the adult Sunday school class. He read his Bible with confidence, skillfully sliding over the strange sounding names of people and places, knowing that only the mission workers would notice his mistakes. That might cause a slight grin and a twinkle in their eye, but they would never let on. They were always pleased and proud of people like Papa. He taught that class for the whole five years I was away at school.

The mission was right up here where those big trees are. We lived close enough that Maggie could stay home until the first bell rang. The teacher always rang two bells for school, one to inform people to get ready and then thirty minutes later the final bell. They always rang two bells for the church services too.

We called the mission school a one-room school, but actually the school was held in the two-story chapel that was built by John Wood. There were two big rooms, one for the first through third grades upstairs, and one for the fourth through the eighth grades downstairs.

The school year went from September until sometime in March. Well, actually there was never a break from school. There were always classes to learn something, anything from Bible classes to sewing. Sometimes groups or classes would get together to make things to help someone. Like, we might have a sewing class where everyone would make clothes for a student who had received a scholarship to go off to boarding school.

The mission charged sixty cents a month for tuition. That doesn't sound like much money, but it was very difficult for most parents to get any money at all. The tuition could be paid in cash, work, food, or almost anything that could be used by the mission. Families mostly paid by bartering. Mama and Papa paid Maggie's tuition, and later Burl's and mine, in tomatoes, milk, butter, eggs, chickens, and by working at the mission.

Before the mission arrived, if the children had any schooling at all, it only amounted to a few months out of the entire year. So the parents were glad to cut wood or give food to cover the sixty cents a month.

During Maggie's first year at school, Mama gave the mission milk for part of her tuition. Every night the mission preacher[7] would come and stay with us while Mama milked. And every night I could hardly wait for him to come. As soon as he sat down, I would jump up in his lap and he would open his big book that was full of pretty pictures and read to me.

It wasn't long before I could read some of the stories. I remember that as if it were yesterday. The first thing he ever taught me was "Yankee Doodle went to town riding on a pony, put a feather in his cap and called it macaroni." He taught me to read "Old Mother Hubbard," "Jack and Jill," and all those old nursery rhymes. I could read every word of 'em when I was four or five years old, well before I started school.

He didn't teach the others. I guess I was always such a tomboy that he was glad just to get me to sit down and be quiet. He might have taught me to read just to keep me from cutting up and aggravating him. I was always ready to aggravate him or anybody, you know—just a plain ol' cut-up.

Everyone said I was just like Papa; he was a cut-up too. He hardly ever got angry with us for anything. My papa was a great big man, well over six feet and weighing more than two hundred pounds. Some people nicknamed him Goliar (Go-lar) after Goliath in the Bible. If

---

7   This could have been Mr. Ralph Freeman, the assistant principal. *The Soul Winner* also listed Miss Bertha Abernethy, Principal; Miss Laura Watt, Primary Department; 65 students in day school and 65 in Sunday school.

they wanted anything, they'd always holler and say, "'Lo, Goliar." Other people called him "Arter" (Au-der) instead of Arthur.

Papa was a gentle giant, respected by most everyone. I never heard Papa say a dirty word but once in my life. That was when I was eight years old. Burl and I were walking with Papa, tagging along after him like we always did, up to his watermelon patch. When we got there, he discovered that several of his melons had been eaten and the rest of them had been hauled off. Every one of his watermelons was gone and he only said one dirty word and took us back home. He found out later who had taken them. He never said anything to them, but I can tell you for a fact that he watched that person mighty close from then on.

We always liked tagging around after Papa or most anyone who would put up with our silliness. We would imitate him, trying to put each of our feet where he had just stepped. Our stride was not so long and many times we would lose our balance and roll off down this hill or that.

Grandpa Hall and Sears Catalog

I had a lot of good childhood memories. I remember one time when I was five years old, Papa, Maggie, Burl, and I were visiting at Grandpa Hall's. We had been up there all that day and, just before we were ready to leave, it started raining and storming something awful— lightnin' a-crackin' 'n thunder rollin' all around in the sky.

Mama was pregnant and expecting the baby anytime now. Papa knew she and Beatrice would be scared stiff at home by themselves not knowing what had happened to us. So he left us with Grandpa and went home that night through the woods. All of the creeks were flooded and the foot logs had been washed away. The water was too deep and moving much too fast to cross the creek safely. The only foot log left that he could find was the one at the house just below the swimming hole. He made it home, thoroughly drenched, but safe. That in itself was a wonder with all that lightning and wind. You know, the woods is not a safe place to be in a storm.

71

That night Grandpa gave me a big ol' Sears Roebuck catalog to look at, the first one I'd ever seen. The next day I dragged that big catalog all the way through the woods. That catalog was so heavy, but I wouldn't let anyone else touch it. It was mine. Grandpa had given it to me. By the time we got home, I was all worn out, too tired to even look at the pictures.

My Grandpa Hall had always liked me best and never made a secret of it. I guess I was special to him because I would always want to be outside with him and follow him around, especially when he took care of the animals. He called me his little cougar and when he would stop at our house to rest on his way to town, he would give us money, a dime for me and all the rest of them a penny.

We Learned to Work Early

There was always so much work to be done to keep a farm like ours going. It was necessary for the entire family to work as a team; even the little ones had to do their share. For example, at canning time we all had special jobs. Like when we would put up elderberries. Papa would bring the berries in, the small children would pick off those fine little stems, and Maggie would help Mama make the jelly.

By the time we were five years old, we were no longer considered babies. We were old enough to get up early with the rest of the family and do our chores. One of mine was to put wood in the cooking stove every morning. Someone a little older, usually Maggie, would help with the cooking. Burl usually helped with the wood for the fireplace, and when I got a little older, I helped him. Sometimes, especially when it was time to prepare the ground to plant the crops or hoe the weeds out of the fields, we would be sent out to the fields, even as young as five or six, to work with the grownups as soon as the sun started to come up. So, of course, breakfast and chores had to be done before it was even light outside.

As soon as each one of us girls was old enough to hold a needle and thread, we were stringing greenbeans. We called beans fixed this way, strung and dried, shab beans. Then we learned to mend and sew, crochet, knit, and tat. Mama taught us a lot, and having the chapel women right there helped, too. They were interested in whatever we were learning to do and would try to help us get material, thread, and other things that we didn't have.

I haven't really kept up with any of my needlework, except crocheting. Every year I crochet myself a little cap. After all these years you can imagine I have quite a few. The caps are not so neatly done, but I crochet them so I won't forget my stitch. I believe I could do tatting yet, if I could find a shuttle.

We were all pretty good about working—Papa made sure of that. There would be no sluggards in Papa's family. We didn't complain because we knew we had to do it.

We tried to raise cotton for a few years, but it took too much time and it wouldn't get fluffy and white like the cotton you'd see in the store. It turned out kind of yellow-like. They said that was because we have such an early frost up here.

Papa and the older children picked the cotton and brought it inside, and the smaller children pulled the seeds out. Each of us was to take one of our shoes and fill it with cotton seeds each night before we went to bed. Of course, that was impossible. It was hard to pick out the seeds, but sometimes we would come close to getting our shoe full. It would depend on how easy it was to separate the seeds from the cotton. Then after the seeds were out, Mama had to card it and fix it in rows. It took a lot of time and she wasn't always well enough to be able to do it.

Charlie and Mary Pack—Mill and Store

There were all kinds of mills up and down the creek. Charlie and Aunt Mary Pack, Papa's older sister, owned the mill and store at the foot of the hill at Mt. Zion Cemetery. They owned all that land up around there. The store and Mary's house were right where the Church of God in the Name of Jesus is now. The mill was down behind the store on the other side of the creek, farther away from their house than L. Conn's[8] is from mine. He also owned land on Sand Hill.

---

8   Larry Conn Myers (11/11/55), Opal's son, converted Opal's barn into a house where he lived until it burned down. The fire occurred after Opal's death, destroying all the pictures, Bibles, and personal possessions remaining of Opal's.

The county owned the land above Uncle Charlie's, next to Mt. Zion Cemetery where Ebenezer Church now stands. At that time, however, there was a little public school there called Mt. Zion, like the cemetery, which also doubled as a church, a Baptist church. That was the first public school that was in this way, but I don't know when it was built. I know for sure it was there when I was four or five years old. Ebenezer Mission's school had been here for maybe ten years before the public school came.

Uncle Charlie would get so upset with the boys from that school because they would throw rocks at his pumpkins and do things to destroy his crops. Many years later, he finally made an agreement with the county—he traded the land that the school was located on for a good piece of his land up on Sand Hill so they could build a new school…one far from his crops.

Mama seemed to be sick a lot, but sometimes on days when she felt better, we would walk to Mary's store. Mama liked Mary and we did too because she would give us crackers and a big ol' handful of brown sugar that we would wad up into a hard lump and eat like it was candy. The crackers back then didn't come in family size packages, but in great big boxes. Mary would sell them either by the pound or a few at a time.

The store was a place people would come to socialize. There was a stove right in the middle of the store. On days when the weather was bad, the men would gather at the store. They would sit around that stove, chewing their tobacco and spitting in the ashes while they told their big tales and played checkers. That's about all the pleasure they had, and all the pleasure they needed, it seemed.

Mary was always good about helping people. Many times people would come in the middle of the night needing something, maybe because of a sick child or wife. Mary would get up and go over to the store to get the medicine or supplies, whatever they needed. She was never cross with them, but instead encouraged them while she slipped a little piece of candy or two down into the bag to surprise the children with. She was a nice woman.

One time we went down there, we saw Aunt Mary and some others sitting out in the yard with a baby that didn't have any clothes on. I thought that was just awful for that baby to be out there with nothing on but a diaper.

We started up towards the house to talk to her, but she said, "Don't be comin' up here too close. This youngun's a-burnin' up with the fever. Think she must have the diphtheria or somethin' like that." I don't remember ever hearing tell who that family was or if the baby got well. People were always coming to Mary for medical advice about what they should do or take for certain ailments.

Aunt Mary—what a hard workin' woman! She'd do it all, even when she was at the store by herself. She might be grinding corn down at the mill when a customer would come to the store and holler for her to come wait on them. She'd say, "You have to wait 'til I get this turn ground." She'd finish the turn, shut the mill off, and go help them.

One time when we were down there visiting Mary, she said, "I've got some of the best tastin', prettiest Irish taters you've ever laid your eyes on. Let me dish ya up some."

She reached down into that barrel and pulled out a plate of big Irish potatoes. "They just don't come no prettier or whiter 'n these 'uns. Don't matter if ya bake 'um or boil 'um whole, they taste mighty good."

They were good all right. I thought since she pulled them out of that barrel she had preserved them sorta like we dried or pickled food and put it in barrels. Like the early pioneers, the mountain people didn't have cupboards, so they used to keep their food inside whiskey barrels or big nail kegs, which were easy to come by. Pickled beans and corn were commonly preserved that way. With big families, there was no place to store all those inside the cabins. Most times they were put, along with other food crops, into the storage buildings.

When we got home, I exclaimed, "Mama, we need to fix us up a big ol' barrel of them taters like Aunt Mary had. They were good!"

I was surprised by her reply: "Aunt Mary didn't have no barrel full. She'd just cooked t'um up and put 'um down in that barrel so she could cover 'um up 'n keep the flies off 'til the next meal." I can still remember her giving us those big potatoes.

You had a great family, Lori. Always caring 'bout people and giving of themselves. That was my Aunt Mary. Wish you could have known her...

6
Living by Grandma Corn
1917–1918

I'd have to say it was good living so close to Grandma and Grandpa Corn. Well, I guess, there were some times we young'uns had second thoughts about that, though. You see, Aunt Florie was tall and big like Papa, and with her and Grandma always there, it was like having a couple of extra mamas around. And believe me, they treated us just like they thought they were our mama. If they saw us doing something wrong or just thought we needed correcting, they didn't hesitate a bit to get a hickory switch and whip us. That was the kind of family we were raised up in. It was like one big family and you respected your elders whether you liked it or not. Yes sir, you showed respect, and if you were wise, you learned that lesson quickly!

My grandma had definitely been one who was able to instill strong values in her children. Not only of showing respect, but the values of sharing what you have—hospitality, and a giving of oneself.

Grandma was a person that didn't get mad or yell or anything like that, but when she spoke, you just knew. You had it in you somehow to know that you had better mind her. She wasn't the type of person to argue with and yet she wasn't overly strict either. I don't know what it was about her. Maybe it was just that we were in such awe of her.

I can recall when we would come into the house from playing and have sand on our feet and she would say, "Look at your feet now." To us it was as good as she if she had whipped us. We knew to get out and get that dirt off our feet before we came back into the house. It was just a rough old floor, nothing special at all, but it was important to Grandma, so we cleaned our feet.

Suzanne Angeline Corn, my grandma, was warm and gentle, even in her strictness. When I was young, I loved my Grandma Corn more than just about anybody. I always wanted to be like her. She was Dutch, only about five foot three—around my height—but she was a lot bigger than I am. She was short and fat.

She always wore a red or blue kerchief over her head, which she tied under her chin. On Sunday she wore a white one. I don't know why. I don't know if it was just the way she was brought up or what. That's why, I guess, I've always worn a cap. I grew up thinking you had to. And then I can remember the mission people reading that part in the Bible, you know, where it says not to pray with your head uncovered. Guess that's where I got that idea and I've always worn something on my head. I hardly ever go without a hat.

After every meal, Grandma would go back in the chimney corner to smoke her pipe. It was one of those corncob pipes they used to make. She had a certain rock on the fireplace chimney that jutted out farther than the others where she kept her pipe and that strong homemade tobacco of hers. That was the only time she would touch her pipe— three times a day after every meal.

Grandma Corn loved to talk about everything. She'd tell us tales about the Civil War and her family and all sorts of things. I'd have given anything if I could have grown up around her and really have gotten to know her in other ways too. But then by the time I was in school and old enough to do things like that, she was sick. She died May 10, 1928, when I was away at school.

Grandma's Stories

Grandma had many wonderful and incredible memories of the past. She would eagerly gather us up in her arms and tell us as much as we wanted to hear about how things once were. Most of the people we knew growing up did not like to talk about the history of their families. Maybe there were too many things they didn't want known. Many were too preoccupied with the hardships of the present day to want to remember times that were even worse. Oh, but not my grandma! She built within us a love and acceptance of our heritage. Kind of like what I want to do for you, Lori.

Isn't it amazing how some people—no matter how much bad happens to them, no matter how difficult the situations life seems to hand them—can come out on the other side even stronger? That's how my grandma was.

I have two favorite stories that Grandma would tell; one about Grandma during the Civil War and the other one is about John Peter Corn and the feisty redhead.

Civil War

In 1863, when my grandma was eight, her life was no different than any other mountain child. She lived with her family in a small one-room log cabin with a half loft and a board lean-to kitchen attached to the back.

She and her sister, Mandy, worked hard helping in the fields, toting water, and caring for Jacob Able, their brother who was only one. In the evenings, Grandma would clear the table, put the food scraps into the slop pail, which stayed in the corner by the lean-to door, and carefully cover it with the rough cut board. She put the dirty dishes into the large pan of water that had been heating on top of the wood-burning cook stove since sometime before dinner. After drying the last dish, she shook out the cloth and used it to cover the leftover food on the table to keep the flies off. Lately there seemed to be more leftovers than usual, but she had also noticed that in the mornings most of them had disappeared. She first thought that her Papa had eaten before he went out to do the morning chores. But Papa had been gone a lot overnight lately, and she knew her mama never ate before breakfast.

For as long as she could remember, there had always been some spaces between the boards in their kitchen, but recently a new hole had appeared in the wall just above the crudely made table. Maybe that ol' coon had been swiping food through that hole. That thought rested lightly on her mind, causing her to be only mildly curious.

After completing her normal chores that evening, Suzanne helped her mama stack some kindling next to the cook stove. Hearing a noise, she spun around, fully expecting to see that pesky ol' coon. Instead, it was a man's hand, large and hairy, feeling its way across the table in search of the leftovers. She was about to scream, but before she could work up half a sound, her mama grabbed her from the back and placed a hand very firmly over her mouth. She looked into her mama's eyes. There was no fear there; only a look that said, "Young'un, you had best not make a sound!" They stood there quietly, and her mama loosened her grip. That hairy hand continued its search across the table, finding the jar of milk and the stack of biscuits.

Recently everything around the community was different somehow. All the grownups seemed to be sharing a big terrible secret that the children were not allowed to question. Polly Ann, my great-grandma, would stand at the kitchen window just watching, sometimes for an hour or so during the middle of the day. You see, my grandma didn't know that her mama was anxiously waiting for the neighbor man, who was a Rebel scout, to signal her. This was the Click's grandfather when he was just a young man. When she saw him wave his big ol' white hat from behind a tree, she would put on her apron and, holding up the bottom corners, would fill it with big cakes of cornbread, onions, sometimes a jar of honey or molasses, along with whatever else might be around. Then she would head out through the back door toward the pig pen calling, "Here pig, pig. Here hog."

One day my grandma asked her, "Why are you feeding those hogs all that good stuff?" Polly Ann told her to hush. Her mama was afraid those Yankees would come through here and she didn't want Grandma telling what was going on. She had heard stories and she was scared to death that the Yankees would kill her and her family for what she was doing. But what else could she do? After all, it was her husband and neighbors who were scouting for the Rebels.

Mary Webb Turner's Grandma

Mary Webb Turner, who lived across the ridge to the east of us, was closer to Maggie's age. Her grandmother also had a husband who was a scout for the Rebels. There were several times when she would cook and carry baskets of food up the mountain to feed her husband and a few of the soldiers.

On one occasion, one of the Yankee soldiers came to her house early in the morning and told her to get out every kettle she had and start cooking up a whole mess of food because there was going to be a crowd at her house for dinner. Sure enough, right at dinnertime they came riding in on their horses. Those soldiers had no regard whatsoever for other people's property or hard work. They raided the barn of hay and threw corn out of the corn crib onto the ground so their horses could eat their fill. It didn't bother those Yankees a bit to waste all that hay and corn. After the soldiers left, Mary's grandma went out and picked up all the corn kernels that were left trampled on the ground so that she could have it ground into meal. It's a wonder they made it through the rest of the year with even some food to eat. Those were hard times for sure.

Another time a man she didn't even know came running into her house. He pushed her out of his way as he told her there was a bunch of Yankees on his trail and he needed a place to hide. How he ever got in there without them seeing him she never knew. It wasn't but a moment after that man had crawled all the way back under her bed that two of those soldiers came into her cabin. One sat down on the bed and the other asked, as he glanced around the room, "Did you see a man running by here in the last few minutes? You haven't had any company recently, have you?"

"Nope, I reckon not." The quilt on the bed went all the way down to the floor, but she was terrified; afraid that man would make a move, or sneeze, or cough, or that those Yankees would turn that bed up and find him hiding there. She knew that if the Yankees discovered his hiding place, they would kill her and him both. When she was sure the Yankees had left, she started screaming at the man, "You get out of this house and don't you ever come back!"

She had good reason to be afraid. She had heard the stories. Some of the people she knew, like the family that the soldiers came upon as they were moving to a new place. Those soldiers stopped them and threw everything off the wagon, took what they wanted, and destroyed the rest. No one in the family dared to even open their mouths. They knew what would happen if they did.

Some other soldiers[9], or maybe the same ones, I don't know, had dragged a husband and wife out of their home and locked their children inside. Then they set the house on fire and made the parents stand outside and listen to their children scream and watch their house burn down and collapse on their children. Then they killed the parents. Whether they were making them pay for something they had done to help the Rebels or just trying to get information out of them was unknown. They had threatened to do the same to a man who lived just over the ridge. They forced him to scout out the farms in the area for food, especially meat. They had told him if he didn't, before they killed him, they would lock his family in the house and set it on fire while he watched. He knew they had done that to a family he had known for years, and he knew they would do it to him. He was able to make arrangements for his wife and children to be moved to North Carolina and as soon as he received word they were safe he disappeared. Everyone had always hoped that he had run off and made it safely to his kin folks.

With all these stories going around of what the Yankees were doing, soon everyone knew, even the children. And when that Yankee

---

9   Most of the atrocities during the Civil War were perpetrated by bands of marauding bushwhackers who had no allegiance to either the Yankees or Rebels. This could be true of Opal's stories of the Civil War.

soldier got killed just over on the other side of Sand Hill, in that log house that sat right out there in a field, everyone was afraid of what the Yankees might do and made plans for protecting their children and food supplies. Polly Ann sent Mandy and the baby Jacob to live with this woman who lived two ridges over and way back in the hollow. It was so far back in there that hardly anybody could find it.

The Yankees Came to Grandma's Cabin

Polly Ann had warned my grandma about the soldiers. "If you see any of them Yankee soldiers coming, I want you to hide. If you're in the house, you crawl as far back under the bed as you can and don't you be makin' a sound or even move until I tell you! Do you understand what I'm a-sayin'—not even if they come in here and kill me, you don't come out from under that bed!"

Her mama was still sneaking food to the scouts, and my grandma worried about the soldiers coming. What if the soldiers found out? What if they found out her papa was a scout?

Then one day the soldiers did come, four of them. Polly Ann and my grandma were both inside fixing dinner when they heard the horses gallop up to the cabin and stop. Grandma immediately got under the bed. She laid on the old dark quilt that had been spread out on the floor for just such an occasion, and grabbing the outside edge, she rolled over, putting her face against the wall. With the dim lighting of the small cabin, they wouldn't see her even if someone looked under the bed. As long as she didn't move, didn't make a sound, she'd be safe.

Before those soldiers had time to come to the door, Polly Ann went outside to see what they wanted. My grandma couldn't hear what they were saying, but in a few minutes she heard the door open and her mama was telling them they could have the food she just cooked. One of the soldiers asked if she had any more meat.

"This here is all I've cooked."

"Go out to the smoke house and see what's there," he instructed one of his men.

"You here by yourself? Where's your husband?" Suzanne couldn't tell what was happening. It sounded like the men had started to fight with her mama. Polly Ann would say, "Stop, you take your hands off me! Stop, you're rippin my dress!" Then she started to cry and scream. Polly Ann only had two dresses and my grandma knew that her mama would be very upset if they ruined one of them.

Polly Ann was terrified; she had heard too many stories of what the soldiers did to the community women. Some had been raped and beaten and then railed. She knew one woman they had taken outside to the rail fence, naked, after they'd all had their way with her. They had forced her to sit on the ground, putting her feet through the space on top of the bottom rail, and then put a heavy rail on top of them. They tied her hands together with one end of the rope and pulled the long end of the rope up and fastened it around the top rail of the fence, pulling her arms up as high as they would go, and placed two big rails on top, trapping her arms so that her bottom barely touched the ground. There was no one there to help her, and she died an agonizing death. Others had died too. She thought that maybe if they did that to her, she would be fortunate enough to escape death. She had Grandma there. As much as she didn't want her young'un to see her like that, she took comfort in that knowledge.

She tried to keep her mind off what was happening to her. One man was holding her down pulling and tearing at her clothes. Then they took turns with her. There was a shot fired somewhere outback. I guess it scared her so bad that it gave her the extra strength she needed to get one of her hands free. She scratched one of the soldiers as hard as she could across his face, making deep gashes there. Being marked like that made him really angry. He cussed at her something awful and then hit her in the face with his fist, knocking her out.

Grandma heard them go out on the porch where they met the soldier who had gone out to the smoke house. She could hear that soldier telling them, "I got all the meat there was and tied it on the horses. Got us a bonus too! That scout we've been looking for was hiding right there in the smoke house. That's one less Rebel we'll have to track down!" Hearing that scared Grandma near to death, but still she didn't move.

It had been quiet in the house, and it had been some time since the men left. She didn't know why her mama hadn't told her to come out. Then she heard her mama moan and the sounds of her pulling herself up into the chair. She groaned again and then called for Grandma.

Grandma was glad to come out from under the bed. "Polly Ann, they found a scout in the smoke house! They shot him, I heard them shoot him! You don't suppose it was Papa, do you?" Suzanne noticed Polly Ann's red swollen jaw. "Oh! They hurt ya! And your dress, they tore your dress all up!"

"I'm gonna to be fine. Now go look outside and be sure they're gone."

Grandma had heard the horses leave and she was sure the Yankees were no longer around. She headed to the smoke house to see how much of their meat had been taken, and as she ran down the path, she tripped over the stick the soldier had hit the scout with. She fell to her knees, and as she lifted her head, she saw him. The soldier had hit him with the stick that was used to prop against the smoke house door to hold it closed, and his head had hit a rock where he had fallen, just to the right of the path in the potato patch. The soldier then shot him in the back. Grandma stared at him in horror. It wasn't her papa. She had never seen him before. His eyes open and staring back at her, yet seeing nothing, and blood trickled out of his nose.

They buried him in an unmarked grave in the cemetery up on Persimmon Hill. He was the third person to be buried there. The first grave was that of a little girl who lived just down the road from the cemetery. After the little girl died of typhoid fever, her sister was heartbroken and in endless grief. She would hardly eat a bite, and her parents found her many times just sitting on the ground by her sister's grave. She would sit there for hours at a time grieving. She soon became ill herself with the fever and also died. She was buried there next to her sister.

Nobody else knows who the scout was or exactly where his grave is, but I do. Grandma told me about that so many times; I know exactly where it is. They buried him by those two little girls in the corner of the cemetery and I could point it out to you today, even though those three graves are unmarked.

I have always believed that the scout my great-grandma buried was my great-grandpa Hall because they were never able to locate him after the war. They claimed the Yankees took him to Chattanooga and put him in a prison camp. Even after chasing rumors and checking Civil War records in Washington and Tennessee, his family could never find any record of him being buried, nor did they have any records of him at the prison camp in Chattanooga.

It's been a long time since that war was over, but there are still reminders right around here—the house where the Yankee soldier was killed being one of them. Why, to this very day it's still called the Yankee House. And for all these years, no one would live in that house. Lawton finally bought it. He even put down a new floor to cover those bloodstains that wouldn't come out. It was a good house, but his family would never live there. Instead, he built that modest house up there in the hollow. Can you imagine, living in that tiny house when they could have been living in that nice one?

Morgan's Raiders would come though here going to and from the train stop over at Whitmore, which was later called West Myers. If you took this path out from my house through the woods, all the way to the river, you would come to the place where the troops got on the train. Of course, now there's nothing here to show that any of it ever existed except the name Morgan Gap and of course Morgan Branch right out here by my house.

I'm glad I didn't live back then. It was a pitiful time to live. How Suzanne Tobey Corn could live through all that she did, bring up all those children, and still be such a happy person, I just don't know.

Corn Ancestors

The other story that I like so well, the one about John Peter, is interesting and funny, too. It's a story about the earliest known Corn ancestors, Matthew and Molly Corn, who came to America with their son John Peter[10], who was only a few years old.

When John Peter became a young man, he fought under Washington at Valley Forge in 1777 and 1778. It is there that our first family tale begins.

John Peter was a good-looking young'un and just as full of spunk and mischief as could be. One day he was attempting to steal apples for his troops when a young woman with a gun stopped him. "Good afternoon, soldier," she said sweetly. "You wouldn't be stealing our apples, now would you?" Slowly he turned around, his arms full of apples, and found himself looking down the barrel of a gun at the prettiest young woman he had seen in some time. Her beautiful big blue eyes framed by a head full of fiery red hair stared back at him. Her tone changed. "If you want to live to see your next battle, soldier, you had best put those apples down nice and gently and walk away like you've never been here!" Well, it looked like she was full of feisty words too, so he figured he had better do some mighty fast talking. He kept begging her and talking to her about his starving men. Well, sure enough, she gave him those apples.

He had only come to steal apples, but while he was there, he stole her heart and lost his heart too. John Peter had for sure fallen in love. He told her, "When this war is over, I'm gonna come back here and get you!" He kept his word. After a short courtship, Hannah Elizabeth Parr's father gave his consent, and they were married in May of 1778. They had a son named Arthur, and my papa was named after him.

John Corn[11], the oldest grandson of John Peter, married Mary Wade Carter, the daughter of Jesse and Lavina Sams Carter, on

10   John Peter was born March 3, 1752, and died on October 14, 1843.
11   John Corn (b. October 18, 1813) was chosen for war, but in May of 1862 he resigned from the army and his eighteen-year-old son John Heatherly Corn went in his place. John Sr. owned 1500 acres of land when he died January 2, 1875. His wife Mary died January 14, 1879. They were buried on top of a hill on the right side of the highway leading from Clayton to Herivassee about one and a half miles west of Upper Hightower Baptist Church.
John Heatherly married Sarah Elizabeth Dillard, daughter of John Barnett and Rachel Matilda (McKinney) Dillard. John H. was the only postmaster the little town of Visage, Georgia, ever had. John and Sarah had a son, Sylvester Barnard born August 7, 1868, who became a doctor. John Heatherly died July 4, 1927, and was buried along with his wife and her parents in the cemetery overlooking the old homestead.

November 10, 1836. The Carters were one of the first settlers of Rabun County, Georgia, after it was organized in 1819. John Corn and Elijah Kimsey were elected as delegates from Towns County, Georgia, to the convention in Milledgeville. This convention was to decide whether or not Georgia should secede from the Union. Corn and Kimsey rode 400 miles to vote against secession, but Georgia voted to secede: 160 for, 130 against.

Grandma and Aunt Jane

When Grandma Corn fell back sometime in 1915 and broke her hip, the mission people came to see her often. They were always helping out in some way, and over the years she grew close to several of the chapel women.

After her fall, she wasn't able to get out much at all, and for the rest of her life she had a great deal of trouble walking. Grandma made the best of it, but she did not like being restricted one little bit. Being as heavy as she was didn't help the situation either. She had always enjoyed going to church and now someone had to be with her every time she got up to go outside. If she went anywhere away from the house, she would have to be taken on a sled or in a wagon.

I don't believe any of us up here, except the chapel people, had outhouses. They were still going off to the woods or behind a bush, and sometimes just around the corner of the cabin to do their business. Grandpa and Papa must have thought up some way to make that easier for Grandma.

It took a long time, but she finally got to where she sometimes could walk a little. I can remember seeing her in the field beside her house a time or two picking strawberries.

Aunt Flora and Jessie were still living at home, but they had to do a lot of the outside work and weren't always able to be close to help Grandma. Even though Aunt Winnie came several times a week to help out, everyone was glad when Aunt Jane came to live with Grandma.

Jane McIntosh was just an old lady who had no place of her own to stay. She was not really our aunt, but we usually called older people "aunt" or "uncle" out of respect. She received a meager pension from the government because of a son who had served in the army. She would always use part of her pension check to buy something to pay for staying at Grandma's.

Back then the old people were always taken care of. Usually they lived with their relatives, but if they didn't have any, someone would take them in and keep them. The older people would try to help out and, if they received a pension like Aunt Jane did, they would also help by paying or buying things for the family.

The chapel women had always been so good to help when there was any kind of sickness, but they were working day and night helping those with typhoid. Several people had already died and many more were very sick.

Mrs. Elsie A. Robinson, one of the chapel women, was a trained nurse and truly an angel of mercy during the epidemic. She went from house to house caring for those with the fever. She gave out medicine and advised the families as much as she could about trying to prevent spreading the deadly disease. She was a great lady, not only concerned about the health of their bodies but also their souls, especially those souls so close to meeting their Creator.

It was that same year when Aunt Jane came down with a bad case of the measles. Aunt Flora, Aunt Winnie, and Mama tried everything to make her better, but they thought for sure that she was gonna die. The measles are so much harder on an older person, and now, with typhoid fever spreading around the community like it was, they were afraid that she might come down with that too.

In the afternoon, Mama and Aunt Winnie had their own homes and chores to tend to. So every day after rest time, Mama would tell Beatrice and me to run down to Grandma's and take care of Aunt Jane; and Grandma kept us busy running for the rest of the afternoon. We would get water from the spring several times to take to Aunt Jane. Grandma said it was very important for her to drink plenty of water. We would wipe Aunt Jane's face and arms to help cool her off and sometimes Grandma would instruct us to sit there and watch her.

Maggie and the Needle

It was customary to have a rest time after the noon meal. The adults who had been working hard in the fields all morning would find a place to lay down while the children played quietly outside. Maggie usually worked inside or around the cabin helping Mama. She did not like to work outside, but sometimes there was so much work to get done in the fields that she simply had to.

One morning Mama had been sewing, making a towel out of a flour sack. She laid her sewing down to fix dinner to have it on the table by noon.

After dinner, everyone laid down in their favorite places. Papa napped on the floor with his head propped up in the doorway. Grandpa took a chair outside and turned it upside down and leaned up against it. Aunt Flora always laid on the bench on the front porch.

During rest time, Burl and I would scoot out to go pick apples or go down by the creek to play. Maggie, who was not as active as we were, liked to stay in the house.

On this particular day, Maggie decided to do some sewing. She had learned how to sew quite well for an eleven-year-old, but Mama wouldn't let her use the needle without asking. She only had one needle and she was afraid that Maggie would lose it.

Rest time was about over when Mama sat down to continue her sewing. She picked up the towel she was making but couldn't find her needle anywhere. She looked everywhere, and the more she looked the more upset she became. Maggie didn't say a word.

About that time Mama heard the hens cackling and went outside to gather the eggs. While she was out, Maggie put the needle back. When mama came in, there that needle was right there in her sewing just as she had left it! Mama looked at that needle and then looked at Maggie. By the look on her face, we all knew she was mad.

I laughed and said, "It was there all the time, wasn't it? You just couldn't find that needle." I knew Maggie had used it, but I was just trying to cover up for her, you know. I thought maybe if I joked with Mama, she wouldn't be so mad. I hadn't said much more than that when Papa came up off that floor and wore me out. Papa had never whipped me before. He would always tell Mama if he thought we needed a spanking and she would take care of it. I believe he was probably afraid that if he ever got mad enough to whip one of us that, because of his strength and size, he might harm us. Oh, he would take off his old felt hat every once in a while and give us a whack across the backside or pull a switch off the tree and give us a few sting marks when we were doing wrong. Even that would scare us half to death; it happened so rarely, though.

In my child's mind, my intentions were pure and I couldn't see a thing wrong with what I had said. I had been covering up for Maggie, not laughing and making fun of Mama. I thought he was terrible to me for whipping me like that. Of course, looking back, I guess that was mean of me, laughing at Mama and saying that needle had been there all along.

We knew better than to say anything hateful to Mama, but I really didn't think I was being hateful. I thought I was being funny. I certainly never did forget that lesson.

Remedies—Doctors

When Beatrice and I got down to Grandma's that same afternoon, Grandma thought I was coming down with the measles because my eyes were red and tired looking. Well, they were tired all right—tired of crying.

I told Grandma I was fine, but she seemed worried because I didn't appear to be my usual self, full of endless chatter and questions. Everyone thought for sure Beatrice and I would take the measles next, but it was actually Maggie and Burl, who were working out in the field and coming in hot and tired everyday, who got them first. Beatrice and I ended up catching the measles from them.

Poor Aunt Jane was apparently not getting any better. Then one day this man told my daddy, "Goliar, you need to go hunt for some sheep manure and use it to make her some tea. That'll fix her up right away."

Well, you can be sure Aunt Jane did not want to take that kind of medicine, but Grandma told him to go get it anyway. Grandma made the sheep manure tea, but Aunt Jane kept her mouth shut tight. They persisted, trying to talk her into taking it, and finally she drank not more than a mouthful. Sure enough, she was better in a day or two.

We sure did have some unusual treatments and cures back in those days. One common ailment was what we called "thrash." It was a breaking-out, usually in a baby's mouth. Their mouths would get so sore they couldn't eat, and sometimes the babies would even die.

Mama said that when I was a baby, she took me to a funeral up here at the Fish Place. I was crying and making a big fuss, when this old woman asked her, "What's wrong with that young 'un of your'n?"

"She's got her mouth sore."

"Thrash, I reckon. Give her to me!" The lady took me down to the barn and rubbed my mouth with cow manure. By the next morning the sores dried up and Mama said I never again had thrash. Though, they used to tease me about having cow manure in my mouth.

I told them, "I don't care what you say. I'm here and I reckon my mouth is a-workin' just fine."

We did have some mighty strange remedies compared to what's available today. It sounds awful, but it was believed that these cows, sheep, and other animals ate all kinds of herbs, and when the herbs had been digested, they turned into a medicinal form. I don't know how they came up with those ideas. There were also superstitions about what caused and cured diseases. For example, if you wanted to cure a baby's thrash, you would have to find a man who had never seen his papa. When that man blew into the child's mouth, the thrash would be cured. I never did understand that one. Though, Mama had some strange practices herself. She'd rub our mouths with a salted meat skin and then give the meat to a dog to eat. The meat skin couldn't touch the floor or ground or anything before the dog ate it. The salted meat would cure the thrash and the dog would eat the germs.

Salty meat was a common cure. Boils were common when we were little, and I still have scars from them on my neck. Mama tied salty meat to our boils as a poultice.

So many of our ailments were caused from bad diets. Of course, the chapel women recognized this and spent a lot of time trying to teach the women about proper nutrition. But many of the people were slow to accept change, if not even downright resentful of the outsiders who would suggest the need for it.

Colored People

Mountain people had funny ideas, superstitions, and prejudices about doctors, foreigners (anyone from outside the community), and "colored people." This was especially true of the old people. They were the most set in their ways, and there was nothing you could do about it. There was no reasoning, no need to argue or discuss anything with them.

A lot of mountain people never saw a colored person until they were nearly grown. When they did see one, I don't think that they felt colored people weren't as good as white people. Most of the people were just afraid because they had never seen someone with skin of a different color before. Prejudice is really just fear based on ignorance. That's all it is.

Others like Grandma Corn were more accepting of all people and considered "colored people" just another variety of human beings that God had created. They were no different than white, or red, or whatever other colors might be out there beyond these mountains.

My grandma even had a colored doctor, Dr. Branch, who came to see her when she broke her hip. My mama, on the other hand, would never have let a colored doctor touch her. She probably got those ideas from her people, as strange as they were. But then again, we rarely saw any colored people up in these parts.

My first experience with a colored person was when I ran into Grandma's doctor. I was by myself running down through the field on my way to Grandma's. About halfway through the field, I came upon this path where I saw fresh shoe prints. I thought maybe Papa had come in from the field to go check on Grandma, so I started following them, trying to put my foot in each of the shoe prints. Now of course, I had to work at stretching my short legs out to step where Papa had stepped. I was concentrating real hard at that and trying to keep my balance. Just about the time I got to the foot log, I ran right into Dr. Branch. I didn't know who he was or why he was black. All I knew was that I had never heard tell of any black people and it scared the wits right out of me. I didn't know whether I should run back home or run the other way.

Over time I realized my folly. Dr. Branch was a very nice man who truly cared a great deal about his patients. His office was in Newport, and when he came up here to visit Grandma and his other patients, he would ride the train to West Myers. From there he would walk the three miles up and over the mountain through Morgan Gap, go past Ebenezer Mission and on down the road to Grandma's place. Can you believe that he would check her and give her medicine for only two dollars, and then he had to walk all that way back! If anyone had need of a doctor for an emergency, someone would have to walk into town to get him. Usually the doctor would come right back with them.

Isn't it something how that man was willing to do all that walking to take care of a patient and charge only two dollars? Nowadays you have to travel to the doctor's office and wait sometimes hours on him and he charges you fifty dollars for just the privilege of seeing him. But not Dr. Branch. He made all the effort in the world for his patients. Times have changed—sometimes for the better, sometimes not.

7
Starting School
August 1919–August 1920

First Trip to Town

*M*y life was a mixture of carefree moments and tough times. You'll go through the same thing, Lori, but never give up. Giving up isn't in your blood. My Grandpa Hall proved that. As he got older, farming became more and more difficult for him. Finally, about four years after we moved into the cabin down from the mission, he decided to get a job in town at the canning factory. He traded his big farm up on the creek for two houses in Eastport where they moved and lived in the first house after you cross the railroad bridge. Grandpa worked as a night watchman at Stokely's and Grandma worked there too, peeling tomatoes by hand. It's funny—Grandpa would let Grandma work at the cannery, but he still wouldn't let her wash dishes or clean house. They always kept a woman in their home to do those things.

Grandpa had promised me that as soon as they got settled in, I could come to town and visit with them for a week. He talked about all the stores in Newport and how he wanted to take me to see them and get me something "store bought." He said he would take me to the place where he worked and show me all around. When I was eight years old, towards the end of the summer, my Grandma Hall came to get me. She spent the night at our place and fairly early the next morning we started our trek across the mountain and down to the railroad tracks. There we saw Miss Ricky Norton walking down the tracks towards us from Del Rio where she had gone to pick up a few supplies. Miss Ricky was an old woman that Grandma had known for years but hadn't seen for some time. Grandma was troubled about her being out by herself, just walking down the railroad tracks like that, so we waited for her to catch up with us so we could walk with her up to where she would head back up towards her cabin. Walking down the train tracks obviously unnerved Miss Ricky something awful.

Every once in a while Miss Ricky would get down on all fours, put her ear on the track, and make a series of strange faces as she listened. Then, when she was satisfied that everything was safe, we would continue down the track.

One time when Miss Ricky checked the tracks, she jumped up a-yelling, "Charity, Charity, we'd better be a-hurryin' 'cause that train's a-comin'! We'd better get to a big wide place and get off the tracks so a door won't fly open and hit us." It seemed like when I was little, people were always afraid of train doors coming open. Miss Ricky was a little more settled when we reached her cut-off place, but I remember thinking, *What a strange person this one is!*

Grandma and I walked the tracks to the underpass going into Newport before we got off and started walking on the road. I wasn't all that far from our cabin, but already things looked different than what I had left back home, even the road. It was much smoother. There were no big rocks sticking out in the middle of it or deep ruts to keep the wagon wheels in. We hadn't gone far at all down that road when I heard something loud coming up behind us. I looked back and saw this thing that looked something like a wagon but it was horseless—nothing was pulling it at all. I'd seen pictures of cars and I knew what it was, but seeing that car come up behind us—coming straight at us like that—scared me nearly to death. I started to run away from it, but Grandma grabbed my arm. The driver was some fancy man that Grandma knew. He stopped and Grandma went to talk to him, but I stayed back as far away from the car as possible. "I'm sorry, Miss Charity, I didn't mean to scare the young'un there like that."

Grandma told him about it being my first time in town, or anywhere else for that matter. I don't know what else they talked about, but a few minutes later Grandma yelled to me, "Come here, Opal, and get in. We've got us a ride to the house. Come here! Come here, Opal, we're gonna ride."

"Ride in that?!!!!!"

"Yes. Come on and get in. It'll be fun, and when you go back home you'll be able to tell everyone you rode in a car! Come on now 'n get in."

I guess that man had wanted to make up for scaring me so badly when he came up behind us like that, but instead he ended up really terrifying me. My first experience in a car should have been fun and exciting. Well, for sure, it was exciting, but not the kind of excitement I wanted. I was so scared and held on so tight my fingers went numb. I don't even remember when we got to Grandma's house that day. Don't remember much at all about that ride—only how scared I was.

My grandparents' house was big, not as big as the mission house, but compared to our little one-room cabin with its lean-to kitchen, Grandpa's house was grand. It had plaster walls and ceilings like the mission house had, and in the kitchen Grandma could pump water right into the house.

That night I was so tired that I could hardly eat. It had been a big day for me and I guess the excitement of all those "first time evers" in one day wore me out. It was the first time ever that I had been more than three or four miles from home, my first time ever going to town, my first time ever to ride in a car, and my first time ever to sleep in a big bed in a room all by myself. As soon as I put my head down on my pillow, my eyes closed and I was asleep, but—the excitement of my first day away from home was not over.

During the night, a horrible, loud noise woke me up. At first, I was so startled and befuddled, I couldn't think of where I was or what that noise could possibly be. I came out from under those covers so fast and jumped up and down on the bed, screaming until Grandpa came into my room and assured me that I would be all right. "Nothin's wrong, Little Cougar. That's just the train goin' by—does that every night at this time." When I calmed down, I remembered seeing the train track next to Grandpa's house and it all made sense.

I didn't sleep through one single night the whole week I was there. Every night I woke up because of the loud noise and vibrations that rattled the dishes and shook the house. To me it sounded like that train had cut loose from the tracks and was coming right through the kitchen. It sounded exactly like that and I never did get used to that train.

The next morning, it seemed that Grandpa was nearly as excited as I was about going into town. "First thing, I wanna take ya by the canning factory where I work. I told 'em all you was a-comin' for a visit and I wan'um all to see my little cougar!"

When we got to the factory, the first thing I saw was this great big barrel, as big as a house. "That's where they make kraut." He took me up some ladder-like stairs to a place where I could look down inside that big ol' barrel. I couldn't believe my eyes. There was a man in hip boots down in there with some kind of a fork pitchin' kraut out into a tub to be canned. I thought that was the dirtiest, nastiest looking thing I had ever seen—that man standing in the food they were going to sell for people to eat! Of course, it wasn't. Everything had been disinfected. But I couldn't imagine eating kraut coming out of a big ol' barrel like that.

After he introduced his "little cougar" real proud-like to everyone he could find, he said, "Come on, Little Cougar, le'me show you what a town is." We walked on down the street; it wasn't far into town. Everything seemed so foreign to me. The stores were wonderful! I had never imagined that there were so many things for people to buy. Grandpa took me into one store that had tables and a counter with stools in front of it. He boosted me up on one of those stools and told the lady behind the counter, "Give us two of them strawberry sodies."

"This is real tasty stuff, Little Cougar. You'll like it." He handed me one of the bottles. I remembered the chapel women warning us about drinking stuff out of a bottle but, of course, they were talking about drinks associated with liquor. I knew there was no way in the world that my grandpa would ever give me anything like that, so I took the bottle. I held it out in my hand and watched the tiny bubbles in the reddish liquid fizzle to the top. It was right pretty. I had never seen a drink in a bottle before; we didn't have Cokes or anything like that back in the mountains.

Not knowing for sure how to drink out of the bottle, I watched as Grandpa put the bottle to his lips. I wanted to be sure I didn't spill any, so instead of putting the opening of the bottle up to my lips like Grandpa did, I put the whole end of the bottle neck into my mouth, resting it on my tongue, and closed my lips around it. Then I threw my head back to take a big swallow.

I don't know what happened. That pretty red liquid shot down my throat with such force and then just exploded back up into my mouth. It made me cough and that in turn caused the soda to back right up through my nose and fly out all over me and Grandpa and the counter. My nose and throat burned so. I couldn't stand that stuff. As I spit out the rest, I thought that was the end of that "new experience"; but it wasn't. Before the soda hit the floor, I let out a burp that made my face turn almost the identical shade as the drink. It tasted even worse than when I first swallowed it, just like the sodie Mama made me drink sometimes when I was sick. I thought that it was the most terrible tasting stuff there ever was. Those chapel women, for sure, knew what they were talking about—nothing coming out of a bottle was fit to drink. Well, that was the end of my drinking. I never did drink anything else out of a bottle, not to this very day.

My visit to Grandma and Grandpa's was truly a wonderment for me. There were so many things I had never seen before, like the spigot in the yard where the water would come out. And I had never in my life seen electric lights or heard anything about them. Grandma and Grandpa didn't have electric lights in their home; they used lamps like we did. I hadn't noticed any electric lights or streetlamps in town either. That's probably because we were there during the daytime. The second night I was there, I noticed the streetlamp at the bridge down from Grandpa's. Of course, I didn't know it was electric, but I was amazed. *How could someone get up that high and light it?* I started watching for that man to come so I could see how he climbed all the way up that pole, but I could never catch him at it—somehow I was always looking at something else when he came. So on my last night at Grandpa's, I decided I would go outside and watch that lamp pole and nothing else until the man climbed up there and lit it.

Guess Grandpa noticed me going out, and after a little while he came out to check on me. He saw me standing there staring up at that pole. "What ya watchin' there, Little Cougar?"

"I'm watching for the man to come light that lamp. I've missed him every night but, I'm catchin' him for sure tonight!"

"Why, Cougar, there ain't no man comin'. They turn that light on from up in town."

"They don't neither. You know good 'n well they can't turn that light on from way up there in town!"

"They do. You just keep watching, Little Cougar, and you'll see when they turn it on." We kept on watching together and sure enough, that light came on all by itself. Grandpa told me that the power to light the streetlamp came through the wires that went into streetlight. I couldn't understand that at all and I don't guess I saw electric lights again until I went away to boarding school for my eighth grade.

The next day, after I'd been at Grandpa's a week, Mama, who at that time was six or seven months pregnant, came to take me home on the train. When we got to our stop, the conductor went to the steps and helped Mama down first. When he reached both of his arms up to get a hold of me and lift me down, I saw that he was a black man, and I was afraid of him, just like I had been afraid of Dr. Branch. I jumped clean over the steps and landed where Mama was standing. She laughed at me about being afraid of the man, but I really was afraid. Guess at that time in my life there were two things I just couldn't comprehend: how fire could come through a wire to light the streetlamp, and why people came in different colors. From the whistle stop we only had to walk three miles up the mountain to get home.

Mama's Pellagra

Mama's name was Flora Louise, but everyone called her Flora Lou-"I"-"Z." She was a petite, beautiful woman. Mama never did weigh much, and at only about five foot three or four inches tall, she looked so little standing by Papa, who was such a great big ol' man.

Mama was not a real healthy woman. She had what they called pellagra, a nutritional disease, and was a semi-invalid for years. I don't know when she got sick, but she was sickly when I was real small, as far back as I can remember. Sometimes she would be up and around almost like there was nothing wrong with her. On those good days she would do the milking and work with her flowers, and sometimes we were able to go on long walks with her.

Mama taught us well, both by instruction and by example. We all knew how to work at home and how to be a good neighbor. Mama was a quiet woman and never talked much. Sure makes you wonder where we all got our tongues! She never went anywhere just to visit or to be sociable, but if there was a sickness you could count on Mama being there to help. She was always quick to do whatever she could. She would do anything in the world for us or anyone else who needed her help. I saw her go to the homes of sick people, wash them, and do all kinds of things for them when she was sick herself. I just don't know if you could get a neighbor to do anything like that for you nowadays.

Usually, when Mama wasn't needed to help the sick, she would just sit right there at home sewing or something. She would go to church with us when she was able. Of course, Papa went all the time, just like Grandpa Corn. We knew we had to get ready to go and, for sure, we had sure better be ready and starting up the road when that first bell rang at 9:30! Nobody asked us if we wanted to go to church. Nobody told us to get ready either. We just knew.

When Mama had bad spells, she would stay in bed, but she could tell us what needed to be done. Like most children back then, we had all been trained to cook and do most everything around the house. And we always tried to do the best we could for Mama.

Even when Mama was feeling well, Papa still took care of her. He babied her, but she always watched out for him too. When Papa went out in the field to plow behind the horse or the mule, Mama would take an old quilt and some sewing and go with him. She didn't like Papa out in the field by himself. Plowing could be very dangerous; accidents could happen easily. The plow blade could get hung under a root, causing the plow to suddenly shift and hit the person guiding it, or the blade could hit a rock and bounce that rock up and over the plow. Men were killed in accidents like that, just as they are today with tractors. That was one of the main reasons why women didn't do much plowing. It was too dangerous and took a lot of strength.

When I was about nine or ten, Mama's doctor started treating her with herbs, and it wasn't long before she was up and working in the garden and feeling much better. One of the herbs he used was blood root, which he crushed into a fine powder. He wrapped it in individual doses like BC Powders and Mama kept them in the clock. She had her last bad spell in 1927 or '28 when I was away at school. This was around the time that Grandma Corn died.

Don't Get Mama Mad

Like I said, Mama was gentle and not easily upset, but if you did say something to make her mad, you had just better get out of the way. If she said "No," that was it, and if you had any idea at all of what was good for you, you kept your mouth shut. We knew better than to argue with her. And when she closed her fist with her thumb out to the side and then with a quick jerk turned her thumb up, we knew she was really angry and we didn't bother her.

Mama was awfully stern; she didn't take well to any foolishness. She was real strict on us and gave us a lot of whippings, not that we didn't deserve every one we got. There was none of this "one—two—

three" stuff that a lot of mamas threaten their children with these days. Mama didn't even think of counting. She told us once and that was a-plenty.

Mama wouldn't let us go anywhere new without first asking Papa. "Go ask your Papa," she would say. Since she didn't get out much, she wasn't always sure what kind of a family our friends might have. Some people drank and others were just plain mean. Neither Mama nor Papa were about to have us close to the likes of that.

Starting School

On the last day of August, three days before Desmer was born, Helen Ellison, Clark's sister, came by to help. She was taking some hot water off the step stove, which had a little hearth-like place around it. I was down on my knees on the hearth greasing a pan when the boy Helen was going with came in from Sunday school. When she turned around to look at him, she spilled the hot water right down on my head. I jumped up a-screaming and Mama couldn't figure out what in the world had happened to me. When they realized that my head had nearly been scalded, they rubbed lard all over it. I looked a sight I'm sure, but my head healed without even leaving a scar. I have always remembered Helen and that day very well. I started school the next day on September 1, 1919, when I was eight years old with greasy hair and a sore head.

Things had changed a little from the time when Maggie started school there. They no longer had the lower grades upstairs. Instead, they used the one big room downstairs for all ages and only used the upstairs for classes in the summertime.

My first teacher was Mrs. Dorothy Anderson from New York. Before coming to Ebenezer, she had been a mission teacher at the John Black's School in the Hartford area, not too far away, where she had fallen in love and married a local man. The mission board wouldn't allow her to stay and teach in the same community, so they were transferred to our mission.

The children who didn't go to the mission school had to go to the public school, which was down where our church is now. Back then most schools doubled as churches and places for social gatherings. The mission church was the first one to be designed and built as a church that would also be used as a school.

I had fully recovered from my episode with Charlie McGaha and was excited about starting school. Of course, to start the school year off right, what did I do first thing but get into a squabble with Miss Dorothy about a book!

Miss Dorothy had a brand new first grade reading book. It was the first new book I had ever seen. When it was my turn to read for Miss Dorothy, I wanted to hold the book for myself and feel the crispness of the pages. Miss Dorothy wouldn't let me hold it. She was just as sweet as she could be about it, but I didn't like it a bit! So I went home and told them all about Miss Dorothy and her ol' book. "How am I supposed to learn if I can't even hold the book?"

Grandpa Hall had stopped by our place and was there visiting when I came in. "Well, we can't be havin' none of that! I'll just have to get my little cougar a book all her own!" He had always called me his "cougar," I guess because he thought I was pretty rowdy. The rest of them were calm and serene in comparison to my wild, independent ways.

Sure enough, a few days later, Grandpa went and got me a book: a second grade reader. I could hardly wait to walk into class with that book. "Why, I'll show her, I reckon!"

"Look, Miss Dorothy, my grandpa got me a new book!" I spoke with a na-nana-nana tone in my voice.

Miss Dorothy took the book, looked at it, and declared, "You can't read a second grade reader, Opal."

"I can too! You just listen!" I read to her from that book without any difficulty at all, and I never did have to go back in that first reader and share her ol' book. I had a book all my own and, since I could already read, I started school in the second grade!

Lunch Time at School

Right at twelve o'clock, Miss Dorothy, Miss Marston, and the other mission workers would go down to the house for their dinner. The students would be on their own until one o'clock with no teacher or mission worker around.

We didn't have many fights or anything like that, and we seldom got into any trouble. We had been taught and we knew that we had better be behavin' when Miss Marston got back. You can't turn forty to fifty children loose for an hour in today's classrooms and say, "You be back here when the bell rings." But Miss Marston did and she didn't have any problem out of them either.

Some of the kids who lived close to the mission would go home for lunch, but we always took ours. Making our school lunch was one of Maggie's morning chores. That wasn't very difficult since Maggie, Burl, and I all shared the same lunch. She just had to fill a Karo syrup bucket with milk, wrap up three big pieces of cornbread in a cloth, and wrap up a spoon in a piece of paper. Maggie would carry the bucket, Burl the cornbread, and I would put the spoon in my pocket and bring it. During the times when Mama wasn't feeling well, Maggie would run to the house and fix lunch for Mama and eat there with her.

At school the students would sit around in groups to eat their lunches. We always sat with the Turner children and shared our food. The Turners had a lot of fruit trees on their land, so they would bring some kind of fruit every day. During the season the fruit would be fresh; at other times of the year they would bring canned or dried apples, peaches, pears, or plums. They would divide and pass around their fruit and we would break up our cornbread and put it in the bucket of milk. Then we would pass that bucket around the circle and everyone would take turns eating. We shared everything. We even shared the same spoon. By sharing our food, we usually ended up with a pretty balanced diet.

I'm sure every school has those few students who think it disgusting to share food. Our school had 'em too, thinking it gross for us to eat out of the same bucket. They were snooty little things and they would say, "Eeeyuck, you eat out of the same milk bucket with everybody else!?!"

I was always quick to answer, "Yeh! And none of us have died of any disease yet!"

After we ate, we would play games or go on a walk. One time when I was a little older, we took a hike during our lunch time right up this hill. We went over the top of the ridge and got way down to Bullfrog Crossing and got lost. I was so scared because I knew we had to get back in time for Bible class or I would be in big trouble, first from Mrs. Marston and then from Papa. Can you believe that—I had lived here for years and still got lost!

At ten minutes to one, someone would ring the bell and we would all line up at the spring to get a drink. We all shared the same cup, taking turns dipping it in the spring, or sometimes we would just pass the cup of water down the line.

When the last bell rang at one, we were to be lined up, ready to go back to class. Depending on the day of the week, some of us would be going to the chapel house for Bible class, where we sat on the floor in the living room. The rest of the students would go back into the schoolhouse. On that particular day, we made it back to school in time for our class, but missed out on that much-needed drink of cool springwater.

Christmas, Santa Claus, and Apples

As the weather got colder and the snow came, we started looking forward to Christmas. The chapel women made Christmas an exciting time, making us feel like we held a very important part in the holiday season. We would make decorations, some to take home and some to decorate the church and school. And there would be hours of practice for the Christmas program.

Our parents brought us up believing in Santa Claus. We would hang our stockings and act like we believed them, but we had already found out who Santa Claus really was.

It happened just before Christmas, two years before, when Burl and I were playing up in the barn and found two fruit jars with candy in them. One was full of chocolate balls and the other one had stick candy. A little later we saw Mama go out to the barn and bring those jars of candy inside. It didn't take us long to figure out what was going on when Santa Claus left the same kind of candy in our stockings. Of course we didn't tell her. We were smarter than that! We just went on hanging our socks each year.

The chapel women always had candy, and fruit too. Can you imagine—we had never even tasted or seen an orange before they gave them to us one Christmas. After we tasted our first ones, we started buying them as often as we could afford to, maybe once or twice a year. As I think back on it now, it was probably the chapel women who had provided our parents with the Santa Claus candy every year.

Grandpa had an apple tree that produced hundreds of big beautiful red apples. Papa had dug several right good-sized holes in the garden where we stored apples. One of those holes was for our special Christmas apples, the very best that came from Grandpa's tree. Each year Papa would put a fresh layer of straw in the bottom of each hole and then place a layer of apples on top of it. Then he added more straw and covered that with boards and then a layer of dirt. He would continue with straw, then apples, more straw, boards and then dirt until the hole was full. He would cover the top of the hole by putting a piece of sod on the top board and we would mark it by sticking a wooden stake in the ground next to the hole. We never opened the hole with the very special apples until Christmas time, but we could eat apples that were stored in other holes anytime Mama would let us. We stored potatoes the same way. We used boards as covers for about everything. Papa and Grandpa would make them out of an oak log, splitting them into boards with a froe. The froe was a very important tool. They used it for splitting shingles, splitting oak logs for wheel spokes, splitting wood for chair legs, and so on.

Our parents never had money for presents, but we still enjoyed Christmas. We had our Christmas stockings filled with apples and candy and we thought we were the luckiest young'uns in the world.

The only presents we got were from the mission. Churches in North Carolina and Tennessee would collect used toys by the barrelsful and send them to the chapel women. Then the chapel women would pick out a special toy or two for each of us and usually give them to us the night of our big Christmas program. They didn't wrap the gifts up or anything like people do now.

Sometimes the church people would send a note or Christmas card with the toys. When I was seven or eight years old, this one little girl sent the doll that I got for my present with a note on it that said, "Whoever gets this doll, please write me a note." Well, we started writing and then exchanging gifts. She would send me store bought presents and wanted me to send her holly and spruce pines. That was easy for me to get for her because we had them all over the place up here. We would send them by train and they kept good in the cold boxcars, but when they started heating the shipping rooms at the train stations they would dry out and be almost dead by the time they got to her. We have written to each other all these years. She's been in the hospital a lot the last few years, but she is still able to write me and send me cards every Christmas.

Christmas Program

Christmas wasn't all about gifts for us back then. We didn't put nearly as much stock in material things as they do today. I don't remember us ever having many new dresses. Every once in a while Aunt Jane, the old lady who stayed at my Grandma Corn's, would buy us a piece of cloth with some of her pension check. We would be down at Grandma's and Aunt Jane would say, "I bought you a pretty!" That's what she called it—a pretty.

We would take that material home to Mama like it was the greatest treasure that ever was and Mama would make us new clothes using nothing more than a needle and thread. The chapel women gave her buttons and hooks to finish some of our dresses. One time they even gave her a bunch of ribbon and lace and I will always remember the church dress Mama made me! It was a long dress that went almost all the way to the floor. It had great big ol' sleeves and was covered with lace, ribbons, and bows. Why, I thought it was the most beautiful dress in the whole world.

Usually a woman or girl wouldn't have but two dresses and we never thought about wearing pants back then. Nobody wore pants. In fact, I never wore them until after I was married and my husband went into the army. My sisters and I each had a play dress and a school dress. It was considered extra special to own a church dress too.

It was the same with shoes. Most of the children back here never had new shoes. The folks were too poor. If any child in the family got a new pair of shoes, it would be the oldest one or the one with the biggest feet and the outgrown shoes would be passed down to the next child who could wear them. I would get Maggie's shoes and Burl's shoes too; even though Burl's shoes were for boys, I would wear them to work in the fields and in the winter when it snowed.

Usually right before school started and occasionally at other times of the year, we would get clothes and shoes from the chapel. But we would all get new clothes and shoes to wear for the night of our Christmas program. Actually, they were never brand new either, come to think of it. They were used ones that had been donated to the mission, but we always called them new because they were new to us. Our new shoes would usually be a couple sizes big for us so they would last longer before they were passed on down to the next child in the family.

The mission Christmas program was similar to the ones we do up here now. We didn't have electric lights, so we would read the Christmas story, sing songs, and say our parts in the program all by lantern light—and we loved it. Every child felt special that night because we were wearing new clothes and shoes and maybe the girls would even get a ribbon for their hair.

Even I liked getting all fixed up for the Christmas program. Mama would spend a lot of time with us curling our hair on corn shucks so we would look real pretty. I remember one year the chapel had received a donation of brand new store bought winter hats to give to the children the night of the Christmas program. An ol' man handed them out and, when he came around to me, instead of handing it to me, he shoved that hat down on my head. I cried and cried because he had ruined my hair. Mama always liked us to look good and after we got a little older, she saved up and got a curling iron that she would stick right into the fire to heat up and fix our hair.

In my first Christmas program with a speaking part, I only had two lines. It started something like, "Why are you so nervous..." Then this boy dressed up as Santa Claus came in with a pair of shoes for me. My next line was, "My new shoes! And Pa bought me a new pair of shoes too!" Then I excitedly lifted my dress and pointed to the shoes from Pa, which were actually the new shoes I had gotten from the mission. Well, everybody just roared and I thought, *Wow, I was great! Everybody's laughing. I did just great!!*

Well, come to find out, I had my new shoes on the wrong feet and these particular shoes were rather big for me and the ends where my toes didn't reach curled up. So being on the wrong feet, they really turned out and kind of pointed up at the audience. I had been so excited about having a real speaking part in the program that I hadn't even noticed I had my shoes on the wrong feet until I got off the stage and got home. That's when I realized what everyone was laughing about. It didn't upset me because I knew I had done a good job.

New House

Mama and Papa had been talking for some time about building a new house just up from the cabin. Since Desmer's birth last September, there was a total of eight in our family, and it was becoming increasingly difficult for all of us to live in that tiny one-room cabin.

Our new house would be much larger, made of planks instead of logs, with two big rooms and a lean-to for the kitchen. There would be a big chimney in the middle of the house with a fireplace that would open to each of those two big rooms. That way, Papa and Mama would have a fireplace to sit in front of and we would have one in our room. Our new house would have windows, real windows, six of them, two in each bedroom and two in the kitchen. Papa was set on having the porch he always wanted—a big one that expanded all the way across the front and wrapped around each side of the house.

Very early that spring, just after I had turned nine, Papa went to the woods and cut down the trees he wanted to use for the house. He had them sawed into lumber and started building right away. He worked on the house all day long, or as much as he could every day. He knew that as the weather got warmer, most of his time would be used up planting and working in the fields, taking care of the animals and the land, and making the needed repairs to the barn.

We were so excited that year as the weather warmed and our little community started turning green. Mama's flowers were coming out all around the cabin bringing color back into the cove. We always loved it when we were able to get outside and run through the fields. At least Burl and I did. It really didn't excite Maggie much at all except maybe 'cause it got Burl and me out of her hair.

Papa worked so hard. By April, when the work had slowed down considerably, the house had been framed in with two-by-fours, the fireplaces were in, the exterior wall planks had been nailed on vertically, the floor boards were down, and roof planks were on. The only thing that had been done on the inside was the partial wall between the kitchen lean-to and our bedroom. It took a lot longer to build a frame house than to put together a little log cabin.

With all those windows, the new house was prettier than the cabin and from the outside you couldn't really tell that the house was not finished. Inside there were no interior walls or ceilings in the rooms, not even in the kitchen, so you could see the two-by-four frame, the ceiling joist, and boards used for the roof of the house.

We were so crowded in the little cabin that we decided to go ahead and move into the new house even though it was not much more than a shell. Papa had wanted to have the house all the way finished before we moved in, but that was not going to be. In fact, it turned out that it would be years before parts of that house would be done and some of it was never finished.

It was quite some time before we even had any kind of a partition between the bedrooms. It was just one extremely big room with a fireplace right in the middle. Papa never did build that porch and we liked teasing him about it. For years, on nice days after a big meal we would say, "It's such a beautiful evening, why don't we all go out and sit on that big ol' porch of ours."

He'd always come back with, "They say when you finally get your house done just the way you want it, you up 'n die. And I ain't dying just yet, so I'm leaving it like this." Why, of course, he was just teasing with us, you know.

The cabin was turned into a storage building, and then later a big window was cut in its side and it was turned into a stall. Now there's nothing left of the little cabin or all of Mama's pretty flowers, except there still may be some old yucca plants that come up. I set one out by the smoke house, and last year, when they plowed that area, they told me it was still there. I don't know if it came up again this year or not.

We were happy with our new house. Mama, Maggie, and I liked arranging our belongings in their new places. We didn't have dressers or anywhere to put our underclothes or special things, so Papa made a box for each of us that we could slide up under our beds. Burl and I made a box with a lid on it so we could lock up our special treasures where nobody could get into them. It was funny—we had a padlock but no key to lock it with. We would just pretend like it was locked up.

We didn't have closets either; no one up here did. That wasn't a problem for Mama. She went out in the woods and cut some hickory sticks about a long as a hanger. She made a little notch in the middle of each one and then she tied hay bale around that notch. Hay bale is a lot like twine except it's nearly as thick as your little finger. She got Papa to hammer some nails into the two-by-fours close to each bed. We could slip our clothes on and off the stick just like a hanger. They were so strong that you could put several coats on one hanger. Papa also hammered in a few nails that we could hang whatever we needed to on them, like our work clothes.

Sometimes when we were changing our clothes and hanging them up on our nails, one of us would think of a story we had read and we would say, "Won't you miss Mary?" and then we would all laugh.

The story was about some children who lived in an orphanage. One of the little girls had died and the teacher there asked this other little girl, "Won't you miss Mary?"

She said, "No, I won't miss Mary."

"Surely you don't mean that. Why won't you miss her?"

The little girl said, "'Cause now I'll get a whole nail to myself."

We just thought that was the funniest thing. We were always saying, "Now we get a whole nail all to ourselves."

Mama's Brother John Visits

That summer Mama's brother and four of his children came back here for a visit. No one had seen or heard much of John since he had left home and lied about his age to enlist in the army. I don't know for sure, but John probably didn't marry until after he got out of the service. I do know though that he and Hattie lived over by Cosby for a while before they moved to Chattanooga. They had five children: Mattie, Elmer, Bernie, Dallas, and Gladys. Mattie, the oldest, was about the same age as me.

I had heard Mama tell Papa that Hattie had died, but I never heard how. Back when I was little, grownups didn't talk about things like that around children. I can only guess that she probably died when Gladys was born. John was left with five little children to raise and no relatives in Chattanooga to help. There was just no way he could take care of all those little ones and a tiny baby too. He had no choice but to give the baby away. I don't know who took her in, but it was someone that he kept in touch with. I don't reckon she was ever adopted by them.

John came to our house in the middle of the afternoon carrying Dallas, who was about two years old, and a big suitcase full of dirty clothes. The other children had little suitcases full of the same. They had been traveling around visiting his folks and whatever other family his wife had and not a one of them had bothered to help him bathe the children or even offered to wash their clothes.

Mama wasn't about to let him take those children back to Chattanooga on the train looking like that. She had us tote in enough water to fill every tub and pot we had. While it was heating, she and Maggie fixed them a big meal.

Mama and Maggie gave all the children a bath and washed their hair and then started on the clothes. It was already early evening, and she wasn't sure that the clothes would get dry outside, so she built a fire in the fireplace and kept the fire going in the cook stove and opened its door. That way there would be more direct heat on the clothes. The clothes were hung on every chair, barrel, and anything else we could find. I helped Mama rotate the clothes. It was a hot job.

With all the walking John and the children had done, they were exhausted and fell asleep shortly after the sun went down. He woke up about nine or ten o'clock and said, "Let those things alone and go to bed. We'll just have to make do someway."

We wouldn't heed him, though. It always made Mama happy to be able to help someone. I guess she was mighty happy that night—we all were. We sat there in front of that stove until we got every bit of those clothes dried, folded, and packed in the suitcases. There was a clean outfit left out for each one of them, including John, to wear on the train ride home.

John later married Mattie Hawk of Chattanooga. John worked at a hospital there for the longest time, but he was forced into retirement at age sixty-one because of that lie he had told about his age. He explained how he had lied to get into the army, but it did no good. The hospital finally agreed to hire him for an outside job working in the parking lot. That got him by for three years until he could get his Social Security, but those years were hard on him. I don't know when Mattie died, but when John's health started failing, he paid some people to take him in and care for him in exchange for his retirement check. John didn't live long after he turned sixty-five. Those people who took him in didn't even let us know he had died; we found out sometime later. It's strange how people do things like that. If they're not kin to them, they just don't pay much attention to them at all.

The First Car to Come into Our Community

Most everyone in our close-knit town cared about one another; even the kids got involved. All of us girls were excited that our teacher Miss Dorothy would soon be having a baby and we loved going up to the chapel house to visit with her. She would take us to the special place she had fixed up for the baby to sleep and show us all the fancy new things she had received for the baby from her family back home. I had never heard tell of so many clothes for one baby. Her home church had sent her a baby bed and a carriage. Why, no one up here had ever seen either of those things before. No one thought of a baby having its own fancy bed, and the only carriage babies here had was a hip. There was always someone glad to tote around a baby.

For sleeping, the families here would usually just put a blanket on the floor and place the baby on it. Some people would make some sort of a box for a baby to sleep in. They couldn't just let a little child sleep in the bed because there were no such things as rubber pants and don't you just know what a mess that would make in those straw tick mattresses.

When Miss Dorothy went into labor, the chapel women sent to town for Doctor Stevenson. There were community midwives who would come to help deliver babies when they were needed, but families up here wouldn't have thought to send for a doctor. Why, Mama had her sixth young'un the fall before and the thought of having a doctor had yet to cross her mind.

That evening, when Mama was up in the barn loft pitching food down to the animals, she heard an awful roaring sound. It was Doctor Stevenson coming down the road in his car, but Mama didn't know what on earth that noise was. She thought the house was on fire and it scared her so bad that she jumped right out of that loft and went running to the house. At thirty-seven, she was a tad bit old for jumping out of barns. You know, it's just a wonder she didn't break her leg or something.

That was the first time a doctor had ever been in here to deliver a baby. Yes sir, that was a night people talked about for years. Everybody remembered the first child to be born at the mission, the first car to come into the community, and Mama jumping out of the barn loft.

Mr. Wyman Digs a Well

During that summer, right before I started the third grade, Miss Marston had Mr. Wyman, a mission worker, dig a well in the dirt floor below the pantry. He was planning to install a pump to run the water to the pantry so the dishes could be washed in the upstairs kitchen. It was a good plan, but the community people got so up in the air that they simply wouldn't have it.

They argued, "You tryin' to kill our young'uns and everybody else? Don't you know that if you drink water that comes from under the floor, it will kill you? It's just plain dangerous! They'll all be dead first thing after drinking that water."

It really would have been beneficial if he could have forced water right out of that well and into the kitchen. But the people then were still so superstitious and afraid of most new things and ideas. And when they got something in their heads, that was just it—no reasoning with them.

It had been less than two years since they had buried the last of the dead from the influenza epidemic, and now there was talk that a few cases of typhoid fever had been reported. They didn't know enough to understand the fever or its causes, and they were terrified that there would be another big epidemic. And it happened just as they feared, only two years after the influenza had laid so many to rest.

For years, some of the community people considered the mission workers troublemakers or intruders and resented being told by them about germs, health, hygiene, and proper sanitation. Now they were the ones talking about the water being dangerous!

Knowing the people, Miss Marston realized that if the mission wanted to continue helping the community in any way, this was not the time to bring in new ideas from the outside world. Miss Marston had us children carry rocks and drop them in that big hole until it was finally filled in.

There were several mission workers like Mr. Wyman who would come from various places to help out. Usually, if they were accepted by the people, they would stay around for a while, but non-acceptance from the community was a little more than most outsiders could handle. It came in the form of rejection so complete that it was as though the outsider did not exist. Greetings and words spoken were unheard. Kindnesses and good deeds were ignored. Nothing could change their feelings; they were final.

Mr. Wyman didn't stay on long after digging that well. He got so puffed up about how the people reacted to what he had done that he decided to go somewhere else. That was the thing about all these remote communities, Lori. If you proved yourself and were accepted as one of them, it was like family. But if you weren't, there was no breaking in.

8
Third Grade
1920–1921

Miss Dorothy's Baby

Everyone just fussed over little Kenneth in his pretty clothes and fancy carriage. All the girls wanted to hold him or push his carriage around, but only Annie, my cousin and one of the older students, was allowed to take care of him without Miss Dorothy there. During lunchtime, Annie would go down to the dwelling house to watch Kenneth. Then after lunch it was Annie's job to go up to the schoolhouse and ring the school bell to "take up books," as they called it. On nice days Miss Dorothy would let her put Kenneth in his carriage and stroll him up to the schoolhouse when she went to ring the bell.

Gladys and I liked to tag along, and usually Annie would let me ring the bell, probably because I was almost always the very first one to grab the rope. When I jumped on the rope, I loved the way the weight of the bell would pull me back up.

The top of the clapper was shaped like a hook and went over a rod inside the bell. If the rope was pulled too hard, the bell would hit the clapper too fast and the force on the clapper would knock it off the rod and it would fall out. We had all been warned about that many times and we knew that it could be very dangerous. Well, one day all three of us had jumped on that rope at the same time and that's exactly what happened—the clapper fell out. We thought the whole chapel schoolhouse was falling down! It was a real miracle, because when that forty-two pound clapper fell, it stuck two or three inches into the two-by-six above our heads. If it had come on down, it would have killed us or baby Kenneth, whose carriage was right under where the clapper was stuck in the wood.

I still think about that 'til yet. Whenever I go to ring the bell at church, I always think about how near that clapper came to killing us or that little baby.

Mama's Apple Tree

That little fuget apple tree that Mama planted just after we moved into the cabin had grown to a good size, but had not yet produced any apples. Finally, after we moved into the new house, Mama noticed the blossoms on the tree. There weren't many, but to Mama it was like a dream come true. She watched those blossoms. Every day, she watched those blossoms. Like the good Lord knows when each little sparrow falls, Mama knew when the fuget tree lost a blossom.

All summer and on into the fall Mama guarded that tree and its precious yield of three nice big apples. Harvest time was almost here, and those apples were the most beautiful forbidden fruit any of us had laid our eyes on. Mama had told us firmly and repeatedly, "Now I don't want a'one of you to pull the apples off that tree. I don't want you to shake those apples off or knock 'em off! I want 'em to get ripe."

Well, I couldn't stand the thought of having to wait to taste those delicious fugets that she had been talking about for years now. So one day when she wasn't home, I slipped out there to that apple tree and ever so painstakingly I tied every one of those apples to the limbs with a white string, making sure that they wouldn't fall off. And then I ate big chunks out of them, all three of them.

When Mama came home, it seemed that was the first thing she noticed. "What *happened* to my apples?!?" she screamed as she turned around and looked directly at me. And when she placed her hands on her hips and gave me that look, I knew I was in a heap of trouble.

Oh, how I wished at that moment that I had not been standing right there by her when she discovered the big bites I had taken out of every one of her apples. I had been very careful not to be disobedient and I had tied them on the tree to be extra sure. "Mama, you said not to pull them off, or shake them off, or knock them off. I, I never—"

"What?" she yelled.

"I never done a-one of those. They're right there on the tree yet!"

She couldn't whip me because she knew I had done what she said. That little tree continued to grow, and for all the years that we lived in the new house, it produced the best tasting apples and jelly.

Peas and Corn

We raised a lot of vegetables too. That year we had so many peas that Papa boxed up the sides of one of the beds and poured the peas in there under the mattress until we could get them all shelled. It takes a long time to shell peas, especially that many.

Of course, now I was always one to look for better ways to get a hard job done while having fun at the same time. So, whenever Mama would leave the house for a few minutes, we would jump up on the bed and dance on those peas. Our dancing shelled them out and we didn't have to do a-one of them by hand. All we had to do was pick the hulls out.

In the fall, we gathered in our corn, shucked it, and after it dried, we would shell it. Every morning Burl and I got up early to take a turn of corn to the mill. We'd each put about half a bushel of corn in a sack and carry it over our shoulders. The teachers understood that even the young children had chores to do. And Miss Marston didn't care if we were late as long as we got back in time for arithmetic class.

We would try to beat everyone to the mill so we'd get ours ground first and get back in time for class. Sometimes Uncle Charlie would let some older person go before us so they wouldn't have to wait so long, even though we'd gotten there first. That would get us so mad; he was supposed to grind ours first if we got there first. I thought that was like a law, like a promise. You had to do what you were supposed to do! You had to take your turn!

The mill took out an eighth of the grain as a toll. Sometimes Uncle Charlie would tease us and make us think he was going to take out three or four tolls and we'd fuss at him.

Winter in the New House

At first the new house was pretty good. We loved all of our windows and the way the light filled the house. Everything seemed more cheerful when we could see the outside—the trees and Mama's flowers. Many times in our former cabin we had to use lanterns even in the daytime to be able to see, especially when the weather was bad and we couldn't leave the door open. Our cabin may not have had pretty windows, but it had been warm in the winter where our new house was cold.

All the wood was green when Papa built the house. It never occurred to him what a problem that would be. During that summer, the green wood started to dry out and by the time winter came, there were spaces between the boards big enough to stick your fingers through.

Our new house did not hold the heat at all. By bedtime it would be so cold that we would have to stand in front of the fireplace to change clothes for bed. It was a tempting thought to climb into bed without changing into our gowns, but I don't know what Mama would have done if she had caught one of us trying to go to bed with our clothes on. We wore the same clothes every day for school and then when we got home we changed into the same work clothes we had worn the day before. Mama was strict about our clothes and how we took care of them. No matter how tired we were or how cold it was, we had to pull off everything and put on our night clothes. Then we would pick up the clothes we had just taken off, hurry to hang them up on our nail, and quickly jump under the covers as fast as we could.

I slept against the wall in a feather bed and Maggie slept on the other side of me. Our bed had a big long bolster pillow that went all the way across the top. I'd put that pillow under the quilts, lengthwise down between the cold wall and me. That extra insulation made it warmer, like sleeping with someone between me and the outside. Then I would pull the quilts up over my head, leaving just a little tunnel so I could breathe fresh air.

By the time we woke up in the morning, the fire had died down to nothing but coals, and the inside of the house would be freezing. When it snowed during the night, the snow would blow right in through those cracks in the walls and in the morning there would be a blanket of snow on the beds and floor.

We would wait for Papa or Burl to build up the fire. When the fire got going good, we would then take turns running to dress in front of it. If it had snowed during the night, we would slip out of bed carefully and shake the snow off our quilts before it melted, being sure we didn't get snow between the covers. There would actually be enough snow on the floor to track us to the fireplace.

We didn't pay any attention to the person dressing or worry about privacy. But then, on the other hand, with eight people living in the same two-room house, we probably didn't realize what privacy was. We just stayed in bed with our heads covered up, trying to keep warm until it was our turn to get dressed.

During the day, the heat of the house would melt the snow and dry the quilts. The next night we'd curl back in bed and it would snow again. It seemed to snow a lot more frequently and the snows were deeper back when I was younger. We soon started stuffing rags and paper in the cracks between the wall planks to keep the snow and sharp winter wind out.

Mama never complained about the coldness of the house; she never said a thing about the cracks between the boards. Cold weather was not surprising in the wintertime, but we did expect it to be at least a little warmer inside than it was outside. We weren't brought up to complain about something you couldn't change. Not much sense in it. We were told, "Don't be complainin'! If'n ya can't find a way to make it better, keep yaself quiet about it."

We wanted our house to look neat and pretty. So at first when the walls were new, we didn't want to ruin them by pasting any ol' kind of paper we could find over the boards like many of the other folks around here did. But it wasn't too long before we decided it was better to be warm than uppity. First, we pasted paper all over the north wall. Before winter was over, we had paper covering every single one, just like everyone else. We even nailed rugs to the wall. After all, things were difficult enough in the winter; there was certainly no need to freeze to death inside your own house.

Even in the winter the children walked to school. Most everybody wore big ol' heavy shoes that they got from the mission. We'd call them "little boots," but they weren't really boots; they were just heavy shoes to keep the snow off your feet.

Since we lived so close, we didn't miss much school because of snow. When several inches had accumulated overnight, Papa would take a broom and walk before us up to the chapel, sweeping a path up the road so we wouldn't have to get in the snow. Papa would also sweep the boardwalks around the dwelling house for the chapel women. That's the kind of man your great-grandfather was, Lori.

Miss Frances Marston

Come a real bad day, when most of the children couldn't get to school, those of us who lived close would go to the dwelling house.

Our teacher, Miss Frances Marston, had come from England with her family when she was twelve years old, and had lived in several different places growing up. She had seen so many things and met so many different people. Why, she had even worked with the Indians in California. Her papa was in some way connected with Maryville College and her brother had a flour mill at Bridgeport. Miss Marston was an older lady who never married and seemed quite content doing mission work.

Somehow Reverend E. V. Tadlock, who was then head of the Presbyterian mission schools, found out about her and was able to convince her to come and head up Ebenezer Mission. Miss Marston was a great teacher and I'm so glad she came to our community. She gave us all a sense of purpose, and encouraged us to follow our desires. Many lives were greatly changed because of her. I know, because I am one of those. Of all the people I have ever known, Miss Marston was the most influential.

On those very snowy days, we would stay inside the dwelling house where it was nice and warm. We could read or look at pictures in the pretty books from the bookshelf. "Pretty books" —that's what we call the books that had a lot of pictures of beautiful places, animals, and things we had never seen before. Sometimes we would write in our journals, and other times we would just meander around, but she wouldn't let us talk.

My favorite thing to do on those days was watch Miss Marston draw or paint. Sometimes she would even show us how to draw things or she would show us other paintings she had done and tell us stories about them. She had some of the prettiest views of the mountains and other places she had been. I'd like to sit and watch her and listen to her talk of those other places while she shared her wonderful stories about all kinds of things. We all thought she talked quite odd, of course, with her accent, which was different than the other chapel women.

She told us about Shakespeare, and the cottages in England with their flowerbeds and herb gardens, and about battles that had happened in England and France. She talked about far away places, and kings and queens in such a casual way, like they were just everyday things. We knew all about the Queen of England and the royal family and Windsor Castle.

Through her stories and tales we traveled the world. We talked of those places and things just like you'd talk about going to Gatlinburg. She created every detail, making our world so much bigger. We were familiar with the world and some of its history before we even studied history in school. We learned a lot more than the students at the public school.

Miss Marston told us make-believe stories too. She called some of them parables and explained how Jesus had used parables to give us a truth with a deep hidden meaning. Somehow her stories always made you think and wonder. Some stories, like this one, I've remembered all these years.

Miss Marston's Parable

"Once upon a time in a land far away, there was a young boy who was a prince. But this prince was not free. His palace had been captured by a cruel enemy who made all the people slaves. The prince was locked up in the palace and forced to work as a servant. He had to work very hard and do things that no other prince would have to do.

"Many times the young prince wanted to complain or do no more than what was required of him to stay alive. But somehow, deep down inside, he knew that he must learn all that he could about everything. Someday he may have an opportunity to escape, and with whatever knowledge he had, he would be able to come back and set his kingdom free. And that's just what happened."

This was how Miss Marston explained her parable: "Sometimes in our country, and even in our community, we can have a cruel enemy too, but our enemy is usually not other people. Our enemy can be sickness and disease, it can be poverty and hard times, it can be ignorance and superstitions. Our enemy may be not having an education.

"So, like the prince, we need to know who our enemy is. Then we must learn all that we can about everything. We must be ready to escape from our enemy so that we can help set the people of our kingdom free."

Germs

The mission people were the first ones we had ever heard talk about germs. Miss Marston had a big poster of a man standing by a tree looking like he was scared to death. There were two little girls on the other side of the tree pulling each other back. The man had just spit on the ground and in the spit there were big ugly germ-bugs with mean faces running around.

There was a caption where one little girl was saying, "Where's your hanky, Mr. Man? Aren't you old enough to know if you spit on the ground like that it spreads disease around?"

The other little girl said, "I learned that in the first grade."

Miss Marston had other posters about holding a handkerchief over your mouth. I had never before heard of germs and I had never seen big posters like that. It was about this time that all the students were given their own tin cup. I guess those posters did what they were supposed to. I'm getting close to eighty years old and I still remember those germ-bugs.

Brush Your Teeth

The chapel women taught us to be careful about washing our hands and told us we should always brush our teeth after eating. That was pretty much out of the question since we had never seen a toothbrush. They thought it was something awful and I guess they wrote off to some churches telling of the need. Before long we had toothbrushes.

Up until that time, if we wanted to clean our teeth, we broke a small twig off a tree and chewed the end until we had made a little brush. We would then turn over the stove eye and rub plenty of soot off into the twig and we were ready to brush our teeth. It made them nice and white. Of course, we did have to rinse a lot to get all the black out of our mouths. Most of the older women used snuff instead of soot. You never heard tell of people going to the dentist. I don't know what the chapel women thought of our method of tooth brushing. Probably not much.

Those poor chapel women, what they must have thought at times. Life was so different back in here, different than anything they could have ever imagined while sitting in their fancy churches back home. Guess most of the city church people felt safe and secure, probably even spiritual, sitting in their padded pews.

Each year churches would send mission workers to help at Ebenezer; most of them had no idea of what they were getting into. It took more than pity and a-tugging at the heart. It took even more than commitment and determination or devotion. It took a deep love and acceptance of the people. That, I'm convinced, only God Himself can give. Miss Marston and Mrs. Henderson had that kind of acceptance. Even though they didn't agree with how the people lived or what they did, they were always able to show real love and acceptance.

The chapel women didn't approve of using chewing tobacco, snuff, or alcohol. They thought it was terrible. But even though they thought so many things like that were a sin, they never rejected the person doing the sinning.

Miss Marston told us about a man who wanted to quit chewing tobacco. He really wanted to quit, but he didn't know how to stop the fierce craving he had for it. Then one day he decided to put a big ol' twist in his pocket and every time he wanted tobacco, he'd get it out and look at it. He would turn it over and over in his hands and then talk to it: "Do you think I'd let a little thing like you boss me? No, you're not going to boss me any more!" And he'd put it back in his pocket. He finally quit.

Almost all of the women used snuff or chewing tobacco back then, even Mama and Grandma Corn. Mama started a lot younger than most. As a baby, she had a problem keeping her food down. When she was about eighteen months old, they started giving her chewing tobacco juice as a medicine. I imagine you can figure out just where that tobacco juice medicine had to come from. It worked, so they kept on giving it to her. Mama would never let us use any of that stuff even though she did.

My grandmother would only chew tobacco that they had harvested themselves. She wouldn't think of using store-bought chewing tobacco. She'd take a tobacco leaf and rub it on both sides until it was soft and smooth. Then she would take it and twist it back into her mouth. She claimed it cleaned her teeth. I don't think she ever saw a dentist in her life; he would probably have told her differently.

After the influenza and typhoid fever epidemics, and with all the other everyday illnesses around here, the mission workers really worked hard trying to teach health to the people. It was so important and the people knew so little.

The mission workers encouraged the community people to build outhouses and to use chamber pots at night. We had always made the bathroom wherever we were at the time. At night we would step outside, maybe around the corner of the house, and go. The public school sent the children to the woods, even years later when I was teaching. Sometimes there might be a particular place where people would go to the bathroom, like the men would go in the barn and the women in the chicken coop.

The chapel women were always going on about worms and how you had to be careful because worms would make you sick. We had never worried about worms because Mama always fed us pumpkin seeds. If you ate ground up pumpkin seeds, you wouldn't get worms. So we were told.

There were still many people who didn't like these outsiders, "them fur'n ers," as they were called. It was not that the mission workers were unlikable, but rather that they were from other places and had different ideas. Some didn't like the way they were so particular about the water or germs, and some could never bring themselves to trust them.

Donations

The chapel women would write back to their home churches and ask that they send different items. The most commonly requested items were clothes, shoes, toothbrushes, hairbrushes, and books. There were several different denominations represented, but most were still probably from Presbyterian churches. Most of the men's clothing donated to the mission was from the wealthy lawyers, doctors, and businessmen of the Presbyterian church.

It was a funny sight to see the men out in the field plowing behind the ol' mule all gussied up in white dress shirts and black or navy vests.

Many of the men and women enjoyed wearing the fine felt hats to shade their heads from the sun.

Weddings and Playing Preacher

Many children had to walk for miles to attend Ebenezer. The children of Jake Hall and some of the Bullingtons walked from near Chestnut Gap. Roy Metcalf and the Myers boys walked from David Carvers; the Frances Click children from up the creek; the David Turner children, the Foxes, and Turners from the T. Hollow; and even the Tobys from Sol Messer Mountain. From time to time, the mission kept some of the children who lived too far away to walk.

Being so close to the mission school, I always had a lot of children to play with. Several of them lived right around here. Like Mont McMahan, who lived in the house where L. Conn lived until he was twelve years old before they moved away to South Carolina. They moved back later, just down the road, and he ended up marrying my baby sister Desmer.

Minnie Fish, the granddaughter of Marion Fish, lived just up the road from us. She was a lot older than I was[12], but we played together with the other children all the time. At the time, I didn't think about how strange it was for someone nine or ten years older than us to want to be around us all the time. Minnie was odd, but it didn't matter to us. We still had fun playing together. Minnie and I would always be the preachers. We put on pants to preach so we would look like men.

One of our favorite preacher activities was marrying people. I guess we started doing that right after the first time we *almost* saw a wedding.

Burl was coming from the chapel when he first saw them. He came running after us loudly a-yelling, "Come here right quick! Come here right quick! Victoria Hall and Regan Jennings is fixin' to get married out here! The preacher's a-standin' up on that ol' stump by the road just a-talkin' away at 'em."

---

12   Minnie Lee Fish was born April 15, 1893. This made her eighteen years older than Opal.

We went flying back down there. But I guess they had already been hitched up because by the time we got there the preacher was sitting on the stump with Victoria and Regan just talking.

Minnie said she had heard that the bride and groom had to jump over a broomstick to get married. So that's how we did it. Whichever one of us was pretending to be the preacher would dress up in pants, stand up on a stump, and say a few things we thought a preacher should say to the bride and groom. Then we made them jump over a broomstick. Why, we married Victoria Hall and Regan Jennings for years after that.

Minnie lived sort of across the road from me. Coming down from the church, which was farther up in the hollow, you would walk by the mission house, which had a fence around it with a gate in front. There used to be a big ol' weeping willow there. Just outside the gate a little ways there was a path that went up and around the hill to the Fish place. I lived down the road from the mission on the other side of the road. Years later, Miss Minnie had a house on the other side of the creek.

Minnie's brother had a big ol' squirrel cage with a big wheel in it. He would catch squirrels and put them in there. After school, the children liked to stop there on the way home to watch those squirrels run around, making that wheel fly round in circles.

When Minnie's brother married the Pack girl, Minnie and I watched with special interest, but we didn't know that we weren't watching the real wedding. I don't know if it was a practice or if they were just goofing around. But the man that looked like he was the preacher started talking to the bride and groom and he ended by saying, "Now in all kinds of stormy weather, I join this minner and gimmer together."

We just couldn't believe that they didn't have a broom to jump over. It was most unusual, after all—you couldn't be married unless you jumped over the stick.

Well, now that we had seen a wedding up close we could marry Victoria Hall and Regan Jennings up right. To all our play weddings we added, "Now in all kinds of stormy weather, we join this minner and gimmer together." And we still made them jump over the broomstick.

I guess it was years later before we realized that they had been making fun of Minnie's brother, calling him a "minner" because his last name was Fish.

Minnie had an older sister with the same name as me, Opal, who married Frank Turner. Minnie said that they got married at their home. The people put Opal in a tub and carried her all the way down to the end of the lane. They put Frank on a rail, made him straddle it, and carried him like that. They also made them eat dried pumpkin.

That's what they called shivareeing. Doing things like that was a local custom back then. Sometimes the bride and groom's friends would go home with the couple the night of their wedding and they would stay there sitting around aggravating the new couple all night long, giving them no peace or privacy; they intended not to let them go to bed. They finally quit that tradition when I was away at high school.

I made up my mind when Minnie told me about her sister that I would never put up with that. Custom or not, I felt it was stupid.

Isn't it interesting how Minnie and I spent so much time playing church and then years later the two of us were the main ones to hold the church together after the Presbyterians pulled out? We preached, taught Sunday school, and held Christmas programs, but, of course, we never did perform any weddings. I reckon God puts some things in your heart early in life and we didn't have a clue how He might use it in the future. Just like planting a seed, it takes time for it to grow into what it was meant to be.

Scalding and Scouring

Once a year, almost always in early spring, we had what Mama called a "scalding and scouring." The chapel women called it spring housecleaning. The entire family worked all day; even Papa took the day off from working in the fields to help.

Mama and Papa got us all up at the first light of day. We woke to the smell of breakfast, which would be our only hot meal of the day. During the rest of the day we would eat leftovers from the extra large batch of biscuits, cornbread, and sausage. Sometimes we would have canned apples or something like that, and molasses to sop the biscuits and corn bread in.

Papa and Burl would carry in enough water to fill the two big wash pots that had been placed on the stove. While that water was heating up, we would take everything we owned outside. Every piece of furniture, all the food, all the clothes, everything right down to the last piece of string went out.

First they would scald everything overhead and then the walls. The older children would go to the branch and start getting sand. We would need gallons of it to sprinkle all over the floor. Mama would mix up a strong solution of lye soap and scalding water into which Papa would dunk the homemade broom and then scrub the floor. When he finished scrubbing the floors, they had to be rinsed off. It was important to get this part of the cleaning done as early as possible so the floors would have time to dry. A hot fire in the fireplaces in the evening would finish drying the floors.

Next every piece of furniture had to be scalded. They paid special attention to the beds because they were afraid there could be bed bugs. The straw ticks were emptied, scalded, and then after drying refilled with fresh straw.

The straw ticks were changed like this more often on the younger children's beds. You can just imagine what it was like to care for a baby with no rubber pants. They would wet or mess in their diapers, which were just large square pieces of cloth or rags. It could run all over and it didn't take long for their beds to smell. That's why having a special little box bed for the young'uns was such a good idea. It could be washed out more often.

By the time everything was moved back into the house and put in its place, we were all pretty tired. The younger children would fall asleep as soon as they got into their fresh beds. The older ones would sit around the fire with Mama and Papa. Sometimes we would sing songs, old mountain songs or songs from church.

My parents were pretty nice people. I never heard them say a cross word to each other. If they ever did have any problems, they kept them to themselves and never said anything about them.

They say that nowadays most married people have problems over money. We didn't have any trouble over money in our family. My parents didn't have any of that to fuss over. Mama had the dollar a week that she earned for washing clothes for the chapel women. We knew that was all she had, Papa knew that was all she had, and there just wasn't anything else to say about money.

Mama and Papa weren't too openly affectionate toward each other. She sat in his lap sometimes, but she usually didn't get much of a chance because we were always sitting in it. He always had one or two of us in his lap as soon as he came in. Sometimes, like after "scalding and scouring" day, he'd say, "Young'uns, I'm tired. Get down." We'd get down a few minutes, then we'd be right back up there. We sat in his lap all the time, right up until we were too big to fit.

After that first "scalding and scouring" day in the new house, Mama stayed up after we all went to bed. She walked around the house probably thinking and planning how she was going to fix up this or that. She really did like her house in spite of the spaces between the boards. She would find a way to fix it. It was home.

9
Fourth – Sixth Grades
1921–1924

Playing in the Franklin House

We all had a considerable amount of work to get done, but as all young'uns do, we always found time to play. Miss Marston would let us girls play in the old Franklin House, which was used to store clothing and other donations. It had not been used as a bunkhouse since Frank Turner got a scholarship and went off to high school in 1915 or 1916. Miss Marston gave us only one condition—we were not to allow any boys to come in when we were playing inside.

One time several of us girls were in there looking for anything that we could use for playing house. I was standing close to the door when a boy tried to come in. I told him boys were not allowed, but he still tried to push his way in.

"Miss Marston said that you couldn't come in here," I announced with authority.

"I don't care, I'm comin' in anyway!"

Well, all I can say is that I warned him twice, then I hit him in the head with a syrup bucket filled with pieces of broken plates. I mean to tell you, I just turned around and slung that bucket at his face.

Miss Marston had told us, "No boys! Don't you let them come in." We meant to do just what she said, and that boy had a face to prove it. He had big patches of cuts all over his face after that incident.

Miss Marston never said a word about me hitting him. Could be that he never told her what happened.

Sunday Afternoons at Grandma's House

Every Sunday after church, we would all go down to Grandma and Grandpa Corn's place for dinner. It was just like it is at my house now. Anyone who wanted to come could. Everyone was treated like family; whether they were or not, it didn't much matter. I grew up thinking I had a much larger family than I really did.

We would start the cooking and baking on Saturday. Sometimes we would go down to Grandma's to cook and sometimes we would cook at our house and take food down there. Most people who came brought something for the meal; some didn't.

If there was a preacher down at Sand Hill, Papa would bring him. Preachers from anywhere always knew they were welcome. All the girls from up the hollow would come with us. There were two Click girls, two Myers girls, and Cletus came with us one time. All of them were teenagers, close to Maggie's age. They were getting to that age where they just wanted to sit around on the porch and look at magazines or swing in the swings. If they felt like getting out and doing something, they would usually walk down and sit by the spring, if you could call that doing something.

There weren't many girls my age. I was younger, but I preferred playing with the boys anyway. Every once in a while the girls would go with us up on the hill and play stink base, but there was just no way that they would ride the calves with us.

When we played stink base at school, most of the time we'd play girls against boys, because it was easier to keep up with and know who was on your side. A lot of times when you were playing you'd get so excited you'd almost catch yourself ... you know.

Stink base was one of our favorite games, but in no way did it compare to riding Grandpa Corn's steers with the boys. There would be George and Clark Ellison; John and Ben Myers; the two Click boys; Harrison, Roy, and Nathan Corn, Uncle Jessie's boys; Clyde Pack; Burl and me; and others would come from time to time. We would ride calves all Sunday evening. We just loved riding the steers.

Guess the only way you could tell me from the boys was that I had to wear a dress. The skirts were full then and about mid-calf in length, but they certainly didn't stop me from getting up on a calf as fast as any boy.

Teasing the Bull

We had one mad bull up on the hill that we enjoyed teasing. We had been told that anything red would make bulls furious, and we were not satisfied until we had found the brightest red piece of material we could. Every Sunday we would go up there and shake that red cloth right in front of that ol' bull. It didn't take all that long to get his attention. When he charged us, we would take off running around behind the cedar tree and climb up in the apple tree to hide before he got there.

That bull never did look up, so he couldn't see us in the apple tree. He thought that we were behind that cedar tree somewhere. He would keep butting that cedar over and over until he forgot why he was doing that in the first place. We would laugh about how dumb that bull was.

Papa got real upset with that bull for ruining his cedar tree. It had been a right pretty tree until that dumb bull butted it all to pieces. Of course, we never did let Papa know why that happened to his pretty cedar. Don't know for sure what Papa would have done if he knew we had caused all that damage.

I was pretty good at playing games and I could usually beat the boys because I could outrun most of them. Sometimes we played less active games, like marbles. We actually played marbles a lot; we called it "rolly hole." Children don't play marbles much anymore.

Playing House

The other girls liked to play house and dolls more than I did. Once in a while, I'd play house with the girls, but even then lots of times the boys would play with us too. We would make play houses and furnish them with old dishes and glasses or whatever we could find. The older children would be the parents and the younger ones would be their children. We had different families and each family had to make their own house. Maggie and Leonard would be the Mama and Papa of one family; Ed and I would be their children. Burl and Ethel would be the Mama and Papa of another family with Audie and the others as their children.

In the early spring, if the hog house wasn't being used, we'd get lots of water and scrub it out real good and that would be one of our houses. When we'd all go to the Turner's to play, our house would be in their barn. We'd play like that sometimes for weeks at a time.

Swinging on Vines

We also liked to run and play around in the woods. We were all the time chewing the leaves of a plant we called mountain tea. It didn't grow very tall but it was just as green as could be. All of us would put a few of the leaves in our mouths and chew them. It tasted like teaberry gum. We swallowed the juice and then spit out the leaves trying to imitate the way men and some of the women would spit out their tobacco juice.

We did a lot of things that would seem pretty strange to kids now. We'd chew on the inner birch bark. Why, that birch sap tasted real good. We even used to chop big ol' places in birch trees and then get down and lick the sap. We liked chestnut sap too. One time Papa was building a fence rail out of chestnut logs. After he'd cut the logs to the size he wanted them, Burl and I would peel off the bark on one side and then we'd crawl down and lick all of the sap off. When we finished with that side, we'd then turn the log, peel the other side, and lick that one.

When we played up in the woods, we would make jump ropes out of grape vines. Two of us would hold the ends and swing the vine and the others would jump. When you missed, you would have to hold the vine. Sometimes when the vine hit you just right, it would knock your feet right from under you.

Whenever we found a strong vine, we would cut one end loose and grab onto the end hanging from the tree and swing. Sometimes our weight would pull the vine right out of the tree and we would land on our bottoms. Of course, our favorite way to swing was out over the edge of a steep bank. This was a lot more fun than swinging in a flat place. Sometimes we would swing out over a bank where we would actually be at the tops of the trees in the valley below us. We loved doing that. We never did think about just how dangerous that could be, but naturally, our papas did and they didn't like us doing that at all. They would warn us about swinging out over the banks or across gullies, but they never did find out who was doing the swinging. Whenever Papa or one of the neighbors found a swinging vine, they would cut it off. They couldn't seem to stop us and they were afraid that we'd get killed. It's a wonder someone didn't.

Papa had fixed us rope swings in some of the trees around our house. He had even tied planks to the rope so we could sit and swing. Maggie and some of the girls liked that but we thought it was pretty dull.

I wasn't your typical girly type. I never had many dolls. In fact, I don't remember having but one store bought doll until I was a big girl. Mama made us some dolls stuffed with sawdust and I enjoyed fooling with those. But come to think of it, the only time I did that was during the winter when the weather was too bad to play outside. I liked other games a lot more. I guess I got used to being around Burl and Jessie's boys and liked them better.

Working at Grandpa Corn's

During the summer, Burl and I spent nearly all our time during the day working down at Grandpa Corn's. Grandpa would put us to work out in the cornfield—Burl on one side of the field and me on the other. We were to each hoe down the row until we met in the middle. To aggravate me, Burl would stop hoeing about three or four hills short of the middle and when I would fuss about it he would say, "Now you know them hills is yours!"

"They're not either mine," I defended myself. "This'un right here is the middle so you had best be gettin' yourself busy 'n hoe to your side of this hill."

We'd get into a lot of silly arguments like that. Then Grandpa Corn would get after us and sometimes make us go all the way back and hoe the other one's row of corn. I don't know what made us do that. I guess we'd just do it for the pure mischief of it, or maybe to see what Grandpa or the other one would do.

Sometimes Grandpa would give us each a section of the corn field to hoe by ourselves. I would work fast to get my part finished so I could lay down at the end of my last row and go to sleep while I was waiting for the rest of them to finish up. Sometimes we worked so much at Grandpa's that it seemed like we only went home to sleep.

Watching Aunt Winnie's Boy

Quite often my job at Grandma's was to watch Estus, Aunt Winnie's boy, so she could help out in the fields. Estus was almost seven years old but he couldn't walk. Most of those in the family thought that Estus was damaged at birth. Ya see, when Winnie was pregnant and close to her time for giving birth, Uncle Hugh was worried about her being at home alone with Swanie while he was out working in the fields. He came up with the idea of using the shotgun as a signal. He told Aunt Winnie, "If your time comes when I'm out in the field and you're ready for the midwife to come, I want you to go outside and shoot the shotgun as a signal." So, when Aunt Winnie started labor, she did exactly that.

Winnie had twins, Estus and Lestus. Lestus was either stillborn or died minutes after he was born, and Estus was born with a nervous condition. As a baby, Estus was so nervous and skittish that you could put a feather down in the doorway and he wouldn't crawl over it. He'd stay there in the house all day. He was scared of everything. No one knew, but they all suspected that her shooting that shotgun had caused it.

I know that it wore Aunt Winnie out trying to keep up with him and she looked forward to coming over to work at Grandpa's during the busiest parts of the season. She and her older son Swanie would work along with Burl and Grandpa in the field and I would usually play horsie with Estus by crawling back and forth on my hands and knees while he rode on my back. He was too big for me to carry any other way.

One day when I was there taking care of Estus, Dr. Branch came by to see Grandma. He noticed that Estus wouldn't walk and asked if he could check him over. That's when they found out that he had rickets. Dr. Branch told them to start feeding him Vitamin D. It wasn't long after that when he started walking. Estus was always short and fat. Even though he was extremely nervous, his mind was good and he learned pretty well in school; his grades were real good in high school and he was always nice to be around.

Things like rickets and other nutritional diseases are diagnosed early now, but back then the people up here in the mountains never bothered about taking their children to be checked for anything. No one was aware of the need for nutritious food, especially for babies and young children. The chapel women had done their best to teach the people, but so many of them never really understood. Most were so poor that even if they knew better, there was no way for them to make changes.

Babies were fed whatever there was to eat and the parents were grateful they had that. The diet for babies back then was finely mashed up pinto beans, corn bread and milk, and gravy. Sometimes they'd give them fatback meat to suck on as a pacifier. During apple season, most families would have stewed apples. We ate Aunt Winnie's canned apples all year round, but they didn't think of fruit as being especially good for a baby so they never gave them any.

All the babies did have the advantage of being breastfed. How long depended on what kind of work the mother had to do. If the mother worked close to the house, she might nurse until the child was two or three years old. But if she worked in the field, she would probably wean him early so she wouldn't have to come in to nurse. Whoever watched her baby while she worked would feed the baby gravy, bread, milk, and things like that.

Most women were soon pregnant again after giving birth. Large families were common. I just don't know how they did it. There is a girl in our church right now who had fifteen or sixteen brothers and sisters. When her brother died last spring, there were still eleven of them living.

Two of Papa's sisters had twins. Aunt Mandy had seven children, her last two being twins named Chester and Lester. Aunt Winnie only had three children; her twins were Estus and Lestus. There was another girl out here, Lizzie Olson, who had twins name Estus and Lestus. I always thought it very strange that Mandy's Lester, Winnie's Lestus, and Lizzie's Lestus all died at birth or as newborn infants.

Winnie died in 1945, and her sons, Swanie and Estus, were killed at the same time in a car accident when they hit a tree just outside Bridgeport in 1954. Estus was probably in his early twenties and Swanie in his late twenties. We never did know what caused the accident. They had just stopped by their Aunt Florie's and the next thing she heard was that they had been in an accident.

Steer Jumped Off the Mountain

When canning time would come, Mama would send Maggie and me off for the whole day to play with the little ones, our cousins and our younger sisters, so she and my aunts could work without them being under their feet. We would pack a box full of food to take with us and eat on that whenever we got hungry during the day. We would always take biscuits, tomatoes, salt, and a knife and whatever leftovers there might be. Papa's watermelon patch was close to where we played, so we would usually go over there and try to pick the ripest and juiciest one in the whole patch. We really didn't know how to do that but we would thump them and knock on them and sniff at there ends. That would probably have been a funny sight for someone passing by to see—all our little rear ends up in the air as we smelled the watermelons.

Sometimes our neighbor Gladys Knight, who was about Maggie's age, would come along and we would play school. Gladys always wanted to be the teacher so the rest of us would be her students. When Burl came along, he and I would climb high up in a tree and the branch would be our seat in school. Maggie didn't like to climb, so she would sit on a low branch or on the ground with the small children. We had a lot of good times playing like that. Children don't know how to play anymore. They would rather watch TV. It's sad.

Sometimes, if any of the older girls were around, they would all join in and play stink base with us, but they really didn't like to play the more active games like we did. Maggie didn't care much about playing anything outside, but Velma was a different story. She always wanted to play with us, but she was still little and Desmer was only about two or three years old at the time.

We didn't have many toys unless we made them ourselves. We always made our own bats out of a piece of board and our balls out of old socks or rags that we twisted and wrapped cord and thread around. We would play for weeks with an old thread ball like that. None of my sisters or the other girls around here could bat a ball, so they just weren't of much use in a serious ball game.

Burl and I were around each other a lot. We played together and we had a lot of chores that we did together. One of those was gathering in wood. Mama liked to keep the land around the house clean, so we would pick up any fallen wood from the trees near the house first. Then we would go into the woods close by. The Turner boys, Leonard and Edward Lee, would sometimes bring one of their steers down and we would take it with us and make it haul our wood.

One time when we were near the peach orchard, that ol' steer got mad because we had tied a great big load of wood on him. He was a stubborn thing and we could not get him to go in the direction we wanted him to go. There was a steep bank there, about as high as a house, and that dumb steer jumped right off that bank, wood and all.

I thought for sure that fall had killed him. We took off running to find a place where we could get down the bank to where he was. Well, that old steer was just standing there on his knees and we couldn't get him up for nothin'.

We ran home as fast as we could, yelling all the way. Mama came out to meet us, wondering what in the world we had gotten into now. We led her back to the spot where the steer had jumped and we all climbed back down the bank. When Mama got down there to that ol' steer, she took a hold of its tail and just twisted it this way and that way, back and forth. Wasn't no time at all before he jumped up. She kept a hold of his tail and that ol' steer went wherever she wanted him to go. We couldn't believe our eyes. Certainly, for a fact, she had to have some kind of magic power to make that steer get up and go ahead of us like it did.

We didn't know then and I didn't find out until years later, when I was watching some men load cattle, that you could get those animals to go anywhere you want them to by twisting their tail back and forth.

Poison

During the summer we went barefooted all the time. This made one of our games especially fun. The game was called "poison" and we played it in the pastures and around the barns. Everyone around here had cows, so you can just imagine what the poison was.

Sometimes while walking through the pasture, we would come up on a fresh, juicy, large, dark green cow pie much too tempting to pass by without playing a game of poison. Once the poison was identified, we would decide where the home base would be.

One person was "it" and all the other children had to walk side by side in a line holding hands. As they walked across the cow pie, they would pull and tug each other trying to get someone to step in it. Whoever stepped in the cow pie had to run to home base before they got caught by the person who was "it." If you made it home, you were safe. If you were caught, then you were "it." And if you stepped in the cow pie, well, you can guess how that was!

I heard one of the teachers when I taught school in Del Rio laughing about that game one time. She had played the same game when she was little. And here we thought we had invented it.

Work Scholarship

I was always good in school and, as unlikely as it might seem, always followed the rules. You weren't mischievous at the mission school, not if you knew what was good for you. I never got a single licking in school, not in my whole life, for anything. Except the one time Miss Marston hit at the girl next to me and got me instead. No, sir, you didn't act up in Miss Marston's class. You didn't even talk in there unless you were called on or had permission. You didn't do anything but study! She was really strict.

Those mission teachers were just as stern as could be, but the public school teachers weren't. They didn't seem to care as much. Down at the public school, my sisters carried on something terrible, just silly stuff, and the teachers would let them.

The school had always been on a paying or bartering basis—sixty cents per month per child plus the cost of renting books. After Miss Marston had been there a while, she gave some of the more promising students jobs to help pay their way.

Starting in the fifth grade, I was given a work scholarship to help with my tuition. Once a week I scrubbed all the steps inside the mission house with soap and hot water. Thirty-eight steps in all for a credit of fifteen cents a week, which completely covered my tuition.

Curtains for Our Windows

One day, when I was at the mission house washing the steps, Miss Marston said, "Opal, we're going to start repapering the mission house. I was thinking that maybe you could use the old paper backing to make curtains for all those windows in your house. I'm quite sure Mrs. Henderson would be pleased to show you and your mama how."

The old paper had a nice, white material as a backing—closely woven and net-like. We boiled the wallpaper in lye soap and water, which loosened the paper. When we lifted the wallpaper out of the hot water with a long stick, some of the paper just slid right off the fabric part. After the cloth cooled down some, we spread it out and carefully removed the remaining paper. Then we washed the material again to make sure we had removed all the paper and glue.

Usually when we washed clothes we would take them outside and hang them over fences, in the trees, and over bushes to dry. On washday clothes would be spread everywhere. The thought of clotheslines never once crossed our minds. The material for our curtains was more delicate than anything else we had ever washed. If we hung it over the bushes or tree branches, it would snag and probably pull or tear, and for sure we weren't about to give the dogs a chance to get a hold of it and play tug of war, so we hung the pieces around inside the house. The material was so light that drying it didn't take long at all.

No one around here had sewing machines. All of our sewing of any kind was done by hand with just a needle and thread. I can't tell you exactly how long it took us to make those six sets of fancy curtains with ruffles, but it didn't take too long with all of us working together. Maggie and I were both old enough to sew a neat stitch. Beatrice watched the little ones, keeping them busy and out of our way. Mama and Mrs. Henderson sewed on the ruffles. Before we knew it, the heading and hems were in and we were ready to hang them.

To hang curtains, most people would hammer nails into the wood on each side of the window. Then they would run string through the heading and tie each end of the string to a nail. But Mrs. Henderson said, "Oh no. No, no, that just won't do for our curtains. They'll end up sagging in the middle in no time at all. We don't have curtain rods, but we can use something like a broomstick until we get rods." So Mama went out and found some young, tall straight trees and trimmed them up real nice and smooth, and those were our curtain rods. We thought that we were right fancy.

The curtains made such a difference in our three-room house. In our entire community there was nothing like them. The only thing anyone had ever heard of making curtains with was old flour sacks or feed sacks. No one except the chapel women would think to actually use store bought material to make curtains or table coverings. That would be such a waste to us. Why, we thought ourselves lucky indeed to have a new dress made out of material from town. Having frilly curtains with fancy ruffles was the most wonderful thing we could think of to decorate our house, and that was all we needed to give us confidence to start our beautification project.

Our house had two doors, one at each end. Whichever door you walked in, you saw the chimney right away, which was about as wide as it was long. There were two fireplaces, back-to-back, with the open fire facing toward each end of the house. All of this was open. Papa still had not built the wall between the room where he and Mama slept and our bedroom.

After we had hung all our pretty curtains, we thought, *Why can't we make some kind of a curtain to hang between the fireplace chimney and the outside wall?* This would separate the two rooms at least at one end.

Mrs. Henderson thought that was a wonderful idea and was able find enough domestic for us to make tie-died curtains. To tie-dye the material, Mama took a handful of the unbleached muslin material at a time and carefully fastened corn shucks tightly around it. When all the little bunches were securely tied, we took the material outside and thoroughly soaked it in a big tub of green dye and then hung it over the bushes to dry. The part that was secured by the shucks wouldn't take the dye. When the material dried and the shucks were taken out, the curtain material looked like it was covered with off-white flowers.

Of course, Mama made a rod to hang the curtain on. No strings for us. Mrs. Henderson said it was remarkable how the window curtains and the curtain dividing Mama's room and ours made the whole house seem brighter. It was wonderful to live in such a *"remarkable"* house.

Miss Marston's New Organ

There were some other additions to the house that made it quite exceptional. Miss Marston's ordered a new organ for the mission, which was delivered in a great big wooden box. The minute I saw that box in the back of the wagon, I started wondering if that box would fit on the other side of our fireplace and work for the other part of our room divider.

"Oh, Miss Marston, it's perfect!" I said as I stretched my arms out to check the width. "Can I have it? Please? Can I have it, Miss Marston?"

At first she thought I was talking about her new organ. "It's the exact size we need for the other side of the fireplace. Maybe Papa could put shelves in it. It'd make a fine little cabinet." I was just so excited about finding that box. Doubt that most children today would be half that excited about a whole new bedroom outfit—bed, dresser, chest, and all.

Miss Marston let us have the box and Papa put shelves in it. We used the shelves to put our clothes and little things on. Nobody around here had any sort of a dresser at all except the chapel women. I don't think we ever did until about the time I married.

The organ box separated the rooms, but it was still not very private because of the open space between the top of the box and the joist in the roof. We didn't have a ceiling; the rooms were open all the way up to the roof.

We decided to hang strings of those little tiny spruce pine cones from the joist to the top of the cabinet. The entire family worked on this project, like we did on most things. Burl and I took the younger ones out to find the pine cones, and Mama and Maggie strung them. Papa tied the strings of pine cones so closely together on the rafters that when they were attached to the back of the organ box, you couldn't see through them.

It was a wonderful time working together like that. It made all of us feel like we had done something really big and important, even the little ones. There is always satisfaction in working hard and seeing the difference you can make. I hope you have the opportunity to practice that for yourself, Lori.

Later we made more improvements to our house. We put another privacy curtain across one end of Mama and Papa's room to make a space just large enough to hold a regular bed and a little table for a washbowl and lamp. We always used that area for the strangers; it was our guest room. We always had room for company.

Gathering Chestnuts and Raising Hogs

Simple living and hard work was a way of life for us country folk. And raising hogs was another part of life. Grandpa and Papa raised theirs together and just let them run loose. In the fall of the year, we would gather chestnuts to sell. We only had one problem with that— the hogs loved nuts and would eat them all day long, if they got half a chance. We would have to get up very early every morning to get to where the chestnut trees were before the first light of day. We would scoot up next to the trees and wait for the sun to come up. As soon as it was daylight, you could count on those hogs showing up. One of us would keep the hogs scared off while the others picked up the nuts. Sometimes the young'uns would line up and keep the hogs back while the older ones hurried to gather the nuts.

The men would take the chestnuts into town to sell. We got ten or fifteen cents a pound for them and that was a lot of money for us. That was about the only time they went into town—to sell something or maybe to pay taxes.

The chestnuts trees were later destroyed in a blight which, I guess, came through here before 1930. We were still in grammar school when we lost our chestnut trees.

Raising hogs has always been an important part of life up here. If you had plenty of hogs, you not only had plenty of meat to eat, but you had lard to cook with. The fat from the hog was also a main ingredient in the lye soap we made.

From the hog we got a variety of meat: bacon, ham, backbones, ribs, chops, liver mush, souse meat, head cheese, cracklings, chitlins, and side meat. I always liked side meat, sugar cured, better than ham and shoulder. It's a stripped or streaked meat just like bacon.

Butchering the hogs was always done in late fall or early winter. We didn't have any form of refrigeration to keep the meat from spoiling as it was processed, so it was extremely important that the weather be cold enough to thoroughly chill the meat.

There were always a lot of preparations to be made before the day of the slaughter. Everything had to be ready and we each had our jobs. Maggie and I had to be sure there were plenty of cook pots, big ol' wash pots, and barrels ready. Papa and Burl sharpened the knives and got together the other equipment that would be needed. Burl and I would gather in plenty of wood and have it stacked ready for the fire. We usually did all of this a day or two before the slaughtering.

Maggie and I would help Mama mix up the seasonings for sugar curing the meat. We used a ratio of one cup white sugar, a little less than one cup of brown sugar, one cup of salt, and just enough pepper to spice up the flavor. The sugars and pepper were for taste, the salt for curing.

Mama liked for everything to be ready; it had to be just so. She always wanted to have a few things cooked up to feed to the neighbors and family who came to help. Of course, they usually brought some food too.

First thing the morning after preparing everything, right at daylight, Papa started building a hot fire outside and putting those big pots full of water on to boil.   When the water was good and hot, Papa hit the hogs in the head with a hammer, knocking them down, and Grandpa slit their throats with a butcher knife.

There's been a time or two when I saw hogs get up and run around after their throats were slit. They'd squirt blood all over the place, but they don't squeal much after you cut their throats.

After I got older, they started shooting them. I didn't like that at all! The hogs would squeal something awful and sometimes it would take a while for them to die. I just couldn't stand to hear them squeal, so I would usually go into the house, cover my ears, and wait until that part was over. That terrified squealing was more than I could handle.

After killing the hogs, Papa tied their hind legs together, and by running a strong pole between their legs, he and another strong man would picked up the hogs one at a time and dip them down into the boiling water. After the hogs were dipped, the hair was scraped off with a knife.

They don't dip hogs like that much anymore. Now they just put the hog out on a board and pour the boiling water over it and then scrape the hair off. If the water is hot enough and the weather is right, it's not hard to get it off. The last time we did a pig, the weather was rainy, and we had such a terrible time trying to get the hair off that hog.

Some years back, someone was helping me slaughter a hog in the rain. When they couldn't get the hair off, they just burned it off. It didn't hurt the meat any—scorched it and turned it a little dark, but didn't hurt the taste at all. I had never seen anyone do that before, and it seemed a funny thing to do at the time.

Next, Papa would cut the hog up into pieces. He put the head, feet, and some other parts into big pans, and Burl and I would take them into the house so the women folk could start fixing the liver mush and souse meat. They would cut the meat into smaller pieces—hide and all—if there was no hair on it. If the men hadn't gotten all the hair off the head, before the women would cook it, they would skin the hide off or cut out the part that had hair on it.

The head meat has a finer grain and is better tasting than any other part of the hog. It still has a pork flavor, but it doesn't taste quite like any other cut of hog meat. Both the head and the feet have their own distinctive taste. The hide or pieces of hide where they couldn't remove the hair would be cut into smaller pieces and fried in oil. A lot of people like to eat those brown skins. Even a lot of the kids now eat pork rinds. Cracklings are the crisp residue left after frying the pork skin. We put that in our cornbread to make cracklin' bread.

The pieces that were to be preserved were carted to the smoke house and prepared for curing. Some were sugar cured and some salt cured. To salt cure you'd put the meat in an open container and thoroughly cover it with salt. After about ten days, you'd turn it over and put more salt on it. It was very important that the salt covered the entire piece until it was cured out real good so that the meat wouldn't spoil.

We always hung our meat in bags from the rafters in the smoke house. Most people would burn hickory, making a smoky fire to flavor the meat after it was cured. I never really did like that smoked taste. We would preserve beef by drying it like beef jerky. I'll tell you, it was a tasty treat, and even today people still love jerky.

Making Lye Soap

We pretty much used the whole hog when we butchered them— everything except the squeal. A lot of people made chitlins from the intestines or used them as casings for their sausage, but we never did. We only used the intestines to make soap. That was one of the jobs I helped Mama with. I didn't like that job, but somebody had to do it. After the hog was cut up, I took the intestines to the branch and, with a knife, slit them open from one end to the other. Then I hooked them over a stick and dunked them up and down in the branch until all their contents were washed away.

Papa had built a little shed about eight or ten feet square for making soap. Inside the shed was a large trough where we put our ashes and the huge iron pot we used to cook the soap. We would pour hot water over the ashes and collect the potash below. Then we boiled the potash with the fat from the hogs to make the soap. We poured the soap into a wooden box to let it set. You couldn't use anything metal. After the soap set, we would cut it into pieces.

The soap really cleaned well, but it was hard on the skin and didn't smell very good. Not many people make lye soap any more. I did make some a time or two for Del Rio Days[13].

Maggie and Annie Courting

Neighbors, family, friends, and children all getting together, that's what I have always liked best. Our parents encouraged us to bring our friends home. "That's what a big house is for, family and friends," Papa would say. Of course, Mama and Papa knew how young people could be and they figured it was best to make our friends feel welcome in our home. That way they knew what we were doing and who our friends were.

From the time Maggie started bringing boyfriends to the house, I felt that, as a younger sister, one of my main purposes in life was to aggravate budding romance as much as possible.

Sometimes I'd put on an old long bathrobe and false faces pretending to be somebody scary. I'd say things like, "I'm going to get you now. I'm old Rumplestiltskins." Other times I would just sit and stare at them and make faces. I'd cock my head to one side, shrug my shoulders, bat my eyes, raise my eyebrows up and down, or do something every time they looked my way. Most of all I felt it my duty to be ever-present and as pesky as I could be.

Aunt Mary and Uncle Charlie would not let my cousin Annie court. But when she came down here to spend the night with us, sometimes Mama would let Charlie Myers, Ben's uncle, come eat with us. She would let him stay for a while to spend time with Annie, which is most likely the reason she was such a frequent visitor.

After supper, Papa would go into their room and either go to bed or sit in a chair by the fire for a while. After putting Velma and Desmer to bed, Mama would usually sit by the fireplace with Papa for a spell before tucking in Beatrice. Mama and Papa usually got up earlier than us, so sometimes they would go to bed before we did. But we were

---

13   Del Rio Days—a small local festival that includes vendors selling or promoting homemade crafts and other items, demonstrations of molasses making, and entertainment such as clog dancing and other music.

usually all in bed a little after sunset in order to get up and start our chores early in the morning.

Maggie and I cleaned up after supper and Burl brought in the wood for the night and next morning. If Mama and Papa went to bed early, Maggie would put Beatrice to bed.

So one night when Annie and Charlie were there, after Maggie and I had finished the dishes, I sat down close by Charlie and started making fun of them. I would pat his arm and look up into his eyes, shake my head and sigh, making silly faces all the while. Annie was getting pretty upset with me. "Opal, isn't it time for bed? Your Mama and Papa have been in their room for an hour already." But do you think her saying that stopped me? I was having too much fun.

I was big enough to know better, but I liked to pester them anyway. And I truly did consider Annie's question as a genuine invitation for more aggravation. So, I reached over and picked up a book and, holding it so they could clearly see the pictures, I said in as grown up a voice as I could make, "Yes, it is time to go to bed. Let me read you a bedtime story."

I sat there and read silly little bedtime stories to them until Charlie had to go home. Annie got so aggravated with me that night.

When Charlie went home, he had to pass right in front of Annie's house, and they were afraid that if Aunt Mary saw him, she would figure out that he had been at Mama and Papa's too. Even though it was dark and almost impossible to see much outside, they soon figured out what was going on. That was probably about the time the next full moon lit up the night sky.

Usually Mama was awake until everyone else was asleep. Even though she was sitting in her chair in the other room, there was no way Mama was going to let anything happen between Annie and Charlie. No sir—between Mama and me they wouldn't get away with that much at our place. And for sure there was no way that Charlie and Annie were going to get much privacy in a three-room house with eight other people right there. And when Mama was ready for us to go to bed, Charlie would have to leave.

Then when I was older, Charlie would bring what they called a "gramophone" and they would wind it up and play records. Sometimes Mama would let us stay up until about one o'clock so Annie and Charlie could sit and talk. Aunt Mary wanted Mama and Papa to stay up too, but they couldn't do that. I can tell you for a fact that Annie's mama didn't have too much to be concerned about with all of us up. I guess it really was true love. Annie and Charlie finally got married. That made my cousin Ben's aunt.

Christmas

Traditions were very important to us as children and none was more special to us than those at Christmas. We loved baking and making presents for each other.

The chapel women always filled the Christmas season with special memories about the birth of Christ so that we would remember those times for the rest of our lives. I always tried to do the same for my school children. I did many of the same things that the chapel women did for us with the children I taught in school and at church. I have always loved having a Christmas play. But when I was young, the most wonderful time of all was Christmas Eve. Every year on that night, Mrs. Henderson and Miss Marston had a big Christmas party up at the chapel for everyone in the community who wanted to attend. It was so much fun! When that party was over, maybe around nine or nine-thirty, all of our friends and some family would come over to our house for the "after party" and we would stay up all night long. We did this every year.

Mama always did a lot of baking for several days before the Christmas "after party," and Maggie and I would help. We would always bake gingerbread cookies and seven cakes—five different kinds. We always had to have two chocolate cakes with chocolate icing, a banana cake, a cinnamon cake, a raisin cake, and two spice cakes. We always had peaches and they had to be our own peaches, the ones we grew and canned. And walnuts—we always had walnuts. We also had backbones and ribs, souse meat, and liver mush from the hog we butchered in the fall. All this was for the all-night party at our house.

After Mama baked the gingerbread, she put it in an empty flour sack and tied it up on the ceiling rafters so the young'uns who came over couldn't get into it. She never had to say anything to us about staying out of her Christmas baking; we knew better. Mama made gingerbread the same way I do, except she rolled hers out in her hand instead of on the table, and made biscuits-size cookies.

With all of our baking done the day before, on Christmas Eve morning Maggie and I helped decorate the chapel with paper sashes and streamers. Some we tied together and the others we pinned with straight pins.

That night when the party at the chapel was almost over and it was about time to leave, Papa snuck out so he could hide and scare people. A few minutes later, Ed Turner decided he would leave a little early so that he could beat everyone down to our house. He knew that Mama would have all the cakes cut and on the table with all the other food, and he wanted to be the first to get to all that food.

It was very dark that night, so he didn't see Papa when he jumped out to grab him. Ed sort of staggered backwards and became all tangled up in the streamers and fell down. Papa wrapped some more of the streamers around him. Poor Ed didn't know what got him. Every time he moved, trying to get loose, the straight pins would stick into him. We just laughed at him as we went by. Finally, he got untangled and came on down to the house cold and worn out and certainly not first.

He was so tired, and probably upset, that upon arriving he fell down on the bed face first with his hands over his head and went to sleep. Well, this was not going to be Ed's night. I got out the needle and thread and sewed his britches up both sides to the bed covers. Then I sewed his coat sleeves to the bed. Before I was done, I had him securely sewed in place.

When he woke up, he couldn't figure out what had happened, he couldn't get loose, so he just laid there and yelled. I guess Mama and Papa got tired of all his noise and told me to get him loose, so I did.

Mama and Papa would spend most of the night in their room, sitting in front of the fireplace, probably talking about how silly we were. We would all be in the other room or in the kitchen. Some of us would usually pop popcorn and make molasses balls. We'd sing Christmas carols and cut up and act the fool. We were silly, all right. After we got to be teenagers, we would give each other presents like handkerchiefs, dolls, and other little things that we could make.

Christmas Eve was such a wonderful time. It's still one of my favorite memories, being able to stay up all night long. We were always so proud that Mama and Papa would do that and I think it eased their minds knowing where we were. They were always so good about us having friends around.

Sometime early Christmas morning, before light, we would go down to Grandma Corn's. We would stay there and eat breakfast before going back home.

At home all the food left over from the night before would be put out on the table where it stayed all day long. People could eat whenever they wanted to and as often as they wanted to. There was milk and coffee to drink and we just had a big time.

Later on Christmas Day, we would always go around to different houses and play special Christmas jokes. If the people in the houses didn't see us before we called out "Christmas gift, Christmas gift," they were supposed to give us something to eat, like apples, bread, apple jelly, stick candy, nuts, or something like that.

Poor Maggie had a lot of problems with her throat and colds, especially around the holiday. One year before Christmas, when she was about fifteen or sixteen, she had such a bad cold and sore throat that Mama and Papa decided that they should take her in to see the doctor. The doctor asked her what was wrong, but she couldn't even get a sound to come out. She kept trying to tell him, but only these little squeaks and whispers came out. The more she tried to tell him, the worse it got. Mama and Papa said that she sounded so funny that the doctor just started a-laughin' away and said, "Why, Miss Maggie, I do believe that you're the first woman I've seen this winter who can wag her tongue at both ends and not make more than a squeak. Looks like you're going to be singing in the mouse choir for the church play this year." We called her "Squeaky" for the longest time after that. Of course, she didn't think we were at all funny.

10
Seventh Grade (age 13–14)
1924–1925

Sent by Mama to Help Others

*M*aggie's place, as the oldest girl in the family, was to help Mama around the house. As the next oldest, I was the one loaned out to help others. I kind of thought of it as Maggie being the one who was called upon and I was the one who was sent.

When someone in the community was sick or needed help, Mama was quick to visit and would do what she could. If she thought someone needed more help and I could do it, she would send me.

Many times she would send me to take care of someone's young'uns or help with chores when the mama was ailing. When I stayed with old people, I would see that they had fresh water and that they ate. Sometimes I would actually have to feed them. Most of them liked being read to or merely enjoyed having someone to talk to them. As you can probably imagine, I've always been a right good talker. I did whatever needed to be done.

Helping people was not easy work, but I enjoyed it considerably, and I didn't mind spending nights away from home. I spent a lot of nights taking care of the sick and old folks, but in the entire time I lived here in the community, I only spent one night at a girlfriend's house.

And I never went out on a date, like you think of a date now, in my life. Mama was always careful about where she sent me and she would check on me or send Burl to see if I was all right.

Mrs. Myers and Family

The only place I didn't like to go was the Myers'. Rosa "Rosie" Myers was sickly a lot when Blanche, her youngest, was a baby. The poor woman was probably just plain worn out. In all, Mrs. Myers had thirteen children; three of them died of hives or something like that when they were real little. It was fairly common back then for little babies to get hives or have little bumps all over their faces. The hives were just another childhood ailment. I don't know why that was; maybe the food or something. I do know that a lot of people dug herbs trying to cure their young'uns who had the hives, but still a lot of them died. Especially when young'uns had what they called "bold hives" it could kill them. Later people started wondering if the hives might have been caused by the catnip tea that was given to fretful babies to help them sleep.

Mrs. Myers's first child was born when she was barely fifteen years old, and now at thirty-three, she had just had her last baby. Her living children were John Thelma, who was age 16; Ben Perry, 14; Columbus Washington, called Lum, was 12; Howard Rhea, 11; Albert, 9; Eddie Oberia Lee, 7; and Herman, Fred, Myrtle, and Blanche were the little ones. The three who died were Troy, Ruth, and Alice. I'm sure you're impressed that I recollect so many names, but for some reason, names always stuck with me. I rarely forget a name.

Marcas Sampson "Sam" Myers (January 30, 1880) was more than eleven years older than his wife. It was not at all uncommon back then for there to be even twenty or twenty-five years between husband and wife. And many girls married young, even as young as twelve or thirteen. The mountain girls didn't have much and could be quite impressed by someone paying them a little attention and buying them trinkets. If an older man had a little money or maybe a pension and would bring her hair bows, a piece of material to make a dress, or even some snuff, why, she would just think that was great.

Sam and Rosie had come from North Carolina when John was a baby. All of these Myers up here came from North Carolina around Flat Creek and Asheville.

The Myers moved around a lot. They never owned their own home or even a piece of land. When I helped out Mrs. Myers, they were living over on the Smith Place. Their cabin was small and, of course, you can just imagine how crowded with all those kids.

In that cabin of theirs, there were four regular size beds: one for Mr. and Mrs. Myers; one for John and Ben; one for Lum and Howard; and one for the younger ones—Eddie, Herman, Fred, and Myrtle. The little ones slept by laying across the bed sideways, their heads at one side of the bed and their feet at the other. Albert had slept in that bed with them, all stacked in there like a cord of wood. But he was growing like a weed and hanging off the bed at both ends, so they had to put a narrow little bed in the kitchen for him to sleep in. Blanche slept in a box with a child-sized straw tick mattress in the floor of the main room by her mama's bed.

When you had a large family, it was not at all uncommon for people to have beds in the kitchen. The Myers didn't have room for a cook stove, table, bed, and enough chairs for them all to sit on. So they had the table pushed up against the bed and the young'uns would sit on the edge of that bed to eat.

Albert loved sleeping in the kitchen. He mostly liked to sleep and eat anyway, that is, when he wasn't running all over these mountains chasing squirrels and whatever else moved. By sleeping in the kitchen bed, he didn't have to get up to eat breakfast—he'd just wake up, turn over, and eat.

Mrs. Myers didn't have any older girls to help her, so Mama would send me down there to help with the canning or whatever else needed to be done, like cooking or carrying water. And sometimes I would watch Blanche and Myrtle.

During that summer when I was thirteen, it seemed to me as though I spent more time helping Mrs. Myers, especially when she was real sick, than I did helping at home. At first it was all right and I enjoyed it. But after a month or so, I wouldn't have gone to their house for anything in this world if Mama hadn't made me. It certainly wasn't my choice for something to do.

Now, I didn't have a problem with Mrs. Myers or Blanche or any of the other young'uns except Ben, the second oldest. I simply could not stand him. I guess he didn't care much for me either. We fought about everything whenever we were around each other. I would see Ben at church sometimes and around the community, and even then we didn't act friendly unless we were absolutely forced to. I was only around him when I had to be, like on business, when I was helping his mother.

A few years later, as I looked back on that time, I began to realize that it really wasn't Ben I had a problem with either. I had played with him and John and a bunch of the other community boys just about every Sunday afternoon from the time I was eight until I was about twelve or so. I never cared a whole lot about Ben, but I guess he was a nice enough boy.

It was almost a month after I started spending so much time helping out up at the Myers' place that some of the boys I had been best friends with for years started teasing us about being sweethearts. Now, that was one thought that had never crossed my mind. There was no way I was going to be called someone's sweetheart, especially Ben Myers's, and for that matter, I didn't even intend to be his friend. They thought I was going down to his place so much because I liked him and that made my blood boil. I guess they were all jealous.

Scholarships to Highland Institute

Between helping out at Mrs. Myers's and chores at home, my summer was pretty busy. Apparently I wasn't the only one working. During the summer, Miss Marston worked hard to find funds for the mission and the Ebenezer High School Scholarship Program. She traveled to several cities in North Carolina and Tennessee to speak to Sunday school classes, churches, women's civic groups, and important businessmen about supporting the mission. Many of the churches would also agree to send school supplies, clothing, Christmas gifts, and other things needed by the mission.

Miss Marston would find a church group or individual who would provide a hundred dollar scholarship for a promising student to attend high school at the Highland Institute in Highland, Kentucky, near Jackson. The first year the scholarship was given to the student on Miss Marston's recommendation, but in order to keep the scholarship, the student had to study hard and do well in all their subjects. The student also had to agree to write to the supporting group or individual at least once a month. When the student left for Highland or a little before, Miss Marston would let those providing the scholarship know the name of the student and maybe some information about the student and his or her family. She would also let them know the student's clothes and shoe sizes in case they wanted to send a special gift at Christmas or graduation time.

She had always been able to raise enough money for scholarships for the best students who were willing to go away to school. Highland, as we called it, was an orphanage and boarding school for the first grade all the way through high school.

When Miss Marston was away from the mission doing her traveling, I would help Mrs. Henderson at the chapel house at night. All the other teachers and mission workers had gone home for the summer. Mrs. Robinson was no longer at the mission either. She left in the spring of 1923, after serving as a nurse there for three years. But even during the time she was here, she only stayed at the chapel house when she wasn't taking care of the sick in the community. Mrs. Henderson did not like to stay alone in that big house and was glad to have me there.

My summer had been busy enough, and it wasn't going to get any easier after school started either. One of those scholarships Miss Marston got was for Burl. Of course, with Burl away at Highland, both Maggie and I had to take over his chores. Beatrice and Velma were getting old enough to be of help too, but it was mostly up to Maggie and me when it came to the hard work.

Seventh Grade

There was no one more excited than I was when it was time for school to start back. I was glad that summer was over. I loved school and I enjoyed being around Miss Marston and Mrs. Henderson more than anything in the world.

I had seen a good bit of them during the summer in spite of the amount of time I worked at the Myers. Since I was also working for Mrs. Henderson, a real paying job at that, Mama let me spend several nights a week sleeping at the chapel house.

I had a whole seventy-five cents of my very own money saved up, and I still had my work scholarship job of washing the steps in the chapel house to pay my tuition.

It was always exciting, to me at least, when the new textbooks and school supplies came in, and I just couldn't wait to get my hands on them. Our textbooks were never the same as the ones used in the county schools and they were never really new either. Some churches in North Carolina and Kentucky would collect books that their local schools had considered outdated and send them to the mission. That made for an interesting variety. We always made do, though, and there was no doubt that we learned much more than the children who went to the public schools around here. Miss Marston would say, "It's not just what's in the book that matters; it's what's in your head and in your heart that makes the difference." The public schools in the community had trouble getting books and supplies too, and still did when I started teaching years later.

I was always impatient about getting my schoolbooks. I guess I was forever raring to go about something. In the seventh grade, I knew for sure that I would have a Rand McNally geography book and a big red physiology book for health. And don't you know, just about every time I looked at that book I thought of Charlie McGaha and the time

I visited the mission school with Auda.

While staying at the mission some that summer, I read nearly every book and magazine Miss Marston and Mrs. Henderson had. Why, it was just amazing to look in a magazine and see pictures of things you couldn't even imagine or dream of. Every page I turned was like discovering something new: the clothes people wore, the places they went, or where they lived in big cities with tall buildings. Now, those were strange sights for a young girl who had only been outside her little community one time when she was eight years old. I had never even been into Del Rio.

Of all the books I read there, I liked the ones with a lot of pictures and the ones that told about the lives of real people best. Mrs. Henderson told me those were biographies and autobiographies. I liked some of the history books too. Reading those books gave me the idea that maybe someday I could write a book myself. That would just be the most wonderful thing, you know.

Of course, the Bible was my favorite book. When I stayed at the chapel house, I spent a lot of time talking to Mrs. Henderson and Mrs. Robinson about the Bible. They would explain to me things about God and what certain passages meant. That's when I learned how important knowing God really was. Of course, my parents went to church and talked about it, but they couldn't read the Bible and explain what it meant. But early in life I learned from Mrs. Henderson and Mrs. Robinson and the others that reading the Bible and knowing God was just the most important thing there was in this life. That was it. And I've been reading my Bible all these years now.

Miss Marston was my teacher again this year and Miss Ivey Hood from Knoxville was the teacher for the younger grades. Miss Hood was older; her hair was almost white compared to Miss Marston's gray strands.

There are many older people who believe that because they are old, there's not much use for them. Why, they couldn't be more wrong! Many of the chapel women were older. If they had not come to work at the mission because they felt they were too old to contribute significantly, the people around here would probably still be living like they were at the turn of the century.

It's really like Miss Marston said: "Being useful is not how much you have to give or to share, because surely that will soon be used up. It's how much the Lord has. And He ever so willingly gives through you to others. All you have to do is give Him control of your life. That's what makes you useful to Him, as well as every single being who crosses your path."

Mrs. Robinson stayed busy taking care of the sick, especially since there was not a doctor close by. One time a girl in the community got badly burned on the leg. I don't know how it happened, but it was quite serious; so bad, in fact, that they said it had started to smell dead. They brought that girl up to the mission house and Mrs. Robinson took care of her leg until it got better. If she hadn't been here keeping the burn clean, the girl probably would have died from infection. Though she did have a lot of scars, it was better than being dead.

Miss Marston was always giving out hope and encouragement. She told us over and over again that we could do anything we wanted to do, be anything we wanted to be. "Just because you're back here in this little community, don't you ever think you can't become something special! God has a wonderful purpose for your life and He will put special dreams deep into your heart to help you discover His plan. Your life work is to listen to God and to do what He says. With His help you can become anything He has planned for you to become. There are two very important things for you to always remember. One, even though it is extremely important to always work hard and do your best, you cannot do these things without God's help because they will be too big for you to accomplish. And two, you must never get ahead of God's plan for you. If you try to make things happen on your own, you will probably end up sorry you did not wait for God to work it out in His own timing. Even though this all sounds very difficult, it's much easier if you just remember: talk to God everyday; listen to God everyday; and everyday do what God tells you to do. It's all about 'trusting' and 'obeying,' and then He works out all the rest and you needn't worry about it." Miss Marston gave us a lot of mini-sermons like that and it always made us feel like we could accomplish anything.

Miss Marston liked to tell us stories or read stories to us, even after we were old enough to have easily read them for ourselves. Some of those were about people who were born poor, but who grew up and made a difference by helping people. Some of them were about people who earned or raised a lot of money and then started schools and churches and orphanages. Dr. Guerrant (1836–1916) was one of those. He founded three orphanages, two colleges, fifty-six churches, schools, and mission houses that touched the lives of 40,000 pupils, 84 salaried workers, hundreds of unsalaried volunteers, 362 evangelists, and 6,304 salvations. She would usually say something like, "With God in your life, nothing is impossible."

My Life's Dream

One day I told Miss Marston, "It would be almost too wonderful to think that I could be or do something special like that."

Well, Miss Marston's face spread into a big grin and then she put her hands on my shoulders and looked me square in the eyes. "Opal, my little jewel, you already are special. There is a wonderful plan laid out for your life. It's up to you to ask God to show you what He wants you to do. Then when He does, Opal, it's up to you to do your part. That means working hard and never giving up—and it will happen. Don't you ever, ever give up on your dreams!"

With her constant encouragement, I found the courage to dream of what could be and the boldness to work at making those dreams come true.

More and more I thought about how wonderful it would be if I could become an author. I wanted to make people feel the way I did when I picked up a book. Finally, one day I told Miss Marston that I really wished to write a book.

"Don't let me hear you wishing, Opal. You find a way to make it so! I know you can do it."

"Miss Marston, you know I can't write a book and have it sound like those books you read to us."

"Well, maybe you can't right now, not like those, but you can one day if you still have that desire. There are other kinds of books too, you know. Start with something you can do right now. You could take pictures of the community and the people and start making a picture book. Who knows—someday it might be a pictorial history book that people will look at to see how things used to be here in the mountains."

"But I don't have a camera, or film, or money for developing."

"I don't want to hear any more 'buts.' Not having a camera, film, and money may be a problem, but problems are for solving. 'Buts' are for excuses."

So, I decided to go ahead and make plans to do a pictorial history of the community. I found a catalog that advertised a Hawkeye camera for $1.00.

I told Mama all about my plans and talks with Miss Marston. "Mama, I have seventy-five cents saved from my work this summer. Please, Mama, if you'll give me the other quarter you can keep the camera and just let me use it 'till I get grown." Mama only earned a dollar a week washing clothes for the chapel women. That was the only cash money we had coming in except for the little tobacco crop we grew. We traded and bartered for everything else.

Well, Mama gave me the quarter I needed for the camera. But knowing that a pictorial history would be an expensive project, I started thinking of all the things I could do to make enough to finance my project. There were chestnuts and blackberries to be picked this time of the year, and this was something our family had done for ages. What I picked for myself would have to be done separately, on my own, in addition to what I picked for the family. The chestnuts and blackberries were seasonal, so I would have to gather enough so my money would last until I could come up with some other ideas. Another problem would be getting what I picked to town. I knew Mama and Papa would never let me take them and there'd be too many for me to carry anyway. But, sure as could be, I would find a way. Papa and Burl would probably help me and they could buy the film for me when they were in town.

Miss Marston had thoroughly convinced me that if the Lord put the idea in my head, He could also put the ideas in there that would help me earn the money I needed. "You never know just how the Lord will provide," she would remind me.

Miss Marston found an advertisement in a magazine for a place in Bristol, Tennessee, where I could send my film to be developed for only a quarter.

After making my historical picture book, I still had hundreds of pictures left. I don't know how we ever got the money, but we had them developed. The Lord really did supply. Everyone in the community enjoyed those pictures. Years later, Catherine Marshall borrowed all those pictures to use in the research of her book *Christy*. Then Ken Wales, a big movie producer from California, came to see about doing a movie of *Christy* and he borrowed those pictures. And those pictures have been reprinted in the newspaper several times. The Lord even protected them from being burned up in a fire.

I'll never forget the day I took my finished picture book, *The Pictorial History of My Mountain Community*, to show Miss Marston. "Here it is, Miss Marston—my first finished book. You said I could do it and I did. I think now I will write other books, real books."

She was so pleased. "Opal, there's another book that you've started without even realizing it. It's called the *Life Book*. It's called that because it's the book you write with your life. Every day you are adding pages. It can be a good book or one that's not so good. Good or bad, it is a book that everyone who meets you will read. Decide what you want your *Life Book* to say. It can encourage, inspire, and change lives, just like the books you have read and studied at the mission have changed your life."

You know, I just heard that kind of talk so much that I really got the idea that I could do something special, and I couldn't think of anything more special to be than a mission worker like Miss Marston and Mrs. Henderson.

Papa Bringing People Home

We always had lots of company—both family and strangers. Papa would invite anybody he saw to spend the night. Papa was an unusual person, for sure; if he thought someone might not have a place to spend the night, he'd just bring them home with him. No one went without, not if Papa had anything to say about it.

It's strange how people have changed from those days. Most wouldn't think of bringing someone into their home that wasn't close family, but they'd bring home a stray dog and treat that dog better that they would treat people. People used to get upset with me something awful because I took in strangers and made my dogs stay outside.

When Papa brought home a stranger, they would sleep in the other bed in the curtained off room. When Aunt Mandy and her family, who lived just down below town in Dutch Bottoms, would come visit us, we'd have people sleeping all over the place. Aunt Mary Pack used to visit a lot too after she moved down to West Myers.

Papa had a lot of fun teasing Aunt Mandy and Aunt Dora, two of his sisters, and their families. Both Mandy and Dora married Crums, so that made them Corn Crums. Papa would say, "Yeh, after these Corns started a-marryin' all those Crums, sure didn't take no time a-tall till we had a whole bunch of Crummy people 'round here."

Papa was the jolliest person that you ever saw in your life. He was tall and big boned, and weighed well over two hundred pounds, but he was not at all fat.

We were taught to be principled and self-respecting. We were poor, but we never thought of ourselves that way. How can you be poor when you have so much to give away to others? Each of us girls had two dresses that were fit to wear out, one to wear to school and church and another one that we wore to work and play in. I can never remember wanting for anything in my life. Now that may sound strange, but growing up, I really cannot remember ever wanting anything more than what I had. Everybody else around us lived the same as we did. My family and the chapel women had always taught us to be thankful for what we had.

If we complained, Mama would say, "You just think of so-and-so," and she'd name off some child; "they'd be glad to have what you've got." It didn't take much to make us realize that we were fortunate.

Grandpa Hall Comes to Live with Us

Grandpa Hall came to visit us several times. He was tall, slim, and had a mustache. He would always bring us surprises and cut up with us. Grandma only came with him a couple times; they were getting old and the trip was too hard on her. When she did come, Mama would clear us out of the kitchen and they would spend a lot of time in there together.

Grandma Hall died in 1924 or '25. Mama was sick at the time and unable to go to the funeral. Not long after Grandma died, Grandpa came to live with us. Papa made the curtained off room a little bigger and moved Grandma's big old-timey bed with the high headboard over from Eastport, along with a few other things. Mama and Papa fixed up a real nice place for him. Next to the bed, they put his table and next to that went his chair. Grandpa was still particular about where things should go and how things should be done. Grandma had told Mama that she wanted her to have that bed when both she and Grandpa died. Grandma's bed first belonged to her grandmother and was over a hundred years old. When my great-great-grandma was eleven years old, she was boarding out to take care of the family of a woman who had died or just had another baby. Actually, I don't know for sure why she was with that family. But anyway, the man couldn't afford to pay her so he built her a bed and a chest.

I don't know if it was losing Grandma, or if he was sick and felt bad, or if it was just his age, but Grandpa was not the same after that. Back then people didn't talk about illness or problems much in front of the young'uns. Grandpa could have been eaten up with cancer and nobody would have told us.

He was hateful most of the time. If he laid down in the daytime, everyone had to be quiet and we were not allowed to play much around where he was. Mama had made a fly chaser by bending paper over a pole and sewing it in place. She cut the paper into little strips so they would make a noise to scare the flies. Velma and Desmer would take turns standing on the table by Grandpa's bed and moving the pole back and forth to keep the flies off him the whole time he was sleeping. We always had problems with flies getting in the house. There was no such thing as a screen door and the outside doors were usually kept open for light and fresh air. Of course, we got plenty of fresh air through the spaces between the boards in the walls. We just had to put up with flies and we always had to keep our food covered up with a piece of cloth.

Grandpa Hall died in July about a year and a half after moving in with us.

In the wintertime, the creek would get frozen solid. A time or two each year Papa would take the little ones for rides on a log sled, which was no more than two log runners with a big piece of wood fastened across the middle where you sat. Papa would pull them over the frozen creek without a thought of the ice breaking, for it was frozen so solid. The water doesn't get that solid anymore; it may be because they tore out all the dams. At one time there were five or six dams by the mills that were all up and down the creek.

Toting water from the spring was not an easy task in the warm weather; but in those cold winters, sometimes it was near impossible. There were times when everything was frozen, even the springs.

Washing Clothes

Mama washed clothes every Monday morning, no matter how cold it was. We would have to bring in buckets of water or chunks of ice in from the branch and heat it in a big tub on the stove.

Mama always rinsed the clothes twice, so we'd have to tote in even more water or ice to do that. We didn't have a clothesline, so we just hung the clothes on the fences, trees, and anywhere off the ground to keep them clean. But in the wintertime they would freeze stiff as a board into the shape of whatever they were hung over and still would be wet when they thawed out, so we would usually hang them over chairs close to the stove. It didn't take them long to dry there—a turn or two and they'd be done.

During the drought in 1925, it was so dry that it was impossible to get a dipperful of water, let alone a bucketful, out of our branch. So Papa would tie the wash tubs full to overflowing with our dirty clothes and the fire wood that Burl and I had gathered to a sled and drag it all the way down to the creek below Grandma's house. We always took along a big box of food that Mama had fixed up for our washing junket. We would usually just have cornbread and biscuits. We never had sandwiches back then. For one thing, we never had loaf bread. Mama never did bake bread. Mrs. Myers did, but she was about the only one around here except the chapel women who knew how to bake bread. Our absolute favorite things to go in the food box were the rhubarb pies that Mama had baked. She would send Burl and me to Mary's store with a couple eggs to barter for sugar for her pies. We would savor every last bite of those pies.

The creek was low, but we were able to get enough water out to get the clothes done. Papa and Burl built a fire close to the creek and we put the tubs right on the fire to heat up the water. Mama boiled the clothes in lye soap and used a big stick to stir them around and then lift them out to dump them into the next tub to rinse them. That water was not quite as hot and she would wring them out with her hands before putting them into the final rinse tub.

Aunt Florie would usually come along and help Mama, so Maggie and I would keep all the little ones entertained. We enjoyed it all, but to Mama and Papa it was an ordeal to make the best of. They usually did just that, making the best of whatever came their way. Couldn't really do any more than that. Did no good whatsoever to complain!

We could hardly wait until all the clothes were washed, rinsed out, and hung around on the bushes to dry so we could eat those pies. After we ate, Mama would let us play down the creek a ways in the swimming hole while the clothes finished drying.

We had never heard tell of bathing suits. Mama wouldn't let us go in the creek unless we had britches on that would cover us up. So we would wear some of Burl's old britches or overalls. Aunt Florie always wanted to go swimming with us, but she was so big she couldn't get into anybody's overalls. She'd have to pin her dress together all the way down between her legs. We thought that was so funny. She was like a big ol' walrus sliding down into that creek and her dress would be all billowed up when she hit the water. We'd always had a lot of fun in the creek. Those were some of my best memories as a child.

11
Maggie at Highland (age 14–16)
1925–1927

The mission did a good job preparing the students in their studies, but it was next to impossible to prepare them for the social and cultural differences they would encounter at Highland. Most of the students were not able to adjust and stayed away from the community for no more than one term.

The mission didn't really consider this a failure; it was a beginning. There was much progress being made in the entire community, and even the students who did not go on to high school benefited from their education at the mission. The influence of Ebenezer Mission went beyond the school itself. There were many families with members who attended the other activities of the mission, you know, like Sunday school, sewing classes, and so on.

In 1925, Miss Marston was able to get scholarships for both Maggie and Burl to attend Highland. Maggie was seventeen when she went away to be in the ninth grade. They were both very promising students, and of course, the whole family was proud of them.

Well, the scholarships were good news for Burl and Maggie, but not so much for me. Oh, I was glad they could go, all right, but their going away meant that I would have to be responsible for their chores. And in order to do that, I would have to quit school. The school and the mission, especially the mission workers, had not only become a part of my life, they were my future and my dreams, a big part of my hope for what could be.

There was a rhythm to the seasons, and each one had its work. Our home life centered around family, work, helping neighbors, and, of course, church. As a family, we had to work hard or we would not survive. It was all very basic. In the spring and summertime, we worked the farm, raising corps and animals for food and to barter or sell. In the late summer and fall, we harvested the crops and prepared food for the family and our animals, which we stored for winter. We gathered chestnuts and took them to town to barter. In the fall, we slaughtered enough of the animals to have meat to last until the next fall. We cured the meat and made soap. During the winter, we did the majority of the sewing and fixing up around the house, and as the weather permitted, we repaired the outbuildings and tools. Of course, we always had to tend the animals. There was always something to do, so when a family member was sick or missing, it made a big difference.

By this time I was almost living at the mission, so I still did have many opportunities to learn from Miss Marston and Mrs. Henderson, even though I did not get to attend classes. Whenever I did finish my chores early, which didn't happen often, I would sit in on Miss Marston's class.

Both Miss Marston and Mrs. Henderson knew I wanted to finish school there at Ebenezer, so I could get a scholarship to Highland. I don't really think they ever had any doubts that I would be able to do just that. They had such faith! "If that's what the Lord wants for you, Opal, that is exactly what will be. So don't worry yourself about it. You just do your chores and be thankful. It's the Lord's part to take care of the rest."

Every night we would talk about school. I was always reading, and even though I wasn't able to attend classes, I had my books and kept up with my studies on my own.

About this time, things began to change at Ebenezer. Of course, I didn't know what was causing it, and, for that matter, I hardly noticed; I was so wrapped up in my own situation. And to this very day I don't know what caused the changes at the mission. Maybe their support was declining because of the economy, or maybe the churches were focusing on other areas of need and no one was promoting Ebenezer Mission. Maybe it was Miss Marston's health. I never did find out.

Many farmers all over the nation, even those with large amounts of land, were suffering and had been suffering since the early '20s when the prices of farm products fell about forty percent. Some farmers had lost so much money they could no longer pay the mortgage on their farms. Around here we were already poor, but we were self-sufficient for food and God-reliant for the courage and strength needed to grow and harvest that food.

The changes at the mission were subtle; when a worker left, no one came to replace her. During the last year, only Miss Marston and Mrs. Henderson remained.

Miss Marston taught all the grades now as well as Sunday school, and Mrs. Henderson took care of the mission and a lot of the work in the community. Both of them were getting older, and I could tell that they were glad to have me spending the nights with them there at the mission. Of course, staying there was a pleasure for me; I loved the mission and the chapel women.

I would get up early every morning, many times before even Mrs. Henderson got out of bed. I usually didn't fool with eating oatmeal and the things they normally cooked for breakfast; I'd just grab a piece of corn bread as I ran out the door to go to my home and start my day's work.

There had always been a lot of work to do and now with Burl and Maggie gone, there was all the more. I worked as fast and as hard as I could all day long; when I finished, I would run to the branch and wash up, pull on my dress, and go over to the mission.

Preparing Food

Most people didn't have many canning jars, but if they found jars for anything, it would be for berries. Sometimes people would dry berries, but most families didn't want to fool with that. There were other foods that were plentiful and well worth drying like beans, pumpkin, apples, and peaches.

Beatrice and I would bend over and pick greenbeans from the garden until our backs ached like they were breaking. Some of them we put into big, tall nail kegs to pickle. We would usually do a barrel of beans, a barrel of cabbage kraut, and a barrel of turnip kraut. Guess not many people hear about turnip kraut these days, but it was fixed much the same way as it was with cabbage. We thought it was good; I guess those who have never tried it would think it had an odd taste.

We also would string beans together with a needle and thread. When our string of beans was about three to four feet long, we would tie the ends together and hang it over a nail on the wall until they were dry and then put them into sacks to keep them from getting dusty. When we were ready to use them, we would take a string out of the bag, soak them a little, or pare boil them. Then we would take out the thread and cook them with fat meat. They're good—most people really like them.

To dry the pumpkins we would slice them in rings and cut off the rind. Sometimes we would run a cord through the slices and then attach or tie the ends of the cord over the rafters. Other times we would run a stick through the rings and hang them. In a few days when they were dry, we would put the pumpkin into cloth bags to keep the dust off them, just like we did with the shab beans. We would tie the bags from the rafters to store them out of the way until they were needed. When we wanted to make a pumpkin pie, we would take out what we needed, wash it, cut it up, and cook it.

We basically did apples that same way too, cutting out the core, then slicing them. Next they were strung across the room on a cord to dry. We stored sweet potatoes in big barrels by wrapping each one up in a piece of paper. The barrel was kept in the chimney corner by the fireplace, where they would keep all winter.

One of my favorite things that we fixed every year was sulfured apples. To prepare them, we put a little pan of sulfur down inside a big barrel and got it burning real good. Then we would put some sticks on to smother the fire and make smoke. The apples were put into a basket, then a stick was inserted through the basket handle and placed across the barrel opening so that the basket was suspended inside. We put a big hood over the top of the barrel and let the fire smolder, tending it from time to time. After the apples had been in there for most of the day, we would take them out and pack them in a big crock or can them. Whenever we wanted to eat them, we would take some out of the crock, wash them off, and fry them. They were so good. Some people would say they didn't like them because of the sulfur taste, but I never much noticed it. We used sulfur all the time for a disinfectant too.

A year or so ago, when I was stringing beans, the mailman came and said, "What in the world are you going to do with them beans?"

When I told him we were going to eat them, he just kind of turned his head and shrugged his shoulders. I reckon he thought it was strange to go to all that trouble of picking out the good beans, snapping off the ends, and pulling the strings out, and then sitting there for hours running a needle and thread through them to sew them together when you could just go into town and buy a can at the store.

Back when I was young, we didn't have much choice. With only a few exceptions, if you didn't grow it or raise it or gather it, you didn't eat it. And that was that!

Ordered from Sears Roebuck

Even though I had to quit school to work, I was not resentful. I was content and felt fortunate to be able to spend my evenings and nights and whatever free time I had at the mission. In fact, I stayed at the mission so much that people would tease me, saying, "Miss Marston must have sent off and ordered you from Sears Roebuck."

The chapel women were always sending in orders for something or other and it just amazed us that people could, or for that matter would, actually order such things out of a catalog. Who ever heard of ordering cookies! Why, one time they even ordered dried fish. Of course, I was impressed, not necessarily with the dried fish, but with being able to look at pictures in the catalog and then just send in an order saying, "I want this and this." Not to mention, I loved all that different food.

The chapel women did eat many foods that we had never seen or heard of. They cooked and prepared their foods differently too, and always made their food look pretty; they called it "garnishing." We didn't have many things at all that were pretty and I don't guess it would have ever crossed our minds to make our food pretty. It wouldn't be pretty for long, anyways.

One time they invited the whole class from Sunday school over to eat dinner with them. They had fixed a pineapple salad. You know, a pineapple ring with a scoop of cottage cheese in the middle with a red cherry right on top. We had never seen pineapple before and we had no idea what we were to do with it. Some of the younger children kind of played with theirs; they usually didn't like to eat strange food. Most of us just watched to see what the chapel women would do with theirs.

One thing Mrs. Henderson and Miss Marston had that I liked was dried peaches. One time they had some of those peaches left out on the table and I helped myself to some of them. It made me feel so bad. I thought that I was just awful because, you see, I felt like I had snitched them. Of course, I had to tell them I had stolen the peaches. They smiled and said that I hadn't stolen them. That's what they were out there for— to eat.

We would always have especially nice and "pretty" meals when the superintendent of the mission would come visit. I always referred to him as "Big Chief," although not to his face. I guess that was because everyone made such a big fuss about him, putting out the best of everything we had—the finest quilts on the bed, the fanciest scarves and doilies on the furniture. And, of course, we always made the dinner table especially pretty with flowers and such. We would even go out and gather fresh flowers to put in vases that would be placed in the bedrooms and in other places around the house.

To me, living at the mission was always exciting. It was like being able to live two lives or in two completely different worlds at the same time. Why, I thought I was the luckiest person in the whole world.

One time when Mrs. Henderson came back from one of her visits home, she brought a big old phonograph. It was the first one any of us had ever seen. She played several records and showed me all about how it worked. I guess we got a little loud, playing the songs and trying to sing along with them. People could hear it all over and pretty soon, before we knew it, the whole house was so full we couldn't get anyone else in.

Mrs. Henderson put on this one record "Swing Low, Sweet Chariot" and everybody wanted her to play it over and over. Funniest thing, they all thought it was saying, "*Somebody carry me home,*" and for the longest time the people around here were singing, "*Swing low, sweet chariot. Somebody carry me home. Swing low, sweet chariot. Somebody carry me home.*"

Almost every night we sat downstairs and played the phonograph and talked until we were ready to go upstairs to bed. Sometimes there would be crowds of people there to listen, but more often than not, it would just be Miss Marston, Mrs. Henderson, and me.

It was during that time in my life when God really became important to me. I had grown up knowing about God. I had learned from Miss Marston, Mrs. Henderson, Mrs. Robinson, and the other chapel women early in my life that God was everything, all-important.

Papa had grown up going to church, and he and Mama went all the time after they married. But it was listening to the chapel women talk about God and what He had done or was doing that made me realize that knowing Him was more than just going to church. They loved Him, adored Him. I knew God loved us and gave Himself for us, but I had no idea that a person could love God so much.

Mary Ellison's Wedding

Mama's cousin, Louis Clark, you know, the Baptist preacher they called Traveling Toe, would stop in at the chapel house most every Sunday. He was still walking and still preaching three or four times every Sunday, first at Shady Grove, then Bridgeport, and finishing up at West Myers that night.

When he stopped at the mission, Mrs. Henderson would always have a cup of coffee and a piece of cake or something for him to eat. Usually Uncle Louis's mind would be on his preaching, and I guess he never would take any time to eat unless someone sat him down and put it in front of him. He was the only Clark who lived right around here, but there were dozens of them living in Slabtown.

I always enjoyed hearing him talk about all the things that "the Lord is a-doin." Sometimes he would tell us about a funeral or a wedding. And you can be sure that ever since the days of "stormy weather," "minner and gimmer," and, of course, Victoria Hall and Regan Jennings, I especially liked hearing about the weddings. They were my first weddings ever and I would never forget them. Most of the people around these parts just slipped off to get married because public weddings sometimes still caused too much celebrating and foolishness.

The first home wedding that I ever knew about was when my Aunt Martha married Isaac Crum. I was there, but that was probably back around 1913, so I was too young to remember much. We children were most likely outside playing and didn't even know what was going on.

We had never heard of church weddings other than what we might read in a newspaper or magazine at the chapel house. The only church wedding I ever saw until after I was grown and married was Mary Ellison's, Clark's sister. The chapel women gave Mary a wedding that was not to be forgotten by anyone, and I was so excited that I was there to help. We spent hours upon hours making all kinds of decorations and food.

The day before the wedding, the chapel women gave an infare supper for Mary and Carl's parents and all those who were in their wedding. Miss Marston called a reception an infare, a word we had never heard before, but then not that many had ever heard of a reception.

The day of the wedding, we got up early and spent all morning fixing up the church. We built a crude frame about five feet wide and centered it at the front of the church. In the middle of the frame, we made a tall window for the preacher to stand behind. Then we covered the entire frame solid with spruce pine branches, leaving only the space where the preacher would be. Around the church we had placed ferns and other evergreen arrangements as well as all the wildflowers we could find. We even picked the chapel house flower garden clean. It was beautiful. We finished a little before noon, giving us just enough time to change into our church clothes before the wedding.

Miss Marston played the wedding march and the couple walked down the isle and stood before the preacher who was behind the decorated window. It seemed to me like they were walking up to the side of the preacher's house and he leaned out his window to marry them. Mary wore a pretty homemade dress; it was white and long, but there was no veil.

It was not customary for the people up here to exchange rings. They did not have the money nor did they get into town much. Mrs. Henderson gave Carl a necklace to give Mary, and Mary gave Carl something that she had.

After the wedding, there was an infare at the chapel house. Before we ate, we played a game called musical paper. We had torn pages out of a Sears Roebuck catalog and put them on the floor. I had always thought that maybe we should have called the game Mail Order Bride. Someone would beat on a pan, just like we did playing musical chairs when we were little. When the music stopped, the person who wasn't standing on a paper was out. Each time you would take up a paper. It was always funny when two people were going around that last piece of paper. Many times they would end up on their backsides on the floor, but the people enjoyed playing it.

Out on the porch we had placed a big table for the food that was almost as long as the porch, which went all the way across the front of the house. There was everything imaginable on that table. We had baked cakes and pies and, of course, best of all was her special wedding cake. To decorate the cake they had beaten up egg whites until they were stiff and put sugar in it, like you would make a meringue. They had made stiff peaks around the cake and placed red cinnamon candy berries on each one. Never had there been a prettier cake in these parts!

The guests brought food for the main meal. There were all kinds of beans, green beans and shab beans, as well as potatoes, corn bread, biscuits, gingerbread, and meats. The food the guests brought wasn't fancy like the mission food, but for sure no one went hungry.

I don't remember seeing any more church weddings until Preacher McKinney came to be the preacher at our church. And I went to all of his weddings.

Christmas of 1926

Right along with the Christmas party on Christmas Eve and the Christmas program on Christmas Day, our Christmas Eve after party had really become a family and community tradition. The day before Christmas Eve in 1926, Daffy Turner came down to my house to help us prepare for our after party and to spend the night with me. We had the best time making molasses popcorn balls and planning what games and things we wanted to do at the after party. One thing we decided to do was spice up the popcorn balls. So we poured a whole big bag of those spicy cinnamon red hots, the same kind we had used to decorate Mary Ellison's wedding cake, into the molasses syrup and melted them.

As usual, we had a houseful of people at the party. Daffy was dating Ben, so he was there along with all our other friends and my family. Daffy and I encouraged everyone to try our molasses popcorn balls— like we were so proud of making them. Those molasses balls were so hot that no one could eat them. Of course, Daffy and I had to pretend that we thought they were fine and ate several.

We sat up playing paper dolls until midnight. Paper dolls were very popular at that time, even with the older girls, and we could get them at the mission. Then we played checkers and dominos and old maids while we dared each other to eat more and more candy, molasses balls, and cake until we were all so sick. Not exactly physically sick, but very close to losing it all. We had eaten so much that we couldn't stand even the thought of food, especially anything sweet.

About daylight I was feeling particularly bad. Daffy and I didn't even want to see food, let alone eat it. Velma and Desmer knew how we felt and took advantage of the chance to tease us. They would offer us a big piece of cake or some other sweet. Oh, just the thought of it would make me sick. They would eat in front of us, taking big bites and letting the food show as they chewed it. Ben had not eaten as much as us, so it didn't bother him. Even Daffy was in better shape than I was.

Miss Marston's Death

Only a week or so after my sixteenth birthday, I learned that Miss Marston needed surgery. I was staying at the mission with Mrs. Henderson in February of 1927, when Miss Marston went into the Knoxville General Hospital to have a tumor removed. She never came back. That was one of the worst times for me. I had never thought of having to do without her.

After Miss Marston died, everything changed. Mixed in with all of my grief were so many questions. What would the mission be like without Miss Marston? Would there even be a mission? Mrs. Henderson had always been more of a helper or an assistant; she would never be able to manage the mission and the school. Would someone be sent to take Miss Marston's place? What would happen to the school? To the families who depended on the mission? What of the sick? The needy? How could we go on? Next to my family, the mission had been my life and I just couldn't imagine going on without it. You see, to me it wasn't just Miss Marston I had lost; it was the mission too, at least as I had always known it. It was almost more than I could handle.

From the time I was little, I had thought about the mission and chapel people and wondered what it would be like here if they had never come to help our community. What would my life have been like? I had no idea. Without the mission, there would not have been a real church and all those wonderful socials and Christmas programs. There had not been a preacher living at the mission for some time, but the Presbyterian Church would send young preachers out to the chapel to preach. We wouldn't have had a school where the teachers sincerely loved us and cared about us and our families.

Mrs. Henderson took care of the people in the community as she had before, but it was not the same, and the mission school never reopened after Miss Marston left. The parents who wanted their children to continue with their educations sent them down to Sand Hill. Even though I had not been able to attend classes, I had been keeping up with my subjects. I was seventeen years old and in the eighth grade. I stayed at home and did the work so my sisters could go to Sand Hill. I guess you could say I was a dropout.

As it turned out, Miss Marston had put so much of herself into me, and even though I missed her something awful, through my memories of her, I always felt as though she was with me. At times, especially when I felt discouraged or was almost ready to give up, I could almost hear her say, "You can become anything you want to be. And with God's help you can do anything you set your heart to do, if you're willing to work for it." Or I would think about where she showed me in Jeremiah that God had a plan for my life and it was to be a good plan. Those words, as well as many others she spoke or read to me, were like a key that opened up the door of my heart and my future. They caused me to have hope and to dream. I have always tried to pass that hope and encouragement on to all my students and the people of my community and I hope that they have passed it on to their children.

My work kept me busy, and most nights I would stay in the chapel house with Mrs. Henderson. When the weather got a little warmer and the trees were beginning to bud, I would go up to the top of the mountain behind the mission almost every day. Everything was coming back to life after the cold winter. I had a favorite spot where I would sit and think about the mission and Miss Marston. It was beginning to look like no one would be coming to take her place, and I had no idea how long the mission could survive without someone. I missed her so much. She had just been everything to me, you know. I didn't want to lose the mission too.

It was one of those times up on the mountain that I knew—somehow I had to get my education and come back here to be a mission worker. I could take care of the people. It seemed like I had always been taking care of someone around the community. I could do it—I just knew it. I could feel it deep down inside of me. And just like Miss Marston had always told me, I would work hard and never give up.

That was the day I made a bargain with God. Sitting up on the mountain, I looked right up at God and said, "If You will make it possible for me to get a scholarship and go off to school, I promise that I will come back here and be a mission worker and take care of my people." And I meant it! And I never once doubted that's just what would be. Oh, there were times when I didn't know how it would, but from that moment on I never doubted that it was God's purpose for my life.

Sand Hill School

The Sand Hill School and the Mt. Zion Baptist Church shared the same small log building. It sat right where our church is located now, except its door faced the cemetery. The desk seats had long church-like benches and each desk held two students. When I was little, I can remember going to a few funerals at Mt. Zion Church. Some of the other smaller children and I sat on top of the desks, because if we sat down behind them in the church seats, we couldn't see the preacher.

The students were all ages and all grades up through the eighth. The teacher did not have a desk or even a chair. He sat on a wooden box at the front of the schoolroom. When it was time to teach a certain class, like maybe arithmetic, all the students in that class would come up to the front of the room and sit on the floor in front of the teacher's box. Some might sit in empty desks at the front of the room if there were any.

Every afternoon when I would finish my work early enough, I'd go to the school to be with my sisters and the other kids. Back then, anyone could visit Sand Hill and sit in on the classes. I came more just to be there than anything. I never learned anything new, but there was something about being in a school that made me feel good…complete.

One day when I was visiting there, something happened that changed my whole life and made me even more determined to get my education and return to help my people. But I doubt seriously that the teacher had any idea that I was even there that day.

Well, on that particular afternoon, when I walked into the school, the teacher had the older students up front and was teaching them geography. He was sitting on the front side of his wooden box, rocking back and forth, just a-teachin' away. He never did seem quite right to me. I just didn't have much use for him at all.

The rest of the students were sitting at their desks working on their lessons. If they were done, they could play what the teacher called "deaf and dumb" games. That meant he didn't want to hear any talking or noise. If he did, someone was likely going to get a whoopin'.

I sat down in the back of the room by this little boy named Ernest. He had brought a grasshopper in from recess so he could play a deaf and dumb game of horsie. He tore off the grasshopper's back legs and handed me one of his pencils so I could play horsie with him. To win you had to get your horsie to cross over the line that had been carved down the middle of the desktop to separate the two students' areas. You could only use your pencil or a little stick to guide your horsie over that line or to keep it from going off the ends of the desk. The other person used their pencil and tried to keep the horsie from crossing over the line.

After we had been playing horsie for a while, why, we just heard the awfulest commotion up at the front of the room. The geography class was just a-rollin' around in the floor and a-laughin'. Then we saw the teacher. There he was, with his tail end stuck in that box and his hands and his feet sticking up in the air.

Well, of course, it took us a while to get our minds back on our game, and just about the time I thought I was going to win the game, there went that noise again. The teacher had fallen in the box again with his hands and feet sticking up in the air. Now all the students were laughin' and almost completely out of control.

By this time, I was certain he was drunk. I had heard one of the men say that he drank with him sometimes. I thought that was something awful, a teacher who would get drunk at school. I decided right then and there that somehow I would get my education and come back here to be a teacher. I looked over at Ernest and said, "I know I could stay on top of that box!" Of course he didn't know what I was talking about, but I had made up my mind. I might not be the best teacher, but I for sure wouldn't be falling down in some ol' wooden box!

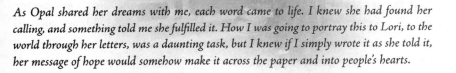

As Opal shared her dreams with me, each word came to life. I knew she had found her calling, and something told me she fulfilled it. How I was going to portray this to Lori, to the world through her letters, was a daunting task, but I knew if I simply wrote it as she told it, her message of hope would somehow make it across the paper and into people's hearts.

12
Scholarship (age 16–17)
1927–1928

Dear Lori,

I hope you have found a dream for yourself to follow like I did that day I decided to be a teacher and work at the mission. It wasn't an easy road, but sometimes the best roads traveled are the slow, steady ones.

By the time Burl had graduated from Highland in May of 1927, he had already been offered a partial college scholarship to the S.P. Lees Collegiate Institute in Jackson, Kentucky, not far from Highland. They even helped him find a summer job there in Jackson. This would be the first summer he wouldn't be able to come home. He knew it would mean a lot more work for Papa and for the rest of us too, but there was nothing he could do about it. Without the money from this job, he wouldn't be able to pay the rest of his tuition. That school became a two-year college in 1927 and changed its name to Lees Junior College.

Maggie was upset something awful. She didn't like the idea of riding home on the train alone, not one little bit. Her eyesight was not good and she was afraid she would get lost or left at a station. It was hard for her. Burl walked Maggie to the train station and told her to tell Mama and Papa that if he could, he would come back home for a short visit before college started.

She told them all right, and almost in the same breath she told us that she was not going to go back to Highland. She didn't want to be that far away from home, not without Burl, and she didn't ever want to ride on the train alone again. I'm sure that not being able to see well had a lot to do with her fear of traveling alone, especially since she had to change trains several times. Maggie's eyesight had become so weak during the last school year that it had been almost impossible for her to see the blackboard, no matter how close they had her sit. The school had even told her that in order to maintain her grades, she would need to have her vision corrected before next term.

Without Miss Marston, there was no one left to get scholarships for the remaining students or to find funds that might be available for special needs, like glasses for Maggie. Probably if someone had thought about it, they could have written to the Sunday school class that provided her scholarship, but no one did. Mrs. Henderson was extremely upset over Miss Marston's death, and her own health seemed to be getting worse also. She was not one to handle finances or business matters, so she probably never would have thought about finding someone to help with Maggie's eyes.

Maggie knew how much I wanted to go to Highland but tried to convince me to stay home. "Opal, you just don't know how far that is. I had Burl with me, but you'd be by yourself and you've never been on a real train ride. You know you wouldn't go all that way by yourself!"

But I didn't care how far away it was. I didn't care that I would be alone. I knew it would be difficult, but going to Highland was more than a mere something of interest. I knew that I was to be a mission teacher and I was determined. Somehow there had to be a way, and I was going to find it.

I offered, "I'll go! I just know I'll go!" Mama didn't want me to go at all either. And Papa—well, Papa didn't say anything.

Even though Maggie was home to do the chores and the other children were old enough to help more, I could not go to Highland without a lot of money or a scholarship. Miss Marston had once told me, "You never know just how the Lord will provide." Even though somewhere deep inside I knew that He would, I still struggled. If only Miss Marston hadn't died. If only the "Big Chief" would send someone to take her place. If only I could have gone to Highland earlier. Mrs. Henderson knew how I felt. She had most likely said some of those same things herself.

Maggie's Scholarship

One day when I was going through my list of "whys" and "if onlys," Mrs. Henderson put her arms around me and held me snugly. Then she put her hands firmly on my shoulders and pushed me to arms length and stared directly into my eyes. "Opal, it just doesn't do any good to sit around talking about what might have been or to start each sentence with `if only.' If you don't do something to make it happen, it never will. Why don't you start by writing to Dr. Guerrant (the son of the founder) and ask him if you can have Maggie's scholarship?"

"What do I say?"

"Just write and ask him if you can have it."

So that's exactly what I did. I got my pencil down and I wrote:

> Dear Dr. Guerrant:
> Can I have Margaret's scholarship?
> Sincerely,
> Opal

That was all I wrote. Mrs. Henderson mailed the letter for me and later, when I thought back on it, I suspicioned that she might have written to him also, explaining my situation. I doubt that from my very brief letter he would have any idea who Margaret or Opal was.

One day in late June or early July, I got a letter from Dr. Guerrant saying that they would give me Margaret's scholarship. I was so happy that I was beside myself, you know. At last, after all these years, I was going away to school!

That letter from Dr. Guerrant and the scholarship, to me, were nothing less than a miracle that proved that Miss Marston was right and that I was going to become a mission teacher. God did want me to be a mission worker and I had the proof—in writing.

There was still one big problem and several of lesser consequence. The biggest being that we didn't have any money, literally—not even a penny. Mrs. Henderson had to pay the two cents to mail my letter to Dr. Guerrant. Even when Maggie was away at school, we always had to go to Miss Marston or Mrs. Henderson every week for stamps, and Mama paid them back out of her wash money.

I needed twenty dollars for the train ticket. I would need clothes, shoes, school supplies, a suitcase, and possibly even a trunk. Maggie would probably let me use her suitcase. If I could get one more dress, that would give me two school dresses, one work dress, and a church dress. And shoes, I would have to have shoes. My church shoes were worn out and the shoes I worked in were men's ankle-high work boots; they would never do for school. There were a lot of needs, but I knew that it was meant for me to go. I was too excited to worry and besides, I figured that if God wanted me to go then somehow He was going to see that I got the things I needed.

Papa had been up at the Fish Place and when he came home he handed me twenty dollars. "I borrowed the money for ya. Now ya can go on to school and make us all proud."

Mrs. Fish, Minnie's mama, was one of the few around here who had any money. She received a pension check from the army because her son had been killed in the service when Minnie was about seven years old. The only person other than Mrs. Fish that we knew of with any money was the old man who lived across the hill. He had evidently been in some war and now received a pension.

Leaving for School

During the summer, Papa had let Maggie and Beatrice go into town with John and Ben to see the fair. During the last two summers, John, Ben, Maggie, Beatrice, and I had spent a lot of time together and had all become best friends. We did everything together and I was so jealous that they got to go to the fair when I had to stay home and work. You see, Maggie kind of liked John and so to get even, just for the fun of it, I had John take me for long walks. John was real nice and I liked talking with him. It made me even madder though that it really hadn't bothered Maggie at all, so I soon figured I might as well just get over it.

Well, the rest of the summer went by fast and slow, both at the same time. When it was time for me to leave, I had everything I needed. It had all worked out. I had done my part; I had worked hard and I had never given up on my dreams. And God did His part. He had most certainly worked a miracle and everything worked out perfectly.

The day before I was to leave for school, Papa hitched the mules up to the wagon and took my trunk and other things to the depot in Del Rio. If we had waited and I had taken my things with me to catch the train, we would have had to leave before daylight and take the wagon over those winding narrow roads full of ruts and holes in the pitch dark. Why, those mules, just as easy as not, would most likely have trotted right off the side of the mountain. It was easier and much safer to take my things the day before and then walk to the train the next day.

That evening all my friends and family came over to our house. Friends and relatives would always make a big issue of anyone in the community leaving or coming home. Most everybody brought something to eat. I guess now we would call that a potluck, but back then that was just what we did whenever we went to visit someone and have a meal with them.

John, Ben, and some others all spent the night at our place so they could walk with Papa and me into Del Rio early the next morning. Even though we stayed awake for a long time talking, we were all up at three o'clock in order to get ready and eat a big breakfast before leaving to walk through the woods down to the river and then on to the depot in Del Rio. I was glad that Papa was going to ride the train into Newport with me. He had planned it so we could have the whole morning together in town.

For sure I would miss my family and all of my friends, and I knew that I would be homesick. John and Ben would soon be going away to work and leaving the community, too. And I wondered if anything would ever be the same again. As Papa and I were getting on the train, just for fun and to get at Maggie, I said, "You'll write to me when you go, won't you, John?"

He blurted back, "No, I won't. You know I don't write letters."

Ben said, "I will! I'll write you for sure, Opal."

On the way to Newport, I studied what the train agent had called my "travel agenda," which I had carefully written down in the tablet I brought along. I wanted to keep notes of my experiences away from home. Maybe someday I would use those notes to write another book. I had thought a lot about Miss Marston lately. I wished she had been there to see me off to school. She would have been so happy for me.

I looked over my schedule, trying to memorize it all just the way I had written it down. I was so excited and very nervous about leaving.

4:00 p.m. Newport to Knoxville arrival 6:00 p.m.
Wait three hours
9:00 p.m. leave Knoxville arrive at next stop at 1:00 a.m.
Short wait
Board train to Lexington, Kentucky, arrival 7:00 a.m.
Change from Southern Railway to L & N
Take taxi to station
Wait one and a half hours
Board train for Oakdale
Arrive Oakdale about 12 noon
Meet Burl at station and walk to the school

When we got off the train in Newport, there was a man selling ice cold lemonade out of a big tub with a large block of ice floating in it. This had become a favorite thing for people to do when they went into town, and there was a long line of people waiting to buy some. Back then people didn't have ice to put into drinks. Some people who lived in town had those old fashioned iceboxes. The iceman would deliver a big chunk of ice to their house and put it in their iceboxes to keep their food cold.

Papa and I walked all over Newport. I felt so special in my new dress walking alongside my Papa. I had the front part of my hair pulled back from my face and tied with a ribbon. The rest of my hair I had curled and it hung loosely down my back. The dress wasn't really new. Mrs. Henderson had found three dresses in the donations that would work perfectly for school. She had found me some shoes too, and ribbons for my hair. I was never the fancy ribbon type, but I wore one that day for Mrs. Henderson. I put my arm around Papa's and he pulled me real close. I knew he would miss me, but I could tell that he was so proud of me. I wouldn't disappoint him for the world. I was determined that no matter how scared I was or how homesick I got, I was not quitting. I would make them all proud.

We got back to the train depot around noon and ate the lunch Mama packed for us. After we ate, Papa had to leave to start walking back home. He had to walk all that way back because he had spent the last bit of his money buying me a big bag of apples to take and eat on the train and the glass of lemonade that we shared with our lunch.

It was sad saying goodbye to Papa and I could tell that it was hard for him too. He gave me one of his big ol' hugs that always took me off my feet and swung me around. We both said goodbye with tears in our eyes.

After Papa left, I looked around in some stores and then went back to the train depot and people-watched. I could hardly believe that it was all true. I had only been to town that one time before when I was eight years old. And now, eight years later, here I was, all by myself, about to get on a train heading for Knoxville, my first of many stops.

When my train finally came that afternoon, I got on and passed the time by writing in my tablet. I made notes about everyone, what they were wearing, what they looked like, at which stations they boarded the train, and where they got off.

My Vinegar and Molasses Man

Right on schedule, it was six o'clock and we were arriving in Knoxville. I put my tablet and pencil back in my little basket suitcase with the food Mama had packed for me to eat on my trip and picked up my bag of apples. When I got out of my seat and turned toward the door, this right good-looking young man came up and asked if he could help carry my suitcase. I refused his offer with a rather too blunt "no." I don't know where I got the idea of being so cautious of young men. I don't remember Mama or any of them ever telling me not to go off with someone I didn't know. It certainly wasn't because I was bashful, so I suppose Mrs. Henderson, along with her other advice about living away from home, had probably told me not to talk to strangers.

There was a three-hour wait until I would board the next train. I spent most of that time watching everything around me and writing in my tablet. Almost everything was new to me. Why, you can just imagine what it would feel like! I wrote a little bit about that good-looking young man—most of that time he was sitting across from me and every once in a while I would catch him looking at me.

When we got back on the train, the good-looking young man was no longer very friendly—in fact, when I spoke to him he was sort of hateful. I added some more notes about him in my tablet, calling him my "vinegar and molasses man" because he was sweet when he wanted to carry my suitcase but bitter after I rejected his offer. I quickly noted in my writing, "I don't want to waste time with someone like that."

The Depot Agent

When I got off at my next stop, it was one o'clock in the morning, and there wasn't a soul there except for two depot agents. I think one of them was just getting off work and the other one had come to replace him. I went in and sat down on one of the long church-like benches to wait for my next train. It wouldn't be too long of a wait and I was glad because, even with the excitement, I was beginning to get tired.

After I had been sitting there a few minutes, the off-duty depot agent said, "Little girl, would you want to go for a ride?"

"A ride?!? What do you mean, a ride?"

"Yah, a ride. We could take a ride while you're waiting and look around. Makes time go faster than just sitting around waiting for your train to come."

He was interrupted by a lady carrying a lunchbox coming in the door. She gave him a disgusted look and she sat down by me. "Kinda late for a young thing like you to be out, ain't it now?"

We talked for a while and she told me about her husband who was a train conductor. Every night she cooked a hot supper for him and brought it to the station, which was about a mile from her house. "Important for a working man to have a hot meal, ya know. They hafta keep up their strength."

I guess it must have been important for her to walk a mile every day at that time of the morning.

She was a nice lady and I was glad she was there, because that ticket agent really gave me the spooks. I told the lady about what he had said to me and she got all riled up. "Don't you never, never go off with anybody strange! There's no telling what that man would do!"

It turned out that I was to be on her husband's train and she made a point of telling him to watch out for me.

It was about 7:00 the next morning, right after daylight, when the train pulled into Lexington, Kentucky, where I was to transfer from Southern Railroad to the L & N. The taxi driver put my trunk and suitcase in the trunk of his cab and opened the back door for me to get in. This was my first taxi ride and only the second time I had ever been in a car. It was a mile to the L & N station, but I wasn't the slightest bit afraid, not like I had been on my first car ride. I had to wait there about an hour or two before boarding the train to Oakdale where I was to meet Burl. He took the train down from Jackson, which was about eight miles away so he could help me get to school.

Oakdale

I was the first one to get off the train in Oakdale, and right off I saw Burl and one of his friends waiting to walk me over to Highland. Burl and his friend carried my trunk and I carried my suitcases, which now held the rest of my apples. They only had a few hours before they had to catch the train back to Jackson, so we had to walk fast. Walking fast up and down mountains and carrying heavy loads was nothing to me, or Burl either, not with all the hard work we did at home.

The trees and land didn't look that much different than at home and it seemed strange that I could really be so far away from Mama and Papa. It seemed like I had waited all my life for this moment and here I was. Why, I was so excited I couldn't have walked slow even up a mountain so steep that my nose touched the ground!

As I took my first step onto the campus, it was exactly like walking into my own dream. I was so excited; I just couldn't believe I was really there. As we walked forward towards the main building, I turned around and around several times just looking, taking it all in. It was all like I thought it would be and much, much more, just like the pictures I had seen and just like Maggie had described it to me. Somehow I had always known exactly what it would look like. I can remember wondering if I was dreaming. Maybe I had fallen asleep on the train and I would wake up and find out I had missed my next stop. Or worse yet, maybe I would wake up at home in my bed or at the chapel house. Even pinching myself didn't help; it still seemed too much like a dream, too wonderful to ever be real. I know that Burl and his friend thought I was acting like a silly girl, but I didn't care, not even one little bit. I was living out my dream!

13
Eighth Grade (age 16–17)
1927–1928

*H*ighland Institute was almost self-contained. They had everything right there: a church, hospital, school, post office, dormitories, and a big farm. They had two dormitories for the girls, one for the older and one for the younger girls, and the same set-up for the boys.

Miles Griffin and Miss Warden

When I walked up to the main building of the school, there was a boy named Miles Griffin sitting at the top of a wide set of steps that led up to the entrance. His sister was sitting at the bottom.

"Everyone's 'bout finished eat'n dinner now. Miss Patty Warden's head of this here dormitory; she'll be back directly. You can sit down with us if you'd like." They were real friendly and it made me feel comfortable.

Miles and his sister lived about halfway to Jackson and had to walk a long way to get to school. But back then it was not unusual for students to walk three to four miles to school and then home again that afternoon. His sister and I became good friends and continued our friendship even after she left Highland in '28 or '29. Her family had decided to move closer to the Jackson school so the children wouldn't have to walk so far. Even though the last time I saw her was when I graduated in 1932, we have written to each other all these years. Then last fall for her 76th birthday, her sister gave her a choice of what she wanted for a birthday present, and she said she wanted to go to Tennessee to see me. They only stayed here an hour or two, but we sure did dig up a lot of old bones in that time. You just can't imagine what it's like knowing people that long!

My First Bathroom with Running Water

When Miss Warden came back she welcomed me to the school. "Miles, help Opal upstairs with her things and show her where her room is."

When I came back down, Miss Warden asked, "Is your room all right? Is there anything you need?"

"Everything is very nice, but I'd sure like to go to the spring and wash up," I told her.

Everyone thought it was funny that I wanted to know where the spring was. Miss Warden sent me back upstairs with this girl named Mary and instructed her to show me where the bathroom was.

Mary opened a door off the hallway, just down from where my room was, and said, "This is the bathroom the girls staying in this side of the building use." She pointed to the spigots.

What do I do now? I thought. Everything was new to me, and even though I was so glad to finally be there, inside I felt like a very scared little girl.

Mary took a glass out of a cupboard and told me that it was mine to use and I should keep it in my room. Then she reached over to the spigot and turned it on, filling my glass with water. "Here, I reckon you're thirsty."

I was glad she did that because I had no idea what to do in a bathroom. I'd never seen running water in a house and I didn't know where that water was coming from. The sink was right next to the toilet and I had figured out what you did with that. I looked at those spigots and then I looked back at that toilet. Well, that thing looked dirty to me and that spigot water coming out so close to it! I looked at my glass and back to the toilet. "No, I'm not very thirsty, but thank you just the same." I poured the water out and took the glass to my room. I was afraid that the water was somehow coming out of the toilet, and you can be sure I didn't want nothing to do with it! I don't know how long it was before I realized that the water was good for drinking.

After I was settled, Miss Warden came to my room to discuss the rules of the school with me. She checked the length of my dresses, which were all three inches below my knees, exactly as the rules stated. Most girls had to let down their hems, but I had always worn mine like that.

For years, over and over I had asked Mrs. Henderson and Miss Marston to tell me about Highland and Kentucky, about the teachers and the students, about what they did and what I would learn there. I don't think Miss Warden told me one single rule that I didn't already know about, and I really didn't think I would have any problems with them or the school. I knew for sure I would get homesick and I did. That improved some with time, especially after the first year, but I never did get completely over being homesick. Things were so different from the way it was back home, but I was determined and nothing was going to stop me now that I had made it this far. You know, I even got homesick when I was in college.

The next day when I met Dr. Guerrant, he teased me, "I liked that nice, brief letter you wrote to me. 'Can I have Margaret's scholarship?'" He emphasized the word *can*. Of course, I should have said, "May I."

Letter from Ben

After I had been there for a month or so, I got a letter from Ben. I was always so excited to get a letter from anyone back home, even Ben. He told me all about his job and how he was called a water boy. He liked living with his aunt and uncle. I had met their daughter one time. Elizabeth was her name and I liked her a lot and I think Ben was her favorite first cousin. Of course, he was just tickled to death about having a job. The Meyers never had any money or anything before.

I was so glad to be getting letters that I never stopped to think that Ben couldn't write letters like those. I found out much later that Elizabeth was writing the letters for him. He'd tell her what he wanted to say and she'd write. Even though Maggie, John, Ben, Beatrice, and I had all been close, especially that last summer, I never did particularly care much just for Ben himself. But as we got to writing letters that first year I was away, I started liking Ben as my friend.

Insist on Staying in the 8th Grade

Well, after the first month, Dr. Guerrant called me to his office. His eyes seemed to be laughing at me, but in a way that made me feel good—accepted. I could tell that he had been looking over my grades, which had been in the high nineties for all my classes. "Opal, I must tell you that I have been watching you with much interest. I'm very impressed with the reports I've received from your teachers and work supervisors. I believe that with these grades you could easily skip over the eighth grade and go on into the high school. I really don't feel that it would affect your grades much at all. You are a very bright young lady."

I didn't need to give it much thought before deciding what I wanted to do. "No, Sir, I won't be doing that. I've never been outside of my community back home and I just don't know anything about anything. Nothing comes easy for me except for what's in these books and I need to have time to learn other things, things about just plain ol' living. So, I'll just be staying in the eighth grade this year."

Even though I was sixteen years old, I knew I was not ready for high school. The other students laughed at me so much because there was a lot I didn't know. I hadn't been out enough. Almost everything that others took for granted was new and usually a surprise to me. If I stayed in the eighth grade that year, I wouldn't have to worry about my grades and I would have time to learn more about life and things that would help me out later.

I'm sure now that was the reason I became valedictorian, too, because by staying in that eighth grade, I had a chance to get caught up on other things.

Study Time and Work Time

The school was very strict about our studies and expected us to take them seriously. There was no messing around—if you didn't do your best, there were always consequences. When students made less than ninety percent in any subject, every weeknight from eight to nine, they had to take all their books and go back to their schoolroom for study hall whether they wanted to or not. Most of the students needed all the study time they could get. Their teacher would be there to work with them individually or in small groups until everyone knew what they were supposed to know. You really couldn't fail at Highland unless you deliberately did nothing.

Highland was only for the poor, unfortunates, and orphans. None of the students came from families who could afford to pay the tuition. Sometimes the school would take a student who had come from a family with money if a parent had died, or had been in an accident and were no longer able to work. There were several girls in my dormitory whose parents were pretty well to do by the standards I grew up with—or so I thought. They were still called poor by everyone else. Looking at those girls and some of the other students, I soon figured out that I must be from the poorest of the poor by money standards, but I was from the wealthiest of the wealthy by standards of family, friends, and values.

All the children who attended the school had to work twenty-one hours a week unless they were on a scholarship, then they just had to work ten. I earned a scholarship every year, but of course I always worked twenty-five to thirty hours when I was only supposed to work ten. If things needed to be done, I'd just go ahead and do it. After all, I was accustomed to being busy all the time.

The school had a big farm. The boys had to feed the cattle, milk the cows, and then bring the milk into the house. It was one girl's job to strain and separate the milk and put it in the cooler. She had to have the milk done everyday before school started, and during work time after school, she'd have to churn the cream to make butter. At night she would have to wait until the boys brought in the milk and then she would work until all of it was separated and put into the cooler.

Molasses Days

We always grew a large crop of cane, more than enough to last the entire year and then some. It seemed like we had a good crop every year I was there. Of course, having a good yield depends a lot on the weather. If the spring is cold and wet, the cane doesn't come up as good or produce as much.

During cane harvesting time, which we always called Molasses Days, the whole school closed down and all of us students would dress in our oldest clothes. Everyone had their jobs to do. Most of the high school students would go out to the cane fields where some of them would strip the leaves off the stalks, which resemble corn stalks. Then a couple of the other students would cut down the stalks and cut off the tops, which are the seed pods. The leaves and tops were used as fodder. The younger students would haul the stalks back to the molasses working area.

One of the older boys helping out at the cane mill would hook up a horse or mule to the pole that went to the grinding wheel. He would make sure whatever animal was hitched up would continue walking in order to push that pole around and around that circle to make the grinding wheel turn. Sometimes when the animal got slow, he would have to walk along side of it coaxing it to keep going. After a while the animal would get tired and have to be changed out and a different horse or mule would be hooked up.

After the stalks were run through the cane mill and had the juice crushed out of them, they were thrown into a pile and some of the eleven and twelve-year-old students would drag them off to the pit silo. There were always a gang of the little children who would follow after them and try to step on a cane stalk pulling it out of the bunch that was being carried. When they got one loose they would just chew away on that ol' crushed stalk to get the last of the syrup out. They would get it all over themselves and end up as sticky as they could be. I'll never forget how one time they got into a fight over the stalk and started throwing dirt at each other. They were covered from head to foot with dirt that stuck on them like a second skin because they were so sticky from that syrup. They were, for sure, just the biggest messes you ever did see.

Next we would strain and filter the juice through clean white cloths into buckets. The juice had to be wrung out of the cloths too and that was quite a job in itself and very messy. Once the juice was strained into the buckets, it was then toted over to where it was to be boiled. There it was poured into great big ol' boiling pans which, I guess, were about six or seven feet long by three feet wide and about twelve inches deep. A fire was built beneath each pan. It was very important that the juice was brought to a boil and maintained at a boiling temperature for six to seven hours or more. The strongest of the boys did this part because it took plenty of firewood. Each log had to be five to six feet long so that there would be an even heat beneath the boiler pans. Each boiling produced about ten gallons of molasses and it took about ten or eleven gallons of juice to make one gallon of molasses.

As the syrup boiled, bright green foam formed on the top. That green foam had to be constantly skimmed to remove the cane residue that came to the surface. When it was done, the foam would be a gold color and the molasses would be a golden brown. Another way to tell when it was done was by the size of the bubbles as it boiled. At first the bubbles are small, about the size of frogs' eyes. When it's closer to being done, the bubbles are the size a bull's eyes. The final test was to look at the thickness of the molasses.

When it was done, the molasses was taken off the heat and right away filtered again through cheesecloth before canning. The stronger boys carried the filtered molasses to the kitchen where it was put into quart jars and sealed. The jars would be left out on the tables until they cooled. When they cooled some, you could hear the tops pop as they sealed. Then the jars of molasses were taken to the storage room.

We used molasses as a sweetener for things like apple butter and in baking gingerbread cookies. I always liked it over hot buttered biscuits.

Working in the School Hospital

My first job was working in the small school hospital, which was used only for students and staff. I had to carry the slop pails into the only bathroom in the hospital, empty them, and then wash them out. I also had to clean up the bedpans, make the beds, do the laundry, and start the fire in the kitchen.

Up until that year, the school had a resident cook who would get up early to start the fires, but she became quite ill, so they hired this old lady to take her place. This lady had her own house and family, I guess, so she could not live in at the school. I had to get up early enough to build the fires for them and get the stove hot before the cook arrived.

Working in the hospital was not the most pleasant job to be had. But I had been waiting on sick people since I was about eight or nine years old so I didn't think too much about it.

One of my first days on that job I was asked to start the fire in the fireplace. I had certainly started many a fire at home and now was my chance to show them I did know how to do a few things. So, I readily accepted the job and proceeded with confidence until I was handed this bucket full of rocks and a box of matches to start the fire with. Well, I had never heard tell of burning rocks, but then again, I had never heard of water coming out of spigots right in the house, where you needed the water to be either. So I put a pile of those rocks in the fireplace and started striking matches, one after another. I knelt there striking matches for the longest time before someone finally came and told me I'd have to start a kindling fire first and, when it was good and hot, the rocks, which where called coal, would start to burn. So much for showing them how much I knew!

Homesick

I constantly fought homesickness. Everything was so different. I didn't want Mama and them to know how difficult it was for me, but I did write to Mrs. Henderson telling her. She wrote back reminding me of the many conversations we had about this:

Dear Opal,

If you want to reach the goals you have set, you cannot let anything stand in your way.

Usually when a person gets homesick, they have their mind on themselves and what it would be like to be back where they felt comfortable and safe.

Think about all the things you are learning, and even though it is difficult, it will help you to understand how hard it is for people to accept change. Understand the fear of change. When you come back here to become a teacher, you will have to help your children accept change. By going through this time, you will be able to better help them.

This very thing is what has prevented others from the community to get the education they needed. The rest of the world is very different than life in these little coves and hollows, as you have well found out. This community can not close out change; it is going to come and the children, the people, must be prepared. They need you to help them.

You must keep your mind and hands so busy that you do not have time to think about yourself. Work hard at whatever tasks they give you; study hard and learn all you can. The time you spend in school now, as difficult as that time may be, is only a short time when compared to the rest of your life. You have a lot to give to others. This is an investment of a few years and the returns will pay off for the rest of your life.

When I first came to Ebenezer Mission, I, too, was very homesick and wanted to go home. Life here was very difficult and very different. I was not always accepted by the people here, and it hurt me too. There were many teachers and mission workers who came and left for the same reason. If they had persevered, they would have made such a difference. If you persevere and finish school, you will do more to help your people than we could have ever dreamed of doing. Don't give up, Opal. Do it for the people you love. Do it for yourself. And most of all do it for God; after all, He is the one who years ago tucked the seed of this dream down into your heart.

It has not been long since harvest time here, and now that it is cold and nothing will grow, we are enjoying the results of the work we have done. We will not be hungry this winter. That seed, planted in your heart by God, was watered by many; it took root and grew and now, as it continues to grow, it will go through a time of cultivating. It is a difficult job hoeing out the weeds, those things that can keep you from growing and producing the harvest that is to be yours.

I think of what I would have missed if I had given up during the hard times and I shudder. How thankful I am that God has given me the strength and He will do the same for you. You don't have to do it by yourself. I must tell you that my greatest loss, had I given up, would have been getting to know and love you. Don't you dare give up, Opal. Remember what Miss Marston used to tell all of you over and over: "You can become anything you want to be. And with God's help you can do anything you set your heart to do if you're willing to work for it."

My prayers are with you, Opal. I love you.

God's blessing,
Mrs. Henderson

That letter I'm sure made a big difference. Every time I wanted to leave and go home, I would read Mrs. Henderson's letter and I could just hear Miss Marston saying, "Just because you're back here in this little community, don't you dare think you can't become anything you want to become. You can do anything you really want to do. All you have to do is go work at it. Start planning. You can do it!"

And with those words, somehow I knew that I could do it. I treasured Mrs. Henderson's letter and kept if for years.

My first Christmas away from home was especially difficult. There were a lot of students who were not able to go home and even some with no homes or families at all. I had a lot to be thankful for, but, oh, how I missed the closeness of my family, the church Christmas program, and the all night drop-in after party on Christmas Eve.

Grandma Corn Breaks Her Hip

Remembering special days and special people was always the hardest, but I guess the most difficult time of all was when I received word from home late in March that my Grandma Corn had fallen off the porch and broken her hip again. She was in a lot of pain, not able to move around at all, and not doing well.

I didn't picture my grandma as a seventy-three-year-old woman who was more than ready to meet her Maker. She was just my grandma and I loved her. So, when she died in May, it was very hard on me, especially since I couldn't even go to her funeral.

There were so many memories that I couldn't help but relive. Sometimes they would make me smile, like thinking of the times I would sit at her feet stringing beans, listening to all the old tales and stories. Other times I could just feel her hands, rough and stained, touch my head or cheek just as real as if she were right there with me, and it would make me cry.

For sure, every year Grandma had to have her "vacation" visiting the kinfolks she didn't get to see all that often. Most of them lived over the mountain there around Edwina about ten miles away. Papa would hitch up the wagon and help Grandma get up on the seat so she could ride next to him. All of us kids would pile in the wagon bed. We would have the best time back there playing games and singing silly songs and Grandma would usually have a story or two to tell us. Then, once we got there. we had a few hours to play with our cousins. Before we left to come back, we would always eat a big meal together.

Grandma would stay for a week, spending a night or two at each place, and then one of my uncles would bring her home in a buggy.

I had no shortage of cousins—about forty-five living and dead. Sometimes Aunt Amanda and her seven children and Aunt Dora with her ten would come together in buggies to stay at Grandma's for a visit. Those were the Corn girls who married the Crums that Papa joked about. I don't know where they slept at Grandma's. I guess the floor was covered with little crums sleeping on pallets. Why, most people couldn't even imagine having seventeen children spending a few nights at their house.

I had heard people saying their grandparents were so hateful, but I never had one like that. I guess Grandpa Hall would have seemed hateful to the other children, but he really wasn't mean. He just didn't pay any attention to them at all, period. But there was no doubt, of all my grandparents, Grandma Corn had the biggest influence in my life and the biggest place in my in my heart.

Winning a Scholarship

My year in the eighth grade gave me time to adjust and learn a new way of life, and that is not at all an easy thing to do. I truly believe my decision to stay in the eighth grade was why I was the valedictorian my first year—that and a lot of studying. That guaranteed my scholarship for tuition and books for the next year. I also won a hundred dollar Bible scholarship for having the highest grades in that class, a five dollar gold piece, and fifteen dollars cash. After winning valedictorian that first year, I was determined I was going to win every year—and I did. Every year I used that fifteen dollars to help pay for my train ticket home. I know that Papa was happy he didn't have to borrow more money from Mrs. Fish for me to come home. But still, every fall he would borrow twenty dollars from Mrs. Fish for my train ride. Then during the rest of the year he would do whatever he could to earn extra money to pay her back. Everyone back home was very proud of me and that made me feel good and study harder.

My scholarship to the Highlands was provided by the Abbie Spears Sunday School Class of a large church in Nashville, Tennessee. Corrine Benson, the secretary of that class, would write to me a lot and the class did all kinds of things for me during the year. They would send me a dress or shoes and little things that I might need. Twice, they paid for me to go down to Tennessee to visit them and Corrine invited me to spend those weekends at her home. She showed me all around Nashville and gave me a chance to get out and see a lot of new things. She took me to church and introduced me to the others who helped with my scholarship. They were all excited to see one of the students they had helped.

When they asked me to speak in the church service, I breathed a prayer, "Lord, I'll be scared to death! You'll have to help me!" That was a great big ol' church and I was only twenty years old then. I had never spoken to that many people at one time, but once I got up there and started talking, I wasn't scared at all. It didn't bother me a bit and I even enjoyed it. But I especially enjoyed going to the Sunday school class.

When I graduated from Highland, the Abbie Spears Class gave me a pair of alligator shoes. They were proud of me for graduating and for making such good grades. That class not only supported me all through high school, they helped me out in college too. They'd just do everything for me. They thought it was an honor to help me.

Corrine and I kept writing to each other. When I was pregnant, she had a shower for me and I named my daughter after her. It's amazing how some friendships can last a lifetime!

14
High School (age 17–21)
1928–1932

I was excited about getting back to Highland. It was my first year of high school and I was seventeen years old. I never told any of the students at school how old I was, and no one would have ever guessed because I was small and looked much younger. Back home we never thought much about how old people were. We never even thought about having a birthday party, not until the chapel people taught us about celebrating our births. But most of the adults never did see much need for doing that. With eight or ten children in a family and all the work that had to be done, there just wasn't time for much celebrating and most of the people thought it to be downright foolishness. I never even learned what year I was born in until they asked for my birth date when I first came to Highland. Isn't that something? I didn't even know when I was born. I had to figure it out mathematically so I could tell them the right year.

Work in the Trade Room

During my second year at Highland, I worked in the trade room. We sent out big mailing bags to churches and organizations all over the country. Then they would collect clothes, shoes, linens, and a variety of other things like personal care items and send the bags by train back to the school. When the full bags arrived at the Oakdale train depot, someone from the school would go over there and tote them back.

There were two or three women who supervised the students working in the trade room. We had to sort through the bags, sizing and folding the clothes and shoes. We organized the personal care items, linens, and other miscellaneous things.

I got all my clothes and shoes, except the ones the Abbie Spears Class sent me, by working in the trade room. Whenever I found something I wanted, I would lay it aside and show it to one of my supervisors. They'd let me have whatever I wanted. This was the only way most of the students and some teachers were able to get the clothes and other things they needed.

Once a week, every Monday, the trade room would be open to the public and then we would work helping the customers. On Trade Day there would be a line of hitched up mules as long as from here to the hog pen. People from all around the community would come—some with turkeys thrown across their shoulders, others carrying chickens or ducks, geese or any kind of fowl that they had. Some would bring berries or various kinds of canned goods. One of the supervisors would establish a price for whatever they brought in and then they would be able to trade for that amount in goods from the trade room. No money was exchanged at all.

It took a lot to feed and clothe two hundred students and staff. Without Trade Day, we would not have been able to feed everyone, even with our farm there at the school. I doubt that the churches had any idea how much they were helping when they filled those ol' mailing bags.

Orphans and Widows

One of the buildings at the school was an orphanage for the young children. It was totally furnished with and run by donations that came in. Some of the orphans were school age, but most of them were three, four, or five. None of the orphans were little babies since it was usually easy to find families who would take them in.

There were many times when the school gave a widowed mother with two or three little ones a job working in the orphanage or the trade room, or maybe as a cook or some other job. There were usually three or four widows living in the orphanage with their children and in the evenings they would help love and take care of all the orphans.

One of the widows, Mrs. Little, was there because her husband was murdered. Some men came to their cabin door and wanted a chew of tobacco. Her husband didn't chew tobacco and didn't have any. Surely, if he had he would have given it to them. Well, that gang of men just shot him down right there before his family. It seemed real strange to me for them to shoot a man over a chew of tobacco. Of course, there probably had been something more than that or they might have been drinking. Mrs. Little didn't know why they would shoot him. She couldn't hear everything they said. The only thing that she could hear them talk about was the tobacco.

Still Homesick

It was good to be back at Highland Institute, but it was not much easier than it had been the year before. There was still a lot I didn't know about life outside of my mountain community, and the girls still teased me and tried to pressure me into doing the things they did. I was no less homesick than I was the year before.

I found comfort in the letters from back home, especially from Mama with news about all the family, and from Mrs. Henderson. I read them over and over when I felt homesick and I read my Bible a lot too. Before I would know it, I was ready to meet whatever the problem was head on—my normal way of dealing with life.

I was even glad to get "real" letters from Ben, who wrote to me every week. After I had gotten home the summer before, Elizabeth told me she had written the letters I had received from Ben. He would tell her what he wanted them to say and she would write them out and make them sound a lot better than his. At first I was furious and swore that if I ever got another letter from him I would tear it into a thousand pieces. Later his letters were looked forward to and he was becoming a good friend. Every Sunday I would write a short note to Ben and slip it into the envelope with my letter to Mama and them. There was nothing personal about my letters. We were just friends, but I could always depend on the girls teasing me about him. One time my roommate even wrote to him—as if I had introduced him to her—just to tease him. But he wouldn't answer her letter.

My Epileptic Fit

I didn't like the way the other girls would tease me and try to get me to go to socials and things. I would tell them, "Well, I didn't come here to date. I came to study!" They would try to get me to go out on dates and I just wouldn't do it. Of course, I really had about as good a time as they did, one night especially.

My room was the first one down the hallway that led from the lobby where all the girls had gathered. From all the chattering and squealing I heard, I could tell that they were up to no good. Then they started calling my name, wanting me to come out to the lobby. There was no way I was about to do that. I wanted to study and had no desire to be a part of their shenanigans. I knew they would soon come to my room to try to get me to go with them, and when they did it would take forever to convince them that I was not going out, so I came up with a plan.

Sure enough, they came charging into my room and plopped down on the beds. As I turned around in my chair to look at them, I rolled my eyes back into my head and fell to the floor. I started to jerk and twitch and acted like I was having a fit. Well, they got up from there real fast and left me alone. They for sure thought I was having an epileptic fit and they were running from me. I scared them good.

They soon figured out that I had played a trick on them and before long they were back to teasing me about not wanting to date. I paid little attention to them. I already made up my mind. I was not going to date. I had a purpose being there and it wasn't dating.

Halloween Bonfire

On Halloween night, I came in from work late. As I arrived at the front entrance, I saw this girl standing on the piano stool just a-waving her hands around. I knew for sure they were up to something the way she was acting—definitely up to something they weren't supposed to be doing. I walked unnoticed behind the group and through the hall door. When I was safely in the hall where I wouldn't be noticed, I listened for a minute at the door. She was saying, "When the clock strikes twelve, everybody is to tiptoe out of the dormitory. We'll meet down the road, where we put the wood for the bonfire. Whatever you do, don't let Miss Warden hear you. Remember, twelve o'clock, and this time we'll make sure Opal goes."

Well, I knew I wasn't going to do something like that. I had never snuck out that way during school and it sounded like they planned to get me to go one way or another. I didn't know exactly how it would set with them, but I had no intention of going. I knew for sure they were going down there to meet up with the boys. They had plans to make a fire and stay all night and that could only mean big trouble!

The school had very strict rules about dating. Boys and girls were never allowed to be together alone. They were always either chaperoned or they could go to the special place the school had for dating, but only at certain times. That special place was no more than several large logs that were lined up on the side of the big hill outside the main building where everyone could see them. At date time there would be two or three couples sitting on each log. I just couldn't understand what they would sit over there and talk about for two hours on those hard log seats. That was the normal date at Highland and I thought that was enough time for dating without sneaking out and breaking the rules. But some of those girls would sneak out all the time. I just didn't believe in it. They were given plenty of chances to date and that should have been enough.

A little before midnight, I got down and rolled back under my bed as far as I could, right up against the wall. Then I took the spread that was hanging down on that side of the bed and put it in front of me so if they decided to look under the bed they wouldn't see me at all. I wasn't afraid of the girls or anything. Well, maybe I was a little afraid because, if they had a mind to, I knew they could get me out of the building and into trouble. Before long I heard them come in and I knew they were looking for me, but when they didn't see me they just took off. I guess they thought someone else had already gotten me outside. After they had been gone for a little while, I came out from under the bed. There were only three of us that didn't go.

I got up early the next morning and went to the kitchen to build the fires. That was still one of my jobs. I was always the first one there and within fifteen minutes the rest of the breakfast crew would arrive, but not this morning.

There were 200 students and staff to cook for and only three of us showed up for kitchen duty. Well, of course, when the bell rang for breakfast, breakfast was not even close to being ready. When the dean walked in and saw the situation, the dining hall became deadly silent. The look on her face could've treed a coon. It wasn't long before Mrs. Holland found out about the girls and their escapade. As she stormed out of the kitchen to find "those ingrate trollops," I couldn't help but feel sorry for them. It was not going to be a pleasant scene when she arrived.

As it turned out, the girls and boys who had snuck out had stayed up almost all night and had finally fallen to sleep just before dawn. They were sound asleep when she found their bonfire. She caught every one of them and marched the whole rumpled group up to her office. She campused all the girls for three months. They were not to leave the campus or go anywhere. No dating, no social activities, nothing!

Teaching Sunday School

Three of the girls who got in trouble were from Shoulder Blade, about three miles from Highland. Even though they were boarding students, Mrs. Holland had been letting them go back to their home church every Sunday to teach Sunday school.

Mrs. Holland called Mrs. Neal, one of the ladies in charge of the mission church, and told her that she was going to have to send someone else to teach Sunday school because her girls were caught sneaking out of the dormitory. Mrs. Neal was so disappointed. She really did think of them as her girls because she was the one who had sent them to school there at Highland.

Then Mrs. Holland called Gladys Bailey and me to her office. We didn't know what she wanted and it puzzled us when she asked, "Do either of you know the way to Shoulder Blade?"

I said, "Yes, I do."

"I'm going to need each of you to teach a Sunday school class over at the Presbyterian Church in Shoulder Blade. Mamie D., Mamie J. and Melber have been campused for three months so they will not be allowed to go home or, for that matter, anywhere else off this campus."

I was a little nervous at first, but I wasn't about to let that stop me. So, from that time on, every Sunday, I walked the three miles to Shoulder Blade and then had to walk all the way back to school after church before I could eat dinner. That is, unless I visited with a family in the community, which I managed to do almost every Sunday. It gave me a chance to see a lot of things, especially the way other people lived. Teaching the Sunday school class gave me a lot of freedom that the other students didn't have. I'm sure that was one of the reasons it really hurt Mamie D., Mamie J., and Melber to lose the privilege of teaching their classes.

I enjoyed teaching that class of eight-year-old boys so much that I continued the whole time I was a student at Highland. For years after leaving that community, I would get letters from some of those boys. One of them was still writing me during World War II, then the letters stopped. He was in the army. I never knew if he got killed or what. Well, that's how I first started teaching Sunday school and I'm still teaching Sunday school here. And I plan to keep right on teaching.

They picked me for several special jobs that year because I was dependable. Mrs. Holland also knew I was a good worker and that I wasn't one to be constantly flitting around with my mind on boys and dating. There were too many things to do and to learn, so I didn't have time to date. I thought it was too much foolishness. But, I guess it would be fair to say that at this time I was right sour on boys anyway because of Andrew Click, Roy Dan's uncle. Andrew and I had always been buddies as far back as I could remember. We spent considerable time together talking and going for walks, but there was really nothing to it. I would go for walks and talk to several boys. They were just my friends and I had grown up with them, especially Andrew, Ben, and John. Well, anyway, before coming back to school that year, Andrew gave me a ring and told me I would always be his special friend. That meant a whole lot to me, especially being so far away from home. Every time I looked at that ring I would think of the good times we all had together. Then a couple months after school started, I got a letter from him asking for the ring back so he could give it to another girl. Well, I thought that was something awful and it really hurt my feelings. I swore right then and there that I would never accept another ring from any boy. So I'm sure Andrew had something to do with my feelings about dating that year at school.

Working for Aunt Bessie

It wasn't too much later that I was transferred from the trade room to a new job. I was assigned to stay with this big ol' fat lady named Aunt Bessie who lived about as far as from here (L. Conn's) to the Click House. Because she was a heavy woman, it was difficult for her to get around much. It was my job to go there in the evenings to cook and serve her dinner and clean up the dishes. I spent the nights at her house and then cooked her breakfast in the morning. Before leaving for school, I'd give her Epsom salts, fix a lunch for her, and make some beer seed beer.

Beer seed beer was a common drink back then. It was made from what was called beer seed, which looked exactly like Grape Nuts. You'd put a handful of beer seed in a quart or two of water along with some sugar and let it sour. It had to be some kind of a fermented drink, but I don't know what exactly it was. We just called it beer seed beer. Most of the families I visited after church on Sundays would have it on their tables to drink with their meals.

Aunt Bessie told me later that the first time she saw me coming to her house she had no idea that I was a student. "Why, when I saw you a-comin' up the hill, you looked just like an ol' lady. I thought to myself, *Lor', what in the world has Mrs. Holland sent me a quaint little ol' lady like that for?"*

She thought that, I guess, because of how my hair was fixed and how I was dressed. I had my hair all pulled up on my head. That's how I usually wore my hair unless I had it down and braided. That first time I went there I had on a gray dress with tiny little flowers. It had a matching jacket just like a little old woman would wear. I guess some older lady had sent it in one of the mailing bags to the school trade room. I thought it was pretty so I asked for it.

Toward the end of that school year, Aunt Bessie's niece and nephew from Newport, Tennessee, came to visit her. They were nice people and especially friendly to me, maybe because I came from close to where they lived. When they found out I had been having a terrible time with my teeth, I told them, "It's only a week and a half until school is out and I plan to see if I can find some work during the summer time so I can have them fixed. I just don't know what Mama's gonna say. My folks are all afraid of dentists. They've heard about people that have been to the dentist and died of infection."

Then Aunt Bessie told them, "I don't know if Opal can make it till she earns enough money in the summer. Mercy, sometimes those teeth hurt her so bad now it makes her cry."

First Dentist Visit

A few days after her niece and nephew left, I got a letter from them:

Dear Opal,

It was nice meeting someone from so close to our home. I hope you won't be upset with us, but we have made an appointment for you with our dentist. He is a very good dentist and has never had any of his patients die on him. This is a gift from us to say thank you for taking such good care of Aunt Bessie.

The appointment is on the third day after your school is out. If you don't want to tell your Mama and Papa yet, you can spend that night at our home. You can have them meet you at the train station in Newport the next day and decide later when to tell them.

They met me at the train and took me to my appointment. The dentist was very nice to me. He kind of shook his head when he looked at my teeth. Four of my teeth were real bad. He had to pull three of those and he filled four teeth.

I had never been to a dentist in my whole life. Grandpa Corn used to pull our loose teeth. He had pulled out one of my jaw teeth when I was thirteen. When I was teaching, I pulled the children's teeth at school all the time. You know, their baby teeth. I'd just pull them out easy as can be. But you just know I had something wrong with my gums or Grandpa couldn't have pulled my jaw tooth out, just like that, with his fingers.

I spent the night at their house and the next morning I expected Papa and them to come to Newport on the train to meet me, but they had walked to town. When I got down to the station, the train was pulling in, and I was going to be there on time so they'd think I was getting off the train. As the train pulled in, I looked under the train and I recognized Ben's legs by his odd walk. I panicked, "They're here, they're here!" I knew then that I would have to tell them that I had been in town since the day before and had been to the dentist. That was my only trip to the dentist until after I married.

Papa's Younger Brother Comes to Visit

That summer Papa's younger brother, Christopher Calvin, came home to visit. Calvin had left here to go into the army when he was young and then became a big shot policeman in Germantown, Pennsylvania.

Uncle Calvin married into a highfaluting family there in Philadelphia and they gave him an important position in the family business. His wife and her family claimed to be direct descendants of Virginia Dare, the first white child born in America. Of course, anyone who has ever read an encyclopedia would have serious doubts about that. But then none of my family ever questioned it and to tell the truth, they really paid it no mind at all. They just figured since the Dares were so snooty about being kin to a baby that it must be some kind of big important deal.

Calvin had not seen his parents in twenty-one years. He most likely felt kind of guilty about not seeing Grandma Corn before she died, and thought if he was ever going to see his father again, he had better be doing it soon. He decided to bring Alice and Virginia, his two oldest daughters, and Alice's fiancé down to see the family.

Aunt Fannie, his wife, couldn't come with him, so she got her sister to bring their two younger kids, Ilene and "Buddy" (Christopher Calvin, Jr.), down so they could meet their grandpa too. At least, she said that was the reason. But she had really sent her sister to snoop and find out what kind of people we were.

Uncle Calvin didn't know if he would ever make it back to these parts again so he had planned to stay here a week longer than the rest of them. That way he would have time to visit with all of his kin people and old friends around here. When her sister got back home, she told Aunt Fannie how Grandpa and the rest of us lived in tiny log cabin shacks and had made her and the children sleep on the floor.

Well, when Uncle Calvin got back home, Aunt Fannie had his clothes all packed and sitting in the hall waiting for him. She said, "I found out all about your family. They're nothing but trash! You can just take your things and go back where you belong! I don't need you here anymore."

Without a home or a job, Uncle Calvin moved back here and lived with one of his sisters. As far as I know, he never saw his wife or children again.

Dr. Blain Comes to Visit

Shortly after Uncle Calvin left, Mama and Papa were surprised to get a letter from Dr. Cary Blain, the superintendent of my school and the pastor of the campus church, Highland Presbyterian. In the letter he asked for permission to visit us for about a week. He said he was very interested in seeing where I lived and meeting my family.

Well, of course, you just know that Papa was all for that idea. He loved to have people stay with us and considered it a great honor to have someone of Dr. Blain's importance visit our home. He decided that for this special visitor he needed to box in the curtained room so that Dr. Blain would have more privacy.

It was kind of funny. Here we were fixing up the house and making everything pretty for Dr. Blain's arrival just like the chapel women and I had fixed up the mission for the Big Chief a few years before. Of course, Mama still had the biggest variety of the prettiest flowers around these parts. My sisters picked flowers, and I arranged them in canning jars and put them all around our house. The biggest and prettiest one sat on the table by the bed where Dr. Blain would sleep.

My family was so excited about a bigwig like the principal of Highland Institute coming to stay with them. My younger sisters would sit on the floor in their room with their backs up against the wall of Mama and Papa's room so they could hear Dr. Blain as he talked to Papa, Mama, and me. They even invited their friends over to see our visitor and to sit with them as they listened to him talk. Why, they were just thrilled to death that somebody like that had come to stay in our cabin.

One day after we had finished eating and were just sitting around the table, Dr. Blain asked me, "So, Opal, why do you want to be a teacher? And what makes you think you would be a good one?"

Well, it made me kind of laugh. And I said, "Well, I really don't know if I would be a good teacher or not, but one thing I do know for sure, I surely can stay on top of the box." He looked at me real strange like and then I really did have to laugh. I told him about the teacher at Sand Hill. We also talked a lot about Miss Marston and the mission and how important the chapel women had been to me and my family and to most everyone else up in these parts. I told him that's what God wanted me to do—get my education to come back and help my people as a teacher.

Burl Won't Farm with Papa

After Burl's first year of college at Lees in Jackson, he transferred to Lees McRay in North Carolina to be closer to home. After two years of college, it was his plan to come back home and help Papa farm. When they were talking about this, Burl asked, "Did Grandpa ever give you a deed?"

Papa answered, "No."

"Well then, I'm not going to put a penny into this land until you get one. He'll drop off and you'll be left with nothing!"

"Oh no, no, Grandpa wouldn't do that!"

Papa never would talk to Grandpa about a deed. Burl stayed for a while and then one day told Papa, "I just can't stay here any longer. I won't tie myself down to a piece of land without having a deed."

Burl hopped a freight train to our uncle's place in Texas where he met and married Annie Sawyer. Her parents were from Tennessee. I have never seen any of his kids except Patricia when she was about six months old and she's a grown woman and married now. The last time I saw Burl was when he came back here for a reunion in 1972.

During the depression, Burl and his little family moved from Texas to California. They lived in a garage and he got a job picking lemons. After the depression, he got a real good job and now he has enough money so that he doesn't have to worry about anything.

He had made the right choice. In November of 1930, Grandpa was walking by the train tracks between West Myers and Bridgeport when a train killed him. They said he was walking too close to the tracks and as the train passed him a door flew open and knocked him under the train.

Papa had never gotten a deed and, of course, Grandpa didn't have a will or anything. The land was divided between the twelve children, so instead of having half of the land he had been paying on for over fifteen years, he had one twelfth. He had to buy two or three of his sisters out just to have enough land to make a living off of.

You just wonder sometimes how they ever made it. They didn't have anything else to do except work. They didn't have any place to go except church. Nowadays, women have so many outside activities, but not back then—and not my mama. If she went anywhere, it was to church or to a funeral.

Everything's Changing

Well, Papa was pretty disappointed and sad about Burl moving away. Of course, he wanted the best for him, but Papa had always hoped that Burl would come back and work with him on the farm. I was sad too. Burl and I had always been real close when we were younger and both at home.

It seemed like everything was changing and nothing would ever be the same again. Miss Marston was gone. Grandma Corn was gone. Mrs. Henderson was gone. The mission was gone, and now Burl was gone too.

An Indian lady had come to work with Mrs. Henderson but she didn't stay long. And then Mrs. Henderson left before the end of last year. Her health was not that good. She still wrote to me and it seemed like she was doing better. She was even talking about going to work at some other mission. It ended up that she worked as a missionary in Mexico for a few years before she died. The steps at the Ebenezer Church were built with money donated by her step-daughter, Winnie Martin, in memory of Mrs. Henderson.

The Presbyterians decided not to continue the mission school or the mission work here. Instead, they planned to use the property for summer camps. They were still keeping the church open and had been sending in a young preacher from the seminary in Louisville to hold the service on Sunday mornings. The rest of the week during the summer he worked at a Presbyterian church in town.

Well, the Presbyterians might have closed the mission, but as soon as I finished school I knew I was coming back here to do mission work,

Presbyterians or not. I was going to be a mission worker and a teacher and that's all there was to it. I had promised God and I knew that was His purpose for my life. And I did not intend to let anyone or anything stop me.

Meet Dorsey

Even though everything else around me was changing, I could always count on Mama and Papa being the same. Papa was still teaching the adult Sunday school class. And as soon as I got home that summer, I started helping out with the children's classes just like I did at Shoulder Blade. Papa told me that the Presbyterians were planning to start holding summer camps at the mission house. For sure, I wanted to do something to help out. I kept thinking, *The mission is going to be used again and maybe I can be a part of it.*

When the workers arrived to get ready for the first summer camp, I was surprised to see a friend from school among them. He introduced me to his friend, Dorsey Ellis, who was from Alabama and very good looking. Dorsey was a good friend of our preacher's and had come to visit with him.

There was another young man named Mark, who came down from New York with his aunt to help with the camp. His aunt had been a missionary here in Eastern Tennessee a few years before. So the Presbyterians knew her and asked if she would head up some of the summer programs. I spent a lot of time working with them and we talked a lot about mission work. When Mark got back home he told his sister about this girl he had met and she started writing to me. She told me, "Mark says he wants to enroll at Highland so he can learn more about the South, but I know he's not being honest with me. He really wants to go to Highland because you're going to be there." He actually put in an application but the school wouldn't let him come because they had money. His family did send clothes and other things that were needed by the school.

That was one of my favorite summer vacations. I loved working at the summer camp and teaching Sunday school and I continued doing that every year during my summer breaks.

The summer of my sophomore year was another good time. During that summer I saw Dorsey again several times when he came here to preach at our church. He was a good preacher and, of course, Papa always made sure that whoever was preaching was invited to our place to eat. Dorsey even spent the night in our special guest room a couple times.

We spent a lot of time together when he was here, mostly just going on long walks all around this area. On those walks I would tell him all about the mission and how important it had been to all of us. I told him about Miss Marston and Mrs. Henderson. I even told him about my promise to the Lord and how I knew for sure that I was coming back here to be a teacher and mission worker.

Dorsey told me his dreams for the future too. After he graduated from the seminary in Louisville, he planned to go back to Alabama and be a minister at his home church there. His church was a very large city church and I could tell from what he said about its big socials and programs that it must be very uppity. He looked forward to going back to his church as if it was something that, like the Presbyterians talked about, was predestined. Sort of like the way I, for years, had known that someday I would come back here to be a mission worker and teacher. It was just understood that it would be so.

We enjoyed spending time together that summer and when I went back to school, we started writing each other. His letters were always full of talk about going back to Alabama and the preaching position he would have there. He always signed his letters "The Minister."

The closer it got to Dorsey's graduation, the more he wrote about his plans and it seemed as though I had become a part of them. He wanted me to go with him.

I wanted to be with him. I had thought for some time that I was in love with him. But I just didn't know how I would ever fit in at a big fancy city church with all of its socials and entertaining. Dorsey thought

I would fit in just fine, but I didn't believe that I would. I had never even been in a big church, let alone a big *formal* church. In fact, I had never been in anything other than small country churches.

Dorsey was from an upper-class family. His daddy was dead, and I could tell from the way his mother and sisters talked about going to all the church socials that they were uppity—and not particularly impressed with me. I saw no way at all that I could go to Alabama and be happy. Besides, I had another year of school left. I used that as my reason for not going.

Well, then of course, Dorsey thought it was an answer to prayer when the Presbyterians decided to send him up to Canoe for another year before sending him back to Alabama. His friend Ted Greenfield had been sent to Newport and preached out here at Ebenezer on the weekends. We continued writing and seeing each other whenever we could, which was not all that often. In fact, the last time I saw him before my graduation was at Christmas. From his letters, I knew for sure that he had made up his mind that he was going back to Alabama at the end of his year in Canoe. He more than likely took it for granted that I would be going with him.

I really did want to go. I would have given just about anything if I could have done that. But every time I'd think about it, something inside me knew I couldn't. I had even thought that if he stayed at Canoe, maybe God would let me go there. It was a country church like Ebenezer, and there were people there who needed the help of a mission worker. But I had told the Lord that I would go back to my people. I had promised to go back there and work and I knew I was going to do exactly what I had promised to do. Just before my graduation, I wrote Dorsey, telling him that *"more than anything I want to go with you, but I can't do that. I just can't."* I knew Dorsey was just as determined to go back to Alabama as I was to staying here. I had known Dorsey for three years and probably loved him for two of those years. It was so hard—the hardest thing I had ever done.

Dorsey planned on coming to see me graduate, but now he had another reason for being there—to "talk some sense into my head." On the last night before graduation, the teacher who lived next to me in my dormitory let Dorsey and Mr. White, the teacher she was going with, come up to her room. Miss Emerson, the dean, never found out. No one ever found out. It was the only time I ever did anything sneaky like that.

Dorsey tried to get me to change my mind. But I was just determined from the very first, years before I met Dorsey, when I promised God that if I ever got a chance to get my education that I would come back and work here. There was no changing my mind and there was no talking "sense" into my head.

I finished exactly what I had set out to do. I had graduated from the Highland Institute, valedictorian of my class, and I received a scholarship towards my first year at college. It was a big day for me, but a sad one too. Dorsey didn't stay to see me graduate—I never saw him again.

I don't know how long the Highland Institute lasted after I graduated. The Great Depression and then World War II came along and changed so many things. Now I don't think there's anything left except maybe a few deserted buildings. I've only been back there once, and that was thirty-eight years later in 1970.

Over the years, Ebenezer sent a lot of children off to Highland. Most of them didn't stay for more than one term. But many of the students that did finish Highland, not just from here but from other missions too, went on to college. Many became teachers, or preachers, and some even foreign missionaries.

So many times I've heard of preachers who graduated from Highland. Not all of them had gone on to college and seminary. A lot of them just started preaching right out of high school. Most of those had come to Highland with plans and commitments like I had—they had made up their minds to do something special with their lives long before they even got there. I'm not saying that everyone that went there turned out well. That doesn't happen in any institution or school. Not everyone turns out the same.

We had two in our family to graduate, Burl and then me. We learned a lot at Ebenezer and a lot more at Highland. Both schools tried to instill in the children that they could be more and do more than they had ever dared to dream and that the most important thing a person could do was to help and teach others. Burl went on to get two years of college. He didn't make a great name for himself, but he made big money. I got a couple years of college and I didn't make a great name for myself either. And, as you can tell, I didn't even make much money. But I was able to accomplish my biggest dreams—I went away to school and got enough education to help my people and to teach school. More than that, I was always able to stay on top of the box.

15
College and My First Year of Teaching
1932–1934

*T*he scholarship I had received was to Milligan College, just outside of Johnson City, Tennessee, and much closer to my home than Highland Institute. My plans were to complete one year of college, which would qualify me to teach in any of the one-room schools in Cocke County. I was so anxious to start teaching that I reasoned I could always pick up another course here and a semester there while I was working and that way complete all of my education.

At Milligan, I lived in a dormitory room on the second floor. There were six of us to a suite. On the first floor where the wealthier girls lived, there were only two girls to a room. Each room was connected to one other room by the bathroom they shared. The four girls directly below us had combined their rooms and made one into a living room and had all their beds in the other room. They brought living room furniture and other things from their homes to make their room look real nice. We really didn't care about all the things the girls downstairs had. We always had a good time—sometimes doing the silliest of things. But that's how I was. Still am that way, I reckon!

One of the things we did for fun was jump rope. I had jumped rope at home from the time I was able to walk, except there we would usually go out in the woods and cut down a vine to use as our rope.

But at school we would take the ropes from around our trunks and tie them together. Then we would tie one end of the rope to the bed and take turns jumping. The girls downstairs would complain because we made too much noise, but we didn't really care. When they complained we would quit jumping for a while and then later we would do it again. After the plaster started falling off the ceiling below and actually hit one of the girls, we knew we had to stop for good. Why, we for sure wouldn't have jumped rope at all if we thought it would hurt someone.

It was the last year of the depression when I was there at Milligan and things grew increasingly difficult for everyone. Around Christmas, our school president was visiting Florida and he couldn't find any money to get back home. Nobody there could or would cash his check and he had no money left at all. He had to stay down there and wait until his wife could get enough cash to send to him. Imagine—the college president!

Postage stamps only cost two cents, but there were many times when I didn't even have enough money to mail a letter home. Because of my scholarship from Highland and the Abbie Spears class, I was able to borrow money from the student loan fund at Highland. All I had to do was write and request it. Of course, I'd write for more than just one stamp at a time, but there were times when I'd have to wait until I'd get some money before I could even send my request to Highland. We just had to do the best we could.

One of my roommates at Milligan was from Newport. She was younger than I was, but she was a senior and I was just a freshman. We always had the best times together. We would sometimes go to school activities and sometimes we would ride the train home together.

Another one of my roommate's lived too far away from college to go home for just a weekend. So, whenever we had extra money at the same time, we would take the train to my home for the weekend. She loved the sulfured apples that Mama made and we would always take big cans of them back to school with us. We would put them in our Frigidaire and use that sulfured fruit for snacks. They never seemed to last long; we would usually eat them all in a week or two. They were so good.

Sometimes there was no money, but money or not, several of us went into Johnson City once a month. We could always find somebody to ride with. If we had money, we might buy a few trinkets and if we didn't we would look around in the stores and just have fun together.

Christmas 1932

That was the first year since I first left home in 1927 that I was able to be home for Christmas. It was so good to be home and help with the Christmas baking.

I had never realized how much our home was in need of repair. The kitchen was leaking before I left for college, but now the roof had rotted even more, leaking something terrible whenever it rained or snowed. On Christmas Day it was pouring rain. Everybody else ate their Christmas dinner in Mama and Papa's room. Ben and I ate ours in the only dry place in the kitchen—down under the table, which was covered with an oil cloth covering. We talked about getting married and we talked about that leaky old roof. I told him as soon as I started teaching I was going to start saving money for tin and make a new roof for Mama and Papa. They just didn't have any money and they had done so much for me and for others.

First Year Teaching at Davis School, 1933–1934

When I first started teaching in 1933, we only had school from September through March. I was assigned to the Davis School and my first teaching salary was fifty dollars a month.

The week before school started I was to report at the county superintendent's office in Newport to pick up the key to the school and my supplies. Papa and I left home early, just as soon as it was light enough for us to see our way. We had to walk all the way into Del Rio for me to catch the train to Newport because the train didn't stop at West Myers that early. Papa would never let us girls walk anywhere outside of the community by ourselves. And usually it was Papa himself who walked with us. It was real important to him to know that we were safe. Years before Papa had let Maggie and Beatrice go into town with John and Ben and that was all right because my sisters were together and there was a group of them going.

I figured by leaving at first light, that should get me to the county office about the time they opened up. I wanted to be at the head of the line to get my supplies. That way, I would have time to take them to my school and maybe still have time to do a little cleaning and check to see what else I might need. If I couldn't carry all of it, I would just send the supplies on to the depot in Del Rio and then Papa or someone going into town with a wagon could bring them on up to Davis.

This was my biggest dream and it was coming true. I was so excited and just jabbered away to Papa all the way down to Del Rio about the things I planned to do. Even though there was no longer a mission, I could do the same work the mission had done. I could be the mission to my students and their families. I could give them hope and encouragement just like Miss Marston had given to me, and then they could pass it on to others. Papa marveled at how that seemed to be true. We do tend to pass on to others what we have received.

Papa just listened and I reckon he sensed that along with being excited, I was also right nervous. He kept reassuring me and telling me what a good teacher he knew I would be. "Me 'n your mama are so proud of you. And don't ya just know that Miss Marston is too. Why, she's most likely leading the angels in a rejoicing fit right this minute."

I wished that Mrs. Henderson and Miss Marston could be there to share this time with me and, of course, it would have been comforting to have them around for advice. I really did think that I would be a good teacher; at least I hoped that I would be. For sure, I was determined to work hard at it. It's not at all like it is today. Nowadays you have to graduate from a four-year college. You take classes designed especially for what you're going to teach and you do what they call practice teaching before you get a teaching certificate.

Even though I was the first and only person there, the woman in the county office acted too busy to help anybody. Without hardly looking up, she said, "Here's your key. The supplies are lined up over there; just pick up the ones marked for Davis School. You get a bucket, a broom, and a box of chalk. Anytime you need more chalk you can come back here to pick it up."

I asked her about teaching books and she said, "Whatever books are in the school building, that's what you'll have."

"What about textbooks and supplies for the children?"

"Like I said—whatever books are in the school, that's what you'll have. Your students are supposed to come into town and buy their books and supplies."

What an ignorant, snooty person you are! I thought to myself. Pleading with her, I tried to explain the situation. "My students won't be able to afford to buy books! Their families are poor and will do good just to get them pencils and paper."

"Like I said, your students are expected to buy their own books. The county will not furnish textbooks for your students!"

"What about my teaching supplies?"

"Those," and she pointed to the chalk, broom, and bucket, "are your supplies. Except for this. Here's your roll book. Anything else you need for you or your students, you will have to buy yourself. Oh, and there's a faculty meeting every month on a Saturday and that's when you get your paycheck. If you want to get paid, be at the meeting."

I picked up my chalk, broom, and bucket and caught the train back. I wanted to see my school.

Checking Out and Fixing Up My School

Davis School had great big steps that led up to the long porch going all the way across one side of the building. When I got inside, I knew I had my work cut out for me. The schoolroom was big and dirty. It would need a good cleaning for certain. I wanted my school to be interesting with pictures and posters just like the mission school had been. I wanted it to be a place where the children would enjoy learning.

There was only one door into the school. Three of the walls had several tall windows, many with broken panes. Going across the front of the room was a big stage about eight or ten feet wide, just high enough for a child to sit on. The blackboard was at the back of the stage; in fact, all of that wall, as high as I could reach, was blackboard.

With only one door, I wanted to be sure the children would be safe in case there was a fire. The windows were about three feet off the floor. I checked them all to see how hard they were to open. They were easy enough; even the smallest child would be able to get out.

There were fourteen double desks. Each had a bench long enough for two students to sit together, and the desk in front of them had a writing board attached to the back of the seats. The first desk in each row had a seat but no writing board. We called these the station benches. When I would call a group or class up to the front, that's where they would sit. The others would be working on assignments at their desks.

We had the same kind of desks down at the mission. But at the mission the desks were made of wood and a two by four was used to nail two of the double desks together. They were very heavy, so, when you wanted to sweep or mop the floor, you needed help moving them. At Davis, the desks came from the county and were made mostly out of metal.

I wondered how many students I would have. The roll book seemed to say they had more students than desks last year, and I was sure I would have more than twenty-eight students too. Were some of my students going to have to sit on the floor? Certainly the county wouldn't allow that. But then there was no desk or chair for the teacher either. I had hoped to find textbooks from last year in my classroom, but all I found was one first grade primer.

So, my starting inventory for teaching consisted of fourteen double desks, station benches, one first grade primer, a roll book, a broom, a bucket, and chalk. I had joked for years about being able to stay on top of the box and now, here I was ready to start teaching and I didn't even have so much as a box to sit on. I knew I'd have to come up with something, so I started to make my list of the things I would need.

For sure, I would get mighty tired standing up all day long. And, of course, I would need something to write on. So, the first things on my list were a chair and a desk for me.

I went back to the school every day that week to get things ready. I must have looked like a pack mule as I toted supplies and the tools I'd need to make my desk in big ol' white sacks on my back. I carried over three pieces of plank, one each day, and on the fourth day I carried over a chair. I could only manage one plank a day because they were long and I had to walk up to the ridge, then straight across towards the Turner Place. Just below their house I crossed the road and cut across there to the school, which was about two-and-a-half miles in all.

For my desk I decided to make a pulpit-like stand with a shelf behind it for my books and school supplies. Well, that pulpit worked just fine. I could lean against it and write on it just like I would a desktop.

First Day of School

The first day of school I got there early, of course, but there were already two children, a brother and sister, waiting on the steps. The boy's name was Herbert. He told me he was ten years old and in the fourth grade. The little girl was very shy. She stood awkwardly on the top step looking down at her feet. She raised only her eyes and introduced herself as Enus Arine. I thought that a rather strange name. I reckon Herbert saw the confused look on my face. "Her name be Edith Irene."

All of my students were from around here, but I really didn't know them because I had been gone from the community for six years. I found out a little later that Herbert and Edith were Franklin Turner's children. Franklin was the boy who was in the physiology class with Aunt Flora that time way back when Auda and I had visited the mission school. He was also the one the Franklin House was named after. I thought that it was really something that the first child I spoke to on my first day of teaching belonged to Franklin, who was the first boy I saw on my first day of ever being in a schoolroom.

I had seen Herbert pass our house several times with his daddy when he was little, but they always called him Bo. I never knew what his real name was and, of course, he had grown a lot since I last saw him. There is no way I would ever have recognized him. Herbert later married one of the Pierce girls and became a teacher himself. His wife got killed in a car wreck. He remarried, but then he died young too. It was a shame; he was so good and helped everyone.

Taking Roll the First Day

Davis School always had trouble keeping teachers. It was only the first day of school and I had already figured out why. If the lack of support and supplies and the number of students hadn't been enough, having two older roughneck boys trying to scare off the teacher just might do it. They were both real big boys. One was a twenty-one-year-old in the eighth grade and the other a sixteen-year-old seventh grader.

That first day there must have been at least fifty children. I had to figure out whose names were not in the roll book and write them in along with the names of their parents. While I was doing that and trying to figure out just who was in what grade, those two older boys decided it was my turn to go. They just started walking up to the front of the room real slow like, just a-starin' at me. Then they grabbed me and tried to get me to dance with them. They had run teachers off before, but this was one teacher that wasn't planning on going anywhere! They might have been a lot bigger than me, but I was going to make sure they didn't want to mess with me for long. I told them to get back to their seats and sit down and behave. They thought they could smart mouth me, so one of them said, "Boy! You won't last here. You won't stay here one week!" I made those boys go outside and cut fifty briars each. Then I made them lay each one out in a row so I could count them and make sure they had the number I had told them to cut.

That evening, I cut some big switches and had them standing up in a box by my desk the next morning. I figured that should say something! At first I had to use the switch a lot but after a few weeks, I didn't. By that time they had figured out that they were not going to get away with misbehaving.

By the end of the week, I had sixty-two students registered. Goodness me! Sixty-two students and twenty-eight desk seats. That meant that I had more students sitting in the floor than at desks. To me, why, that was just something terrible! I was used to the mission where we always had enough big desks and plenty of books. The desks might have been homemade, but the children never had to sit on the floor.

I knew for sure that I had some big challenges ahead of me! Here I was with all these students and I had no books and no supplies. There were twenty-one children in the first grade and only one primer between them. In the rest of the grades the children were pretty evenly divided except the seventh and eighth grades, which had fewer children.

It seemed that there was no way of helping the children to get books and supplies except begging. I had begged the county, but that did no good at all. They didn't even seem to care. My next plan was to write letters to all of my old teachers at Highland and at college, and of course to the Abbie Spears class. I also wrote to Dr. Blain to see if he would have the trade room send out some mailing bags to the churches and ask them to send me books, newspapers, posters, the white cardboards out of nylon hosiery packages, and school supplies.

My old gym teacher was the first to send me a big barrel of books. They were no particular grade level and I don't think any two of them were the same. They were everything from grammar school to college. Just everything. But they all had ABCs and they all had words in them. I was forced to be creative in my lesson plans. Some of the college textbooks I would never be able to use for their intended purposes with first through eighth graders. So I tore out the pages and wrote several words, maybe five or six, across the top of each page. Then I'd give a page to each of the younger students and they would see how many times they could find those words on their page. Then they would write the words and learn to spell them. Another activity might be to find a word on the textbook page for each letter of the alphabet. I came up with all kinds of games and lessons for them to do. They loved them and learned quickly. Many times I would hear the students talking about how they were in the third grade but that they were so smart the teacher had to give them college books to study from.

In a couple weeks I started getting bags of books and supplies from all over. Some even sent clothes and shoes.

School Slates

I used the white cardboard out of hosiery packages to make what I called slates. I'd sit up every night and write on them things that the students needed to learn or assignments for them to do.

For my first graders I would print their name and they would have to learn how to write it. I would write out the ABCs, and the numbers to one hundred. We would work on them together in class and I would have some of the better older students work with the younger ones.

For the students who were a little older I might write the multiplication tables to ten times five and the Roman numerals to ten. I might have sentences with facts that they would have to learn, like, "My state is Tennessee and its capital is Nashville." I'd fill those cards up on both sides with things they had to learn or do, and then I'd mark them off when they learned them. I made a slate for every one of my students, and when they finished one, I would have another one ready for them. They always knew exactly what they were supposed to learn.

The children also knew where to sit. The younger grades sat on the floor on the stage and when they got up to get a drink of water or go out for recess, they would put their slates in their place with their names up. When they went out to go to the bathroom they had to hand me their slate before going out the door and get it from me when they came back. That way I always knew who was outside and how long they had been there.

Before long we had books for most of the subjects and most of the grades. We studied English, math, geography, and Tennessee history. When we didn't have the right books, we did a lot of "making do."

Teaching Goals—Reading and Writing

My youngest child that year was barely five years old. She was probably too young for school, but she always wanted to come, especially when the weather was good. I wasn't about to tell her she couldn't. Her two big brothers were in school and if she didn't come with them, she would be alone at home while her mama and papa worked out in the fields or with the animals. Her papa carried her on his back to school every morning and after school on the way home her brothers would take turns carrying her when she got too tired to walk. When she would get sleepy during the day, usually after lunch, she would lay in the corner of the stage and take a nap. She was real good and learned many things that year.

That first year, I wanted to teach them all that I could, and my main goal was for them all to be able to read and write, especially the older ones. But there was no reason why even the youngest child would not be able to learn to read some, and to at least write their name. Back then, they moved teachers around however they wanted. I didn't know how long I would be there to work with those students, or how much the next teacher would care. By the end of that year, every student would know their ABCs and know how to read and write. I wanted them to have the foundation. Then, whether the next teacher helped them or not, if the children really wanted to learn, they could go on and learn a lot more on their own.

Not many of the parents could read or write enough to help their children with homework. They wanted their children to be more educated than they were so they did all they could to see that their young'uns attended classes every day. Of course, there were a few parents who just couldn't care less. Most of the students did want to learn, but we had a family or two of children that would skip school and stay out in the bushes all day.

It was like down at the church, you know, when I started teaching Sunday school. Hardly anyone in my class could read or write. I thought that was such a terrible thing, so I decided to teach them right there in Sunday school. See, I'd call out a Scripture reference and help them learn how to find it. Then I'd read a verse and have them read after me. They learned to read by reading the Bible. They learned to recognize all the names of the books of the Bible and memorized a lot of verses.

One of the girls I taught to read like that was nearly as old as I was. Her parents couldn't read and they were so proud of her.

Not Much Sleep for Me

I don't see how I ever made it that first year. Guess there's a lot to be said for being young. Every night I stayed up until eleven and sometimes longer than that working on the lessons for all of the grades, first through eighth, for the next day so my students would have something to read and assignments ready for them to do. School started at eight o'clock and turned out at four. I always got up at three in the morning and I usually got to the school by seven thirty. A lot of mornings I had to walk in the dark and many times it would be dark or getting dark by the time I got home.

After school, I stayed there to see that everything was clean and to do whatever needed to be done. Of course, the students had certain chores that they took turns doing too. Then I had to come back home and take care of my chores and help cook. I usually baked the bread for supper. My main chore was milking the cows and I helped with whatever else needed to be done.

Every day I walked a total of five miles to and from school with my book satchel, supplies, lunch, and assignments in a white sack. Everyone made fun of me, the way I'd tote everything on my back in that ol' white sack. They called me Traveling Toe just like they had called Uncle Louis.

Bathrooms

The school didn't have any real bathrooms, not even outhouses, and that was a big problem. At first, I didn't know how I was going to manage it.

The first day of school, after I had taken roll, I had all the students go outside and stand at the bottom of the steps with the girls on the right and the boys on the left. I stood at the top of the steps and gave them the rules for using the bathroom. "Now, boys, you can take the left hand side. You see the rags I've tied around those trees over there? That's where you'll go, in that area beyond those trees. And don't you let me catch you to the right of that last tree I've marked right there!" And I gave the same instructions to the girls and told them to stay on the right hand side.

I had marked off an area in each direction where the boys and girls could walk down behind the hill to be out of sight. They used leaves to wipe with. Those woods had a lot of good leaves; even in the winter you could find something to wipe with. But in the winter, I also had a Sears catalog that they could pull a couple of pages out of on the way to the woods.

With that many students, the bathroom area couldn't be small. There was plenty of land around the school and they had the whole woods out there in the direction I had marked off for them to use, but they still had to watch where they stepped. Those marked off portions were only for that purpose and the students were never allowed to go into them to play or for any other reason. At first, I thought that those big boys might be hateful or try to bother the girls, so I always had the girls go out in pairs to be sure they were safe. But the boys were good about it and no one else bothered them either.

Later, when I taught at Rowe School, the side windows of the school faced the direction of the girl's bathroom area. Everyone could see the girls go off into the trees and thought it was the funniest thing ever when one of the girls came back out to pull some leaves off a tree and then disappear again back into their area. Those boys would just giggle and snicker at that. I'd tell them, "My lands, you know everybody has to do that. There's nothing funny about it. It just makes sense to use the leaves. After all, it's better than not having anything to use." I guess the boys did the same thing when they went out, but they still always joked about the girls.

People from town would laugh when I'd tell them we didn't have bathrooms or even outhouses at the schools up here. I don't know if they didn't believe me or were just embarrassed by the subject.

Chores

I made up a list of the chores that needed to be done and then assigned students to certain jobs. Getting water from the spring, which was a good ways off, presented a bit of a problem, but the older boys were strong and could easily carry a bucket full of water that far. With so many children, they would have to get water two or three times a day. We only had one bucket and one dipper that everyone used.

Cutting wood was another job for the older boys. The younger children would go out in the woods and find downed wood and tote it back for the older ones to cut up and stack. Some of the men in the community would bring in logs for us to use for firewood too. Sometimes they would even split and stack it for us. Other times the boys would have to split the logs.

The older and more advanced students would be assigned to grade papers and work with the young or slower students. This really helped me a lot. Of course, they all helped me by doing the other chores like sweeping the floors, cleaning the blackboard, passing out papers and supplies, cleaning windows, ringing the bell, and just anything else I could think of that needed to be done. If we didn't share the work, I would have to do it all and I usually didn't have time to do even one more thing.

The children were eager and real good to help. I never did have any problems with any of them except my sister's girl. Her daddy wouldn't let her sweep. That was the only one I ever had in all the years I taught that wouldn't work in the schoolhouse.

Teaching Class and P.C. Williams

At school we always had memory Bible verses. In the morning, the first thing was our devotional and then we would memorize Scripture verses. At dinnertime, we would say the twenty-third Psalm and after the recesses we would recite the states and their capitals. It wasn't too long after school started that I got a Bible teacher to come around once a month. Of course, not many of the one-room teachers cared much one way or the other about having Bible teachers at their school and simply wouldn't invite them to come, you know. But I was always glad to have them come to my school.

After our Scripture memorization, I'd start working with the individual grades. I'd usually start out by calling my first graders up to the station benches because they didn't need extra time in the morning to study. When I got done with them, the second grade would have all their books and assignments ready to come to the front. We didn't have any problems with study periods. The students would study and do their homework while the other grades took turns at the front with me. I would have the better students helping the younger ones and that worked out real good.

One day while I was teaching sixth grade English, not quite a month after school started, I looked up and glanced out the window. I saw a man coming right out from where the girls went to the bathroom. I thought he might be trying to harm the girls, hit them with rocks or something like that, which had me scared. The thought never crossed my mind that he might be trying to molest my girls. You just didn't hear of things like that. We didn't even know what perverted sex was. Of course, I heard plenty about it a little latter.

I calmly told the children, "There's somebody outside. You stay right here at your desks, look at your books, and don't pay any attention to him when he comes in. Don't even look up!"

I went on with what we were doing as best I could. I waited and waited and finally the man came up towards the schoolhouse. He came up on the porch and just looked around. I didn't know what to think of him and it scared me when he finally did come on into the schoolhouse.

He slipped on in and sat down beside someone in the back, just like he belonged there.

Now, I was really starting to get scared and then I saw him take a little black book out and start writing. I thought, *Lord 'a-mercy, that's one of the officials checking on what I'm doing!* He was writing down notes. I didn't have any idea of what I was doing wrong; but then I didn't know what I was doing right either.

And directly he walked up to the front and said, "I'm P. C. Williams, the superintendent of Cocke County Schools."

I thought, *Lor' me alive!*

I didn't even know he was a man. I knew the superintendent's name was P. C. Williams, but I had thought P. C. might just as easily be a woman. When I went down there to pick up my supplies before school started, I only saw one person.

He said, "I was just checking the window panes. You've got thirteen or fourteen out. You can pick them up in town when you come to the faculty meeting. We'll provide the glass, but you'll have to see to it that they get put in."

The students and everyone else who heard about it laughed at me about that man scaring me so. It scared me so badly that I didn't even think to ask about desks or books for the students. Of course, we were getting in a lot of books by that time. But after that, you can be sure that they heard plenty from me at every monthly meeting about not having enough desks and not having an outhouse.

Potty Platform

Not too long after P. C. Williams' visit to my school, there was this woman—Ruth Webb O'Dell was her name—and she was running for superintendent. She's the one who wrote *Over the Misty Blue Hills, the Story of Cocke County, Tennessee,* and served as a State House Representative from 1937 to 1941. Everybody called her "Lady Ruth."

Well, we had never had a woman run for superintendent before. I liked her from the first time I heard one of her campaign speeches and she talked about how one of the things she was going to do was build toilets for our schools.

All the men really acted stupid about having a woman in the running and heckled her when she talked. "Don't you just know, if we elect a woman superintendent, all she'll think about is building pretty toilets on the sides of all these mountains. She'll probably even want to plant flowerbeds around them so they'll smell better." They made it sound like it was just something awful that one of the planks in her platform was to build toilets for the rural schools.

I defended her, saying, "Well, there are a lot of planks in your candidate's platform that need mending! I'm teaching at Davis School and we don't have any bathrooms, not even an outhouse. At every recess time I turn out sixty-two students to go squat around in the woods and wipe with leaves and you just know that can't be very sanitary! I have to allow more time for recess, because with that many children you know they don't all want to go at the same time right next to each other. I'm sure you enjoy your privacy. My students would like a little privacy too."

Everybody thought it awful that I would say things like that. But I'll tell you what—if they had come to visit my school, I would have taken them for a little walk in the woods and they would have known what it was like. I thought her wanting to build toilets was a splendid idea. If I had been able to, I would have voted a dozen times because I knew firsthand what an important improvement that would be. But her opponent and the men who supported him said that toilets were not a part of education. Well, it most certainly was education. It was teaching the students health rules, teaching them to be clean. They could have then taught their families.

Combining the 7th and 8th Grades

My going to the faculty meetings every month was going to be hard on my parents. They wouldn't let me walk by myself, especially at 3:00 in the morning. They wouldn't even let Ben walk me into town.

The morning I got my first check, Papa and I had to walk all the way into Newport. The train didn't come early enough to get me to my meeting on time and if you missed the meeting you missed your check. Well, I had already walked one hundred miles to and from the schoolhouse and to get that check a few more miles wouldn't make that much difference. After the meeting, I paid twenty-five cents to take a shared taxi back to where you turn there on Highway 107 in Del Rio. Papa was there to meet me and walk me home. Can you just imagine all that work and walking for fifty dollars a month!

At the faculty meeting, besides bringing up the problems of not having enough desks and not having outhouses, I had a question about how my students starting Newport High School next year would be transported to the bus stop in Del Rio. "My sister, who's in the eighth grade at Sand Hill School, said that the county provided a driver to pick up the children who had finished her school. The driver picks them up close to their homes and drives them into Del Rio to catch the Newport High School bus. She's been told that next year the county will do the same for her and the others going to the high school. I haven't heard anything official about this. Are you planning to do the same for my students?

No one from Davis had gone on to high school for years and I wanted to be sure that my students would be able to go on with their schooling. When I was away at Highland I know that two or three of Doctor Turner's young'uns would walk across the mountain every morning, carrying a lantern to light their way. They had to walk to the railroad tracks to Bridgeport to get a ride to the high school.

The officials told me we would have to have at least five students going into the ninth grade before the county would pay someone to pick them up. Well, now of course, I wasn't about to tell them I only had three in the eighth grade. I had to think up some way to get those kids to high school. I thought about that all the way home and came up with the idea of moving six of my other students into the eighth grade. I was sure that they would be able to do that. There were other students who could be moved a grade or two higher also. Many of them were already older than they should be for the grade they were in. It would mean a lot of work, but I thought my students could do it, and I was determined to make that happen. Of course, I never did tell anyone at the county office. After all, they really didn't need to know. I couldn't see where there was anything wrong with what I was planning. If the students were prepared and able to move up a grade or two, it would benefit them to do so. For sure, when you have a twenty-one and sixteen-year-old in the seventh and eighth grades, you know that's certainly not a good thing.

I tutored those six students until I was sure that they would be ready for high school. So, my first year, I had nine students who finished the eighth grade. The county said we had to have at least five students but we had even more. Then when it was time for school to start the next year, all those students, except the twenty-one year old, went on to high school and did just as well as anybody else.

Thanksgiving 1933

After my last faculty meeting before Thanksgiving, I ordered and paid for the tin for Mama and Papa's new roof. Papa took the wagon into Del Rio and picked up the tin from the train station. Meanwhile, Ben and I went out in the woods looking for tall trees that were about four inches across and cut them to replace the rafters that were not solid. A week or so before that, Papa had cut down a big tree and taken it up to the sawmill to be cut into planks for the roof.

While we were off in the woods looking for trees to cut, Ben asked me playfully, "Don't you think we should get married?"

"Under one condition." I snapped.

"What's that?"

"If you'll promise you won't buy me a ring. I won't accept a ring and that's all there is to it. I've heard so many things and read stories about how a girl would get the ring and then later the boy would want it back. I don't intend to be givin' anything back, and I won't have to if I don't go takin' anything to start with."

I didn't really take his proposal seriously. I had just answered him as a pure joke, you know. But I was serious about not accepting a ring. I had already vowed years before that I wouldn't because of Andrew Click wanting me to give him his ring back to give another girl. I wasn't going to be hurt like that again.

I made sure that everything was ready to start working on the roof as soon as my Thanksgiving vacation started. The first thing we had to do was take off the old roof. We put the rotten wood in the woodpile with the other firewood and the good wood we put in the shed by the barn. We would use that later for repairs on the outbuildings. We replaced all the bad supports with the trees Ben and I had cut and put the freshly cut planks across them, and then the tin went on top of that. At ten o'clock Thanksgiving night, we finished the new tin roof on that kitchen by lantern light, a new roof that wouldn't leak. We were so proud of that. We never did have enough money to finish putting a ceiling in the house. But with the new roof, we never did notice it being as cold.

Hall Top

I had promised my students that at the end of the school year I would take them all to Hall Top. I don't know exactly how far that mountain top was from the school. I've always heard people say it was about eight miles from Davis and about ten miles from here. You just don't realize that it's that far away when you love walking though the woods as much as I do. I don't believe I've ever gotten as tired walking the paths as I've gotten walking on the roads, although I've heard it said that walking cross country is supposed to be much more difficult. Back then, no one really would have thought of walking the road to Hall Top. That road just wound back and forth and twisted and turned through all these little dips and hollows. It didn't seem like you got anywhere; the footpaths were a more direct route. The ones we took to the top were all straight up, and coming back it's all downhill. I enjoyed walking those paths, but I guess they're all grown over by now.

There's a fire tower way up on Hall Top that was probably built around 1934. You can actually see Hall Top from the front of Roy Dan's place when you stand up there on top of that big rock and look straight ahead to the highest top out there. And when the sun is shining, you can see the glistening of the fire tower's roof. About the only time someone stays in the fire tower at night is during dry weather in the fire season, and sometimes during that time of year you can actually see the light in the tower.

Of my sixty-two students, probably about fifty of them went to Hall Top with us. There were about ten little ones whose parents wouldn't let them go that far. The youngest one to go was the little girl who was five. The only way her brothers were able to go on the trip was if they agreed to carry her when she got tired. She did give out on us a few times and have to sit down and rest or have one of her brothers carry her for a while. Then she'd walk alone until she got tired again.

The students each brought their own lunch, but every time I took my students anywhere, I'd always take a little extra for the families that couldn't afford to send much with their child. I always took crackers and peanut butter, gingerbread cookies, and things like that, but we didn't have a lot to carry. We didn't take a thing to drink, but everyone had to bring their own old tin cup to dip water out of the springs along the way. Nowadays you can't take kids out anywhere without having sodas and potato chips and stuff like that. We never thought about taking little paper cups and paper plates or napkins either. I just wonder how people got to doing all of that kind of stuff.

I have these friends who will go to a parkway causeway campground to camp and have a picnic. They just have everything with them and they won't camp anywhere unless there is a bathroom and clean picnic tables. I said, "My goodness, if you have to have all that, why don't you just stay at home and enjoy your luxury?" To me, that's just not camping.

"Oh! You mean you'd just use the bathroom on the ground!?!"

Well, my goodness, people around here lived like that for years. Growing up, we didn't know what it was to have a bathroom. Why, I can remember down at my Grandpa Corn's, they had a big chicken house. One end of it had poles for the chickens to roost on and the other end was where the women folk used the bathroom. The men had to go in the barn. I don't know of anybody back then that had an outhouse except the mission people, and they had two, one for the men and one for the ladies. Even in all of my grown up years, we've never had an indoor toilet—not one that flushed anyway.

We used that old outhouse out from my place up there for years. Then Jack and some others made that fancy log outhouse chinked with cement up on the hill there across from L. Conn's. There was this one little city girl named Heather who came up here all the time with her parents and brother. She always loved to help me make biscuits and mud pudding. Well, she was up here visiting with me when they were building that outhouse; she was just standing around there watching them for the longest time. You could see that she was up to something and determined about it too. To this day you can still see her initials H.D.L. written right next to her hand print on the backside of that outhouse. Heather didn't think a thing of using that outhouse, but I don't think she ever cared too much for the one out from my house.

Not having taken a group that far before, I was afraid that the young children would get tired and need to be carried. So when a couple of my friends, John and this other boy, offered to go with me to help carry the food and help with the smaller children, I was all for that. John was about my age and we had been friends for years. He was such a big help and wouldn't let me carry anything on our walk to Hall Top and back. I guess he was a little sweet on me and I was thinking maybe I would like to spend more time with him. So as we came back up the road and down to Chestnut Gap, right down there toward the schoolhouse, I said, "We're having a special program for the children at the church tomorrow. Would you like to go with me?"

"I can't. Sunday's Easter and Daddy wants us all to be there at his church with them."

I was a little disappointed about the rejection, so I just said, "It doesn't matter anyway."

For the longest time I had thought John was a second cousin or something like that to me, but it had turned out that he was not kin to me at all. He was mixed in with all those Corns that had married Crums, so naturally I just figured he was one of our family. Sometimes there was so much marrying between families up here that it was difficult to know who was related and who wasn't.

Why, I never will forget when Auda started dating and her second cousin kept asking her to go out with him. She'd said, "Clifford, we can't date because we're cousins," and Clifford answered with, "We ain't enough kin for it to matter none." I thought that was so funny.

A few of the younger students needed some help climbing the steep trails, while others ran and played all the way to the top. They would run past us and soon be out of sight. Then we would catch up to them and find them climbing trees and swinging from vines. They would take off again and the next time we caught up with them they might be chewing the leaves of the little green plant that tasted like teaberry gum. Sometimes we would find them with big handfuls of birch bark and they would walk along the trail with us for a while just a-gnawin' on that bark. Birch sap does taste real good, ya know. Then, directly, they would run off again. This time we might find them licking sap from a hole they had made in the bark of a chestnut tree.

All of my students were excited. They had worked hard all year and learned much. For many of them this would be a rare day of having pure fun, because Monday morning they would be working hard, repairing buildings and fences, getting the fields ready, and planting crops.

When we got to the top, everyone was ready for lunch. I put the extra food I had brought on the huge round tree stump in the middle of where we all sat. There was plenty for everyone. Most of the children sat around in circles and shared their lunches with each other just like we did at the mission when I was little. We couldn't stay long on the top, only an hour or so because we had to be back to the schoolhouse by four so the children could get home in time for dinner and chores.

When it was time to leave, I stood up on top of the stump where the food had been and announced that it was time to start back to the schoolhouse. "Children, be sure to pick up any trash you have and put it back in your pack to take home. We want to keep our woods clean."

Then I looked at the older boys and said, "Boys, this has been the longest week I've ever seen in my life!"

Of course, they all wanted to know why I would say such a thing as that.

"Well, at the beginning of the school year, you told me I wouldn't last a week, but I've been here the whole year!" and everybody laughed.

I reminded them of all that we had accomplished in spite of all the things that stood in our way. I told them how proud I was of them. "It just goes to prove what I've been telling you all year. 'You can do and be anything you want to be if you're willing to work at it.' We have been able to get nine of you ready to go to high school next year." I loved saying the same things to my students that Miss Marston once said to me. It made me feel that I was a good teacher and I really believed that their lives could be changed just as mine had been.

It was a good year. I had made it though and it was just like Miss Marston had said: "If you really want to do something bad enough—and work hard enough—you can do it." I was proving that to be true.

I felt good about keeping my promise to God, even though for a while back there in high school it had been a difficult choice. Over the last year I had also learned that even when you're doing what He wants you to do, you still have to depend on Him for the strength and wisdom to do it. It was like together we were working His plan—a partnership—a relationship that I never dreamed possible.

We all had such a good time on our trip to Hall Top that I decided that I would do this with my students every year. And I did. I took children from all the other schools where I taught to Hall Top. That was somewhere the children could go without having to pay for it. The groups I took from Sand Hill and Rowe were a little smaller, probably about forty students. We would go at different times of the year. They would be teaching trips: sometimes we would collect leaves; other times we would identify as many plants and trees as we could.

After the first year, Ben helped me by bringing the littlest ones up in a truck. Some of their parents wouldn't let their six-year-olds go unless they could ride. We'd start at seven or eight o'clock, get there in time for lunch, and we'd play around and start back so we could be at the schoolhouse by the time school usually let out.

The children didn't complain about the long trips we took. In fact, I had a time keeping up with them. They'd run and climb trees and do everything they could think up, and then even on the way back they were still full of energy. They were being children, and it reminded me of my own childhood. I hope you, too, can look back on your childhood with such fondness someday, Lori.

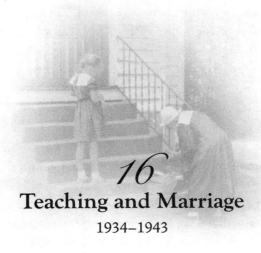

16
Teaching and Marriage
1934–1943

Easter Sunday 1934—Ben Asks Me for a Date

*B*en was still working up there by his aunt and uncle's, but usually he would be down here at our place on the weekends. Well, this time when he showed up at our house, early on Sunday morning, he asked me for a date.

After all these years of writing letters and spending time together and even talking about getting married, that was the first time he had ever asked me for a date. Why, we had done things for years that most people around here considered dating—and there was no "asking" to it.

There was a history between us two. We started writing to each other when I first went away at school in 1927, but we weren't anything more than sort of friends at first. Then, at the end of every school year, Ben came with Papa to meet me at the train station. Oh, and then when I was home during the summers, we went to parties and socials at the church. A lot of Sundays he walked with me to church services up here at the chapel and sometimes down there to the service at Sand Hill. That's one of the main ways people dated back then. But usually when we got to church, the girls would go inside while the boys would stay outside and talk or do whatever it was they did. Sometimes we would go for walks around here and talk. I had never thought much about it. I would go for walks with different boys, you know. I never felt obligated to any of them. They were just good friends as far as I was concerned. So, you can see where it would seem pretty strange to me for him to show up and ask me for a date to do what we already did most every Sunday.

I don't even remember when Ben first started talking about getting married. I guess that's because he talked about it several times and I really wasn't interested, so I'd just let it pass on by. And then, for a while there I had my mind on someone else. I know we talked about getting married when I was home from college the Christmas of 1932—the time when it rained and we ate dinner under the kitchen table to stay dry. And we talked about it again just before my Thanksgiving break in 1933 when we were in the woods looking for trees for the new kitchen roof. That was one time he asked me to marry him.

Well, for our "date," he spent all of that Sunday with me. In the morning we went to the mission church and afterward he ate dinner with us. That afternoon we went to the church that was held in the Sand Hill School and then we went back to church there again that night. We usually went to church three times on Sunday: morning, afternoon, and night. When you were dating, that was a good chance to get out and talk. It was better than just sitting at home. It was better than staying at home even if you didn't have a date.

Before he left that night, Ben asked me again to marry him. This time it was an official proposal.

I accepted his proposal but told him that I would still not take a ring. And I meant it for more than the reason I had given him before. I had seen too many people go into debt to buy a ring. We didn't have anything to start a marriage with and I for sure knew I didn't want us to be in debt for a ring. I was making fifty dollars a month and I thought that was big money. But I had to pay fifteen dollars a month on the money I had borrowed for college, and I helped out Mama and Papa every month. I used some of my money for my teaching supplies and things I wanted to buy for my students. There wasn't any extra money to be spending on a wedding. We didn't know when we would get married, but I had thought it would be sometime soon. I know it sounds strange, but we never talked about it again after that.

Teaching

For sure, it had been a hard year of "making do," but I had made it through my first year of teaching and I felt fulfilled. All of the children had learned to read, and that was my biggest goal. Even my little five-year-old could write her name and read a few words. She could even count past twenty and knew the alphabet.

I didn't know if I would be asked to teach at Davis again the next year or not. But I knew for sure that I didn't want to have to go through collecting textbooks again. Even if I was assigned to teach another year there, I didn't want to chance leaving all of my books and supplies at Davis and then have some hooligans come in during the summer and tear them all up. After all, it was not uncommon for school houses to get broken into, not because the vandals wanted to read schoolbooks or learn anything, but just for the shear meanness of it. And if I was assigned to another school, there was just no telling if there would be any books there to teach from. There was no way of knowing what the county would or would not be providing for the next year. So I decided to pack up all the books and the teaching supplies and store them in boxes in Mama's barn.

As it turned out, I only taught that one year at Davis. I don't reckon anybody ever taught more than one year in that school. I never did find out why except for the older boys trying to scare off the young teachers. I can imagine that a lot of teachers just didn't want to go back, but I would have, if they had given me another year.

My second year, I was assigned to the Sand Hill School. The week before school started, I picked up my key and roll book from the county office and rode the train back to Del Rio. Papa had hitched our old mule to a wagon and loaded up all my boxes from the barn. I had also set aside some boards I wanted to use to build bookshelves and the frame and legs for a sand table. He put all of that on the wagon along with my hammer and nails and cleaning things and met me at the depot. The school was on our way back home. We passed it every time we took the road to or from Del Rio. Coming from the depot, it was on the left at the top of the hill before you get to the big curve by the church. Papa unloaded all my things and put them inside the schoolhouse and left me there at Sand Hill.

There were a lot of briars around the school that would need cutting. The spring where we would get our water was farther away from the school than last year. Sand Hill was smaller than Davis, but it had more desks. After Papa left, I walked back into the schoolhouse. There at the back of the room I sat down in one of the desks. I traced the carved-out line going down the middle of the desktop with my finger and remembered back to when I had played "horsie" with Ernest. I smiled as I pictured the teacher with his legs and arms sticking out of that ol' box. Well, I had stayed on top of the box last year and I didn't figure this one could be much harder. I spent the first couple days of that week cleaning and building my bookshelves. I put all the books on the new shelves with the ones for the younger children at the bottom so they would be easier for the young'us to reach. Before building the sand table, I decorated the walls and around the blackboard.

Sand Table

My students at Davis had the best time with the sand table. They thought that they were playing, but I do believe they learned more about history right there in the sand than they did out of their books. Oh, we used the books all right, but then we would playact it out in the sand. My first year at Davis, the students and I had made animals and people out of papier-mâché and log cabins out of twigs and bark. This year we would add to the collection. I made the frame for the sandbox, which was five or six feet long and two feet wide and about one foot deep, with short legs so the little ones could see and reach inside without standing on their toes. I waited until school started and had the students carry buckets of sand to put in the table. I didn't have to worry about finding sand. There was plenty of that; that's why it was called Sand Hill.

The first thing we did was make more animals and people and things like trees and mountains to add to what I had left from the year before. We made them out of papier-mâché and cardboard and things like that. For the trees the children had to go out and collect leaves from all the different kinds of trees. We attached one or two leaves to a twig, and when they needed a tree, they would push the twig into the sand. They had to learn to identify each kind of tree by the leaves. The children loved working with the papier-mâché. When we used the things they had made in an illustration, the children would stick them into the sand so they would stand up. It worked real well.

The first time we used the sand table at Sand Hill was for an illustration about pioneers and how they cleared the land and built their cabins. Then we added onto it to make a farm scene. We made barns and outbuildings.

I got so tickled at this one little girl. I was explaining each step and the children were so excited about getting everything, all the animals and buildings, in the sand table that they were getting way ahead of me. I said, "Wait a minute. Hold your horses, just hold your horses!" and this one little girl reached over and picked up all the horses that we had. She stood there holding them and everybody roared. She thought I meant for her to actually pick them up and hold them, you know.

Ben and I Decide to Get Married—9/21/34

The worst thing about teaching for me was the monthly Saturday meetings in Newport. Plus, most months I would have to go back into town on another Saturday to buy supplies for some project or other. Making the most of those trips, whenever I was in town, I always bought whatever groceries we needed.

Every time I went into Newport, either Mama or Papa would walk me all the way to Del Rio where I would take the train on into town. Then that afternoon the other one would come back for me. Usually Papa and I would take the short path over the mountain early in the morning, which was only four or five miles. But that was much too difficult for Mama. It was easier for her to come the seven miles by road. That made a total of about ten miles for Papa to walk and fourteen miles for Mama every Saturday that I went into Newport. Mama usually rode on the mule instead of walking all that way. Then on the way back she would sometimes hold a bag of groceries while she rode and I would carry the rest. Other times we would put my supplies or groceries into two cloth bags that I then tied together and put over the mule's shoulders.

I just hated more than anything that Mama and Papa had to go all that way with me. That was too much for them to do! They had already done that for one year and I didn't want them to have to do it anymore. Mama and Papa were getting old, but Papa was so stubborn, even more stubborn than I was. He was not about to allow one of his daughters to walk all that way alone and I for sure couldn't convince him otherwise. It was something that simply wasn't permitted.

One Friday, on my way home from school, I stopped at our mailbox down there where my grandparents lived. There was a notice in the mail from my eye doctor in Johnson City saying my glasses were ready for me to pick up.

The next day was when I was to go to my faculty meeting in Newport and pick up my check. After that I could go into Johnson City to see about my glasses and it seemed to me like the perfect opportunity to get married. That would free Mama and Papa from having to walk everywhere with me.

If we got married, it would have to be kept a secret because when I signed my teaching contract, I had to agree to a whole sheet of rules. I had promised to resign from my teaching position if I got drunk, went to a roadhouse or a dance, smoked, or rode in a carriage or car with any man excluding members of my family. Married teachers had to agree to resign for the rest of that school year if they became pregnant and if single teachers got married during the school year they also had to agree to resign for the rest of the year.

Ben and I could get married in Johnson City and that way no one here would know about it. Seeing about my glasses would be the only time I would have a reason to go there. I wasn't going to go another time and have to lie about why I was in Johnson City. Thinking about it now, I don't really believe it would have mattered to the superintendent or anyone else in the school district. They didn't seem to care anything at all about what went on back here in the coves and hollows.

Well, after I got the mail that day, I started walking up the road to my house, thinking about how I was going to tell Ben that if we were going to get married, it would have to be the next day. It was the funniest thing. I was just walking along thinking and I looked up and there he was, coming towards me from the field there at my grandpa's place.

Here I thought I was going to have to go all the way up in the hollow that evening to talk to him and instead, I ran into him on accident. Ben had quit his job and was no longer living with his aunt and uncle. Instead, he had been living with his brother John who had married my sister Beatrice. He was doing odd jobs around here and helping build a fence or something there at John's.

It surprised me when I saw him there like that. The first thing I said to him was, "Are we going to get married this year or next?" That was the first thing I said. No "hi" or "how ya doin'?" I didn't build up to it or anything. But that's the way I was—if I thought something, I said what I thought.

He looked at me so foolishly. I guess I shocked him because we hadn't even mentioned getting married since he had proposed. I knew he loved me; I wasn't worried about that. Looking back, I guess that was pretty funny just walking up to him and saying that. It wasn't like it is now; back then girls didn't say things like that.

By his response, I knew I caught him off-guard. "What? Well, I hadn't thought much about it. I don't…I don't know."

"Well, I haven't thought much about it either."

I wasn't even especially interested in getting married and I had told him so several times. But then, I had always told Ben that I would marry him—someday—and then I would always put him off. I loved Ben, but my work came first. I had promised that I would come back here to work and for sure I was going to do that very thing. I was going to teach and Ben knew exactly the way I felt about it. "Now it's up to you if you want to marry me. I don't care if we do or not. But if we get married now, Mama and Papa won't have to walk me into Del Rio all the time. It's just too far for them to have to walk. When we're married, you can go with me. You could even stay in town all day if you wanted to and then we could walk back together. But if we do get married, we'll have to slip off somewhere so no one around here will know." I told him about my plan:

"I don't guess I've got any clean britches."

"Well, forget about that. That's nothing. Beatrice can get you some washed and get them dried someway tonight." I continued on, "If we're going to get married this year, it will have to be tomorrow when I go to see about my glasses. We can go to Johnson City, stop at The Grange, and get married while we're over there. You know we can't let people around here know what's going on. We can't let them find it out because I'll lose my job and won't be able to teach anymore this year. I just think this would be a good time, that's all—and we won't even have to tell a lie about it."

"I don't have any money yet hardly. I haven't got but eleven dollars comin' from workin.'"

"That'll be enough."

"I'm going to go get it now."

"You're going to have to get back up here tonight in time to ask Papa. I told you a long time ago I wouldn't marry you if you didn't ask him."

I left him there and came on home. Ben went down the creek on the other side of the church and up across that hollow to where he had been cutting the tops out of trees to get the money they owed him.

Asking Papa

When I got home, only Mama and Papa were there. Ben came over later that night, but by then Papa had gone down the road somewhere so Ben went down there to hunt him.

While he was gone, Swanie Turner came over just about as it was getting dark. Swanie was at our house a lot. Sometimes I'd help him write letters to his girlfriend that he had met in South Carolina just like Ben's cousin had done for him. Other times we would sit around there and talk and laugh. When I heard Papa and Ben coming back up the road talking, I told Swanie he had better leave because Papa was coming and would be tired and want to go to bed soon after he had eaten. I wanted Swanie to leave because I didn't want to chance him hearing about our plans.

I put the food on the table and stepped out the door like I was going out to the bathroom as Ben and Papa came in. I didn't want to be in there because I didn't know what Papa was going to say or if he was going to tell Mama then and how she would react. When I did come back in, Ben was still back in the kitchen eating and Papa had gone to bed. I quickly sat down in the chair next to him and whispered loudly, "What did Papa say?"

"Your Papa said that he didn't care."

Ben went on home so he would be sure to be ready for the next morning. Mama and Papa were both in bed and I didn't see any more of either of them. I don't know if he said anything to Mama that night about talking with Ben. Mama knew she was going into Newport with me the next morning and then on to Johnson City so I could get my glasses. But did she know about the change in plans?

The Next Morning

Papa always got up first. He started the fire in the kitchen stove so that it would be hot enough to cook breakfast. That was one of his chores and he did it everyday right up until the week before he died. No matter how hot it was, we always had to have a fire started to cook our meals.

By the time I got up the next morning, he had told Mama, but she didn't say anything to me about it. I know that sounds strange that her daughter was getting married that day and she didn't talk about it. She just didn't talk much at all, but that didn't mean anything; she was always quiet. Mama was a lot of fun if you got her to talking. She would play games with us sometimes, but she was never much of a talker. I definitely took after my papa in the respect!

Mama never did "carry news," or gossip, either. Maybe it was because she just didn't talk that much, but since she never let us talk about people, I'd say it was because she just didn't believe in carrying tales. So that morning, Mama and I got dressed and ready to go. I wondered if Ben was even going to show up, but when it was time to leave, he was there and ready to go. We went into Newport and then got a ride to Johnson City in the back of Jumping Spider. The same man who took the children from Sand Hill to meet the school bus in Del Rio used his truck that we all called "Jumping Spider" like a taxi, charging a quarter per person. He would take groups of people into Newport or Johnson City. Sometimes there would be ten or fifteen of us packed in the back of the truck. When it was snowing or raining, he would put up a tarp to cover us. He was kind of a handyman too and helped people out on different projects. He and his wife lived with us for a while later on when we lived in the mission.

After we got to Johnson City, we walked over to the court house, but Mama didn't go in with us. She didn't say a word to us—she just stood there crying. She wasn't going to tell anyone we got married, and if anybody asked her, she'd just say she didn't see us get married. We were married by the justice of the peace. I didn't have to make up big wedding plans; all I said was "I do" and that was it. After we got married, we went down the street and I got my glasses.

On the way back home, Blue John Smith, one of the men riding with us, suspicioned that we had gotten married and started singing to us. I guess he assumed that because we were sitting close together on the same feed sack. We had never sat that close to each other before. That ol' man sang "In the Pines" all the way home.

When we got back home that night around ten, we counted our money and together we had two dollars left. That's all we had. It was a good thing we weren't going to start housekeeping yet, and we teased each other about that. Our plan was for Ben to stay at John's and I would stay at Mama's.

I didn't figure we would be able to set up housekeeping for ourselves until the end of the school year. I felt torn inside. I was glad that Mama and Papa would no longer have to walk me everywhere outside of the community and I would still be there to help them. But I was afraid if word got out about us being married, especially since now Ben was walking me into the train depot or into town, I would lose my teaching job for the rest of the year.

There was nothing I loved more than teaching and community work. I felt that I was really making a difference in the lives of my children and their families, even when it came to some of the more unpleasant parts of teaching and training my students.

Chores and Discipline

One of the biggest problems we had around all the schools up here was briars. They were anywhere from being a mere nuisance to being extremely dangerous, especially for the young children. There were a lot of wild blackberry plants that the little children didn't notice when they were out running around playing until they ran right through a patch of them. They'd come back with scratches all over their little legs. Those briars had to be cleared away! There were also briar plants with long shoots of thick, strong thorns that could tear a child's arm or leg wide open.

A big bottle of liniment that I made up out of turpentine, lamp oil, and castor oil was always a part of my first aid supplies, along with bandages I made by tearing up old sheets. When the little ones would come in with briar cuts, I would shake up that liniment real good and apply some on one of those bandages and wipe their legs off with it.

When it came to discipline, I intended that a punishment should do as much good as possible and should always be of practical use. Like the week before school, when I first started teaching at Davis, I noticed how many briars there were when I was marking off the bathroom areas for the boys and girls. I decided right then and there that those briars needed to be cut down. I didn't have time to do all of that, but I was sure that I would be having some students practically begging for a job like that. And sure enough, the first day of school those two older boys showed me that they needed something more constructive to do than smart-mouth and dance with the teacher. Before long, the briar problem was under control, but those ol' briars grew fast so there were always plenty around. Cutting briars became one of the punishments I used at every school.

The number of briars they had to cut would depend on what they had done. They might have to cut twenty-five, thirty, or fifty briars. For fighting or hurting another child, they always had to cut at least a hundred. After they cut the briars, they always had to lay them out in a row so I could count them. Then they had to pick them all back up and carry them to the briar stack. The children were usually real nice about doing their briar punishment. Maybe they just didn't want to have to cut more, because if they fussed or complained, I would double the number they had to cut. A lot of them laugh 'til today about how they had to cut briars.

Sometimes if one of the students teased another child, or done something to them, they would have to do the other child's chores. Of course, they still had to do their own chores too.

One time there were about eight students who were to be punished and I gave them the choice, as I usually did, of getting a whipping or cutting briars. The first boy, a mischievous little one and usually a troublemaker, took the whipping. Then he went outside and told the rest of them, "Don't take the briars; she'll make ya do a hundred or more. I took the whoopin'n she just 'tended ta whoop me. Just hit the bench, she did." So the next little boy came in and told me he wanted the whipping too. Then he turned around and leaned right over that bench and I wore him out. After I whipped him, he looked at me with those big ol' eyes of his, just sobbing away, and said, "Robert said a-ya wouldn't-a hit me, but you'd just a-hit a-da bench."

Mrs. Pierce and Her Children

Sometimes I wouldn't give them a choice. They just automatically got the whipping anytime a student did something that was dangerous or could harm another student—like what happened with Curtis Pierce.

You see, one day Curtis found a big ol' lizard and started chasing the girls with it. Of course, they were all running around screaming and squealing. Well, he caught this one little girl and pulled out the collar of her dress and put that lizard down her back. It was a big lizard!! That poor little girl took off running in circles screaming. I had to catch her before I could get the lizard out of her dress. Then I found me a switch and whipped Curtis. Of course, he went crying home and told his mother.

There was one house between the Pierce's and the school. The lady who lived there said she saw Curtis coming from school crying. And then the next thing she knew, Mrs. Pierce was coming back towards the school just a-talkin' to herself, saying, "I'll whoop 'er! I'll whoop 'er! I'll whoop 'er! I'll whoop 'er! She whooped Curtis 'n I'll whoop 'er!"

A few minutes later she saw Mrs. Pierce heading back home saying, "I'll whoop 'im when I get home! I'll whoop 'im when I get home!"

The neighbor asked her, "Mercy, me. What's the matter?"

"She whooped Curtis 'n I thought she beat 'im fer nuttin' 'n I got up thar 'n foun out he'd put a lizard down that little girl's dress. I'm gonna go back 'n wear 'im out!"

She didn't say a thing to me. I didn't even see her. When she got up to the schoolhouse, some of the girls told her what had happened and said that he for sure deserved every whack. Somehow, I believe that Curtis most likely got two whippings that day.

Mrs. Pierce was not a well person. People said she had had some kind of a stroke that messed up her mind. Others said it seemed like somebody shot off a firecracker too close to her and it messed up her nerves. She was always terribly nervous and easily upset. Mrs. Pierce raised a big crowd of children. I don't know for sure, but I think there were about ten in all. I hafta say, she raised them all with morals. She was strict with her children, especially when it came to treating other people right and keeping up their responsibilities. She meant for her children to do right, but you had better believe she wanted to make sure people didn't do wrong by her children either.

The Pierces owned a real big place right down below Lawton's and back up in the hills. In the 30s and 40s, it was hard to get money. Even though Mr. Pierce was a good worker, they had it pretty tough getting all that land paid for and raising all those young'uns. The Pierce children all did real good in school and were usually well behaved. Troy was a little slow at first, and he couldn't talk real plain when he first started school in the first grade. One day I was trying to teach him this poem:

> Birdie with a yellow bill
> Hopped upon the window sill
> Cocked his shiny eye and said,
> "Ain't you ashamed, you sleepy head?"

When I taught the little ones poetry, I would usually say each line and have them repeat it. So when I said to Troy, "Birdie with a yellow bill," he covered his mouth with his hand and started snickering. So I repeated, "Troy, say 'Birdie with a yellow bill.'" He looked around at Bertie Ellison sitting over on the other side of the room and snickered, "Bertie ain't got no yellow bill!" I had to explain to him that his poem was talking about a little bitty bird and not Bertie Ellison.

Troy was real good; all the children were, even mischievous little Curtis. Troy grew up and married a Christian girl and his son is now a minister. Dorothy, one of the girls in the family, stayed with me for a while after Desmer got married and took care of Corrine. Later she married a man that worked for the light company.

Mami was the only one of the Pierces who went on to high school. I always talked to all of my students and encouraged them to get as much education as they could. I told them about boarding schools like the one I went to. But the Pierces didn't want any of their children to go on to high school. I don't know why. Maybe they wanted the children to stay there and help them work the land, or I guess they could have been afraid that they would get out of the community and never come back.

I don't know how Mami got to go, but she did real well in high school, and earned a scholarship to go on to college. She became a teacher and met this man who was a meteorologist and married him. He had a good job and she taught for a long time. They both retired about two years ago and have been traveling all over the United States. I just got a letter from her and she told me about how they went to Switzerland and some other places this last summer. That child has been just about everywhere. I guess Mami bought out all the other children, because she now owns and rents out all the land that her folks owned.

They all married and made for themselves a decent life, except the oldest girl, who married a boy from the community. He never did do much or own any property or anything. He tended to move around from here to there. They said he was sick a lot and he's been dead now for several years. The best way for a girl to make it back then was to marry someone from outside the community with a good education who knew how to work and do things. The oldest girl's daughter lived up here in the Click House for a while. She married the man who handled snakes down at the Church of God in the Name of Jesus. He raised copper heads and kept them in a box up there in their home. I didn't like the idea of having so many snakes that close.

Setting Up Housekeeping

Ben was at our house a lot and ate with us most every night. One day when I came home from school, Mama looked sickly and Ben was sitting there doing the churning for her. I thought that was the funniest thing he'd ever pulled. Papa and Burl never worked in the house but Ben would cook and churn and wash or do anything that needed to be done. He was a big help to them.

After a while, Ben and I started talking about setting up housekeeping. A good friend of mine who knew we were married said, "If you'uns want to move to that house down there closer to the school, I'll rent it out to you. I won't tell anyone you're married and livin' together there, won't say a word."

That was for sure something to consider because if the children got to school before me, they had to stand out in the snow and cold until I got there with the key. It would be almost as cold inside the school as it was outside until I got the fire going, and even then it would take a good while for the school to warm up. If we lived there close to the school, Ben could slip over and make a fire early in the morning and they'd never see him. We could have the room hot or at least a lot warmer by the time the children came. It seemed like that would be a good thing to do, so that's exactly what we did.

We didn't need too much more to set up housekeeping. After living away at school for six years, I already had a lot of what our home required. I had my own bed, two sheets, two blankets, two plates, two cups, and two saucers—two of everything. I didn't have too much, but what I did have would be a good start.

The next time I was in town I found a cabinet, stove, and several other things for only twenty-five dollars. That was pretty cheap. Then there was some old lady down here selling out and we got some more dishes, pans, mops, and other things from her. We also bought six white plates, some white soup beans, and a big pot. I got some domestic and made us two good straw ticks. We bought things like that here and there as we had the money.

The cupboards I bought were like kitchen cabinets now, except that they were just shelves; they didn't have doors. I took paper and notched it out with scissors making all kinds of curlicues, holes, and flowers in it and put it on the front of the shelves to cover them up and make them pretty. When it got dirty or wet, I would put up new paper with maybe new designs. I put some more of that pretty paper around our medicine shelf. One night, a while after we moved in there, I was sick so I went to my medicine shelf to get something to take. I put my candle on the shelf so I could see better. Guess I didn't set it down just right, because it fell over and the paper caught on fire. That's when I decided to tear it all down and not to use paper to decorate with anymore.

In February of 1935, the Presbyterians let us rent the mission house. After we moved in we decided to make another bed. That way, when we had other visitors we'd have somewhere for them to sleep. We used the old pieces of wood that we had taken off the kitchen roof at Mama's to make the boxlike frame and the slats. Then we cut down trees to make four posts, one for each corner of the frame. We put one of our straw ticks on that and then all I needed were the pillows and quilts.

The county officials never did say anything about me being married. They may never have found out, or maybe they just didn't care and I had done all that sneaking around and worrying for nothing. It was during my second year teaching at Sand Hill that I became pregnant with Corrine.

Kitchen and Feeding Program at Rowe School

When I started back teaching after Corrine was born, I was assigned to Rowe School. Desmer, who was still living at home with Mama and Papa, said that she could help me with Corrine while I taught. I had to get up before daylight to get ready, feed Corrine, get her things together, and take her down to Mama's. Then I'd have to walk back home to get the things I needed to take to school. It was just too much to take Corrine and everything else in one trip. And then I would have to walk all the way to school, which was a long way off. Late fall through mid-winter I walked most of that way in the dark.

Starting around the first part of October, Desmer would come over every evening and spend the night at my house. That way I didn't have to be concerned with getting Corrine up and ready. She could sleep later and Desmer would take her on down to Mama's after the sun came up and it got a little warmer. That made it so much easier for me. Desmer was so good to help me and help Mama too. Desmer and I had never been real close. I had always liked her, but I guess because of the eight-year difference in our ages, we just never got to know each other. She was still a little girl when I left here to go to school in Kentucky, and when I was back home during the summers, I was always busy working or doing something. But in the end, Desmer has been closer to me than all of the rest of my sisters. Beatrice and Velmer moved away. Desmer did move off for a few years too, just after she married, but she came back. And for a while Maggie lived close, but later she moved too. Since then it's just been me and Desmer for all these years.

Things were pretty much the same at Rowe as they had been at Davis and Sand Hill, except I had a lot more children whose parents didn't take very good care of them. I told Desmer how the condition of some of the students was pitiable. "I know some of those young'uns don't get enough to eat at home and they hardly have enough in their lunches to give them the strength to make it through the rest of the day. I just don't know what I'm going to do about it. We've got to think of some way to help them!"

Well, Desmer and I started cooking food for me to take to school. We'd make big pans of biscuits, corn bread, and sometimes gingerbread cookies. Of course, we had to give food to all the students so that the ones who really needed it wouldn't feel bad or embarrassed about someone giving them charity.

Before long, others began donating food. Some would bring a bushel of beans or maybe corn. The Freemans, who owned a store and the furniture shops, lived up there not far from the school and they sent food. Mrs. Freeman even canned fruit for the children and sent fresh apples. Her own twins, Rolland and Roger, were students at the school, and though they had plenty and would be considered by any up here to be rich, they acted just like all the other children. They were real nice and didn't consider themselves to be the least bit better than anyone else.

We did that both years I was at Rowe, and when I was moved to Sand Hill again, we started a food program there too. I found out that if we had the backing of the school district and a kitchen at the school, I would be able to get food from the government. The superintendent and school board didn't want to listen to me, but I knew if I kept pushing I could make it happen. It took a lot of work to get the meal program started. It took getting the whole community to go in and get a-hold of the superintendent. You know, it's really a shame that the school district didn't come up with this idea themselves. The eighth graders helped me build a lean-to kitchen onto the school. In no time I was able to get food like eggs, flour, raisins, and dried peaches from the government welfare program. The parents brought food too. We had dozens of jars of canned tomatoes, and in the fall they would bring in dried peas and beans. Pretty soon we were getting so much food from the government and community we had to build storage shelves. The government even paid Desmer and three other girls to cook. They got thirty-eight dollars a month and they thought they were rich. Desmer was thrilled. Being the youngest in our family, she always got the old hand-me-downs. That was the first time she had ever been able to buy a dress for herself. Miss Minnie and Mrs. Click were good to help me with Corrine. I just couldn't have made it without them.

In 1939, Papa was having some serious money problems. He was in debt and went in more debt to buy a cow. Then when the crops didn't make it that year, there was nothing else he could do but sell his part of the original Corn Place. He sold his sixty acres to the McMahans and a little later they sold it to Frank Turner. Mama and Papa moved into a log house just off the highway, back up in the hollow down there by Stone Mountain Recreation Park. Papa farmed some with a man who lived down there, but his health was deteriorating. Papa was so unusually heavy that it was really hard on him to do too much.

After Mama and Papa moved, Desmer stayed at the mission with us a lot until she married Mont McMahan in October of 1941, when she was twenty-two years old. Mont was closer to my age, about seven years older than Desmer. She and Mont had dated on and off for five years. She had dated this boy named Henry who was in the army, and she was actually engaged to him for a while. He deserted the army, and she tried for a while to get him to go back, but he wouldn't do it. She wouldn't have anything to do with him after that. Mont was a good worker and always provided for Desmer and their family. The McMahans had moved to South Carolina when Mont was twelve years old and then moved back and forth from South Carolina to here for several years. After they married, she and Mont moved to South Carolina and stayed there until 1943. When they moved back, they lived just across the hill from us for a long time. You know, up there where the peach orchard used to be. They lived on across that little ridge and still lived up there when the mission burned. Even after Desmer and Mont moved into town, I would visit her every chance I got. Now, when one of the boys needs to go into town for groceries or some other shopping, they always take me down to her house to visit. We talk on the phone a lot too.

Boys Go Skinny Dipping

When I was teaching at Rowe School, I had three boys who would sneak away from school to go skinny dipping. I knew I had to think up something that would keep a thirteen, fourteen, and fifteen-year-old from going swimming during school time. Boys that age can be pretty easy to embarrass, so I thought that if I could sneak down to the creek and grab their clothes that just might do it. But I had to make sure that I wouldn't catch them out of the water or I might be the one who was embarrassed. I came up with a plan. One day I told the girls that I was taking them on a field trip to see how many different leaves we could find. I told them I had something to do and that I would catch up with them down the road. The directions I gave them would take them right past where the boys went swimming. The boys would be able to hear them coming but the girls would not be able to see them.

I waited a few minutes after the girls left, then headed down the road. Sure enough, when the boys heard the group of girls go by, they hit the creek and I went down the bank and picked up all their clothes. "Let us have our clothes!" they shouted. "Let us have our clothes!"

"No, sir. You come and get your clothes."

"Not me!"

"You either go without them or you come get them out of my hand." So I turned my back and hung out a pair of pants and said, "Whoever these belong to, you come and get them. I'll keep my back turned until you get them on, but I'll not give them to you until you come and get them right out of my hand."

It just tickled the life out of me because I knew those boys were so embarrassed that they were just dying when they came out of the water and got their clothes. They put the clothes on their wet bodies and took off down the path. The girls saw them coming out the path and had a well-deserved laugh at them.

One of the boys lived pretty close and he was still wet when he got home. But I never did hear anything from the parents, so they must have agreed with the way I handled the situation. But most likely, those boys didn't say a word to their folks about what I had done. Usually, if the parents didn't like what you did or the punishment you put on the children, they'd send a note. I never heard a word from anyone and the boys never went to the swimming hole again during class time.

Special Children

In all the time I taught in one-room schools, I only had one child who was retarded and couldn't learn the way other children did. This retarded child lived where Roy Dan lives. At that time, there were sixteen or seventeen people living in that little cabin. It only has two rooms with a loft and a kitchen. I guess the children all shared the loft. I would have given anything if he could have received special education. I believe he could have learned a lot to help himself if there had been someone to work with him.

After the schools consolidated and I worked at the school in Del Rio, a lot of the students acted like they were retarded because they wanted to get into special education classes. I called it "social education" because it was nothing but socializing. There was no special education to it. They just sat together in class doing crafts and things like that. Those classes are good for children who really need them, but only hurt those who are lazy or those who are just slow learners. I had a lot of slow learners, or children from families that just never taught them anything before they started school. I would always give them "special attention," not special education. I found out what they were good at and helped them feel good about themselves. And I taught the other students to respect all people.

I had one little girl at Sand Hill whose parents told me, "I don't know what you'll do with Lois 'cause she just can't stay in the house or sit still for long periods of time. She has to go outside and move around."

I told the little girl, "That will be fine. We've got papers and trash out there that need picking up anyway. So when you get tired of sitting, Lois, you just go outside and pick up papers and bring them in and let me see how many you got." Pretty soon she got so she could stay in her seat as good as anybody else. When she had to pick up papers, she discovered sitting at her place wasn't too bad. It turned out that Lois would much rather be in school than work outside.

The Dirty Little Girl

There was this little six-year-old girl that came to school so dirty it was pathetic. She smelled of stale urine so bad that the other students couldn't stand to sit by her. I don't know if she wet the bed at night or if some of the other children sleeping in the same bed did. Her parents never changed her clothes, not even her underwear. She slept in the same clothes she wore to school and then would wear them to school again the next day.

I started bringing clothes for her to wear at school. When she got to school, I would take her into the kitchen, clean her up, and put clean panties and clothes on her. When it was time for her to go home, I'd put her dirty clothes back on her. Sure enough, that little girl would show up again the next day in the same clothes. Sometimes when the sun was shining enough that it would dry her hair before she got home, I would get some of the eighth grade girls to take her outside and wash her hair. I just don't think the mother knew enough to keep her clean. The little girl was just as bright as she could be. After her mother died, when she was about sixteen, she went to Greeneville to some of her mother's people. I hope they took better care of her.

Teachers Aides

I had several mamas who would come and help me listen to the little ones read and say their ABCs and times tables. Usually they would stay the whole day. I had one mother that would come and stay whenever I needed her, and if I had to be off a day she would teach the classes. I'll tell you, that was wonderful when something urgent came up. I didn't have to go through a lot of rigmarole finding a certified teacher. To be a certified teacher in a one-room school you had to have one year of college and to be a substitute you were to be a high school graduate. But it wasn't easy finding someone with those credentials to come in on short notice. Somehow God always provided for every occasion.

17
1944 – 1946

Buying Land

Sam, Ben's daddy, never owned land. Like everyone else, they did have a garden, but he really didn't want to work the land to raise larger crops grown for food or to barter with in town. Instead, he was content to work for someone else and earn just enough money to buy their food and the other things they needed. For a long time Sam worked for a large landowner doing odd jobs, this and that. The landowner had what was called a company store on his property where his workers could purchase food and other things on credit. That is why the Myers always had more variety in their food and ate more uppity than we did. But they never did have any money or any property of their own or anything else to show for it as far as that goes. They had biscuits and yeast bread when everyone else up here ate only cornbread. But when the "due bill" was deducted from Sam's pay, he hardly had any money left at all, barely enough to pay their rent.

He worked all his boys the same way. As soon as John, Ben, Thomas, Howard, and Albert were big enough, he took them out of school and sent them out to work. Being young, they were hardly paid anything at all and what they did earn was used up at the company store to buy food for the family. Those boys did all that hard work and never got any of the money for themselves. They never had anything. That's the reason all of the boys left home as soon as they got old enough to get a better job and make it on their own.

I guess Ben was like Sam—he never saw the need of owning our own land. We had rented from the time we got married, but I had always had the dream of owning my own place. Desmer knew how much I wanted to own property. So, when she heard her brother-in-law say that he was planning to sell the McMahan Place, she could hardly wait to tell me. The place included a house and fifty acres of land. It began on the other side of the road from the mission house up there at my little toilet and went all the way up to the top of that mountain, all the way up to the Click House and then up in that hollow.

Back when I was going to the mission school before the government took back all the land leases and made the people move, there were dozens of families living back here in this community. Now there weren't many houses left at all. Coming up here from the Old Fifteenth, there were a couple houses that could be seen from the road, a few more were back off the road about halfway up to the top of the mountain. Then there was the mission house and across from it and down a little bit was the McMahan Place. At the very end of the road, right up against the national forest, was the Click's cabin.

Even the church-schoolhouse was gone. We had decided back in the early '40s that it just made a whole lot more sense to move the church over to the old Sand Hill school location down there next to the cemetery at Persimmon Hill. One of our biggest problems had been trying to conduct funeral services with the church and the cemetery that far apart. About the only thing we could do was have a graveside service, and in bad weather that was terrible for everyone. So we got permission from the Presbyterians to dismantle and rebuild the church at the new location. We used the old wood to rebuild and the Presbyterians paid for the nails and other expenses like that. The pastor, who the Presbyterians were then sending up here to preach, and his sons, my papa, Ben, and a few others did all of the work themselves. It really turned out to be very good for everyone because the church was much closer for most of the people and not all that far from us either. It was even closer for the preachers who lived in town. They for sure were glad they did not have to travel that last mile or so of road which was still not much more than ruts and rocks. With the church in the new location, we were able to have funeral services in the church and then immediately take the casket out to the cemetery and have the burial.

Well, I kept trying to get Ben to agree to buy the McMahan Place, but he was not at all interested. He would just say, "Aw, we don't need it."

"Yes, we do!" I declared. "What if something happens to you? What would Corrine and I do then? We don't know how long they'll let us rent the mission. And if they ever decide they don't want us living here anymore, there's no other place around here to rent. We can't go outside the community to find a place. We don't have a car and that would be too far for me to walk to school. How would I teach then?"

I kept after Ben about buying land and finally I talked him into it. The land would cost us eleven hundred dollars. That sounded to me like a whole lot of money. I was making sixty-nine dollars a month and only got paid eight months out of the year. But I figured up that I could pay two hundred dollars a year on the land and Mont's brother agreed. Before I finished paying for that property, the county started dividing our pay over ten months.

Buying that property was one of the best decisions we ever made. Just after Desmer and Mont moved back up here, Mama and Papa moved into that house, the Old McMahan Place, and they lived there until they died. It was good to be able to provide that for them. They had always done so much for us and for everyone else too.

Mission Condemned

Ben left to go into the army on February 14, 1944. He hadn't been gone hardly any time at all when one day, when I got home from teaching school at Sand Hill, there were six or eight men waiting for me at the mission house. They were all dressed up in suits and I didn't know what in the world they wanted. It turned out that they were big shots from the Presbyterian Church in Kingsport and wanted to see the mission. Why, that just worried me to death because I never did have time to keep things cleaned up and my beds made. Everything always seemed to be in a scattered mess or in dust covered stacks of things that needed to be sorted. I told them, "You know, that with teaching school and everything else I do around here, I just didn't have time to do housekeeping."

"Your housekeeping is not what we came here to see. We're establishing a summer camp program and want to inspect the mission house to see if it's suitable for that."

That was rather interesting, I thought. We had already been doing that for years and they're just now thinking of it. Why, how silly could they be! Maybe we should have asked for their permission, but it had never crossed my mind that we might need approval from any of the higher-ups. Whenever the preacher from town would tell us he wanted to bring a group, we would tell them to come on and then we would get everything ready for them. I couldn't quite understand why they had to go through all this rigmarole now.

Those men acted real uppity and snooty, high 'n mighty like. They shook their heads and made clacking sounds as they looked at the steps and around the outside of the house. When they went inside and looked around, they seemed to get more upset. I had never heard such fussy talk from grown men! The floors screeched and they panicked over it. "This building is dangerous! Law! Three stories high and listen to that! Do you hear that floor? Listen to that! This building is not at all safe. Not only will this not do for a summer camp, I'm afraid we'll have to have this mission house condemned."

They said it wasn't even safe for me to live there and that it should probably be torn down right away before someone got hurt. Why, I had lived there since 1935, nearly ten years, and I had spent much of my childhood in the mission house. I owned the property across the road and I could live there with Mama and Papa. But I didn't want to move and I for sure didn't want it torn down. The mission was too important to me. I was so afraid—I had to think of something. Maybe if I were willing to take it off their hands, then perhaps they wouldn't care about its condition. If I owned it, then there would be nothing they could do to the mission. So I just up and said, "Yea, well, I'll pay you five hundred dollars for the mission."

They said I could have it with certain stipulations and told me I would have to sign a fifteen-year contract saying that I would keep and take care of any Presbyterian preacher or worker who came to help out in the community. I thought it was strange that they would want their preachers and workers staying in such an "unsafe" place. But I guess safety wasn't such a big issue if the liability was mine and not theirs.

Well, of course, that was just fine with me. I'd only been doing that most of my life. Since we first started renting the mission, we had always reserved a room for people who came to visit in the community, whether they were preachers, workers, or someone just needing a place to stay for a night or two. It was called "The Preacher's Room" and even when Corrine was just a little girl, I told her not to go in there because it was a room for special guests to stay. It was the only room in the house that was always clean and the only room that had linoleum flooring. The linoleum went almost from wall to wall. All the other floors were just wood planks. There was a nice rug by the side of the bed and a vase on the table for flowers when a preacher or someone special came during warmer weather.

Most of the families up here had more grownups and children than they had places for them to sleep and there certainly was no extra place to put visitors if they should happen to have any. I was the only person up here who had something like that, you know, and I'd invite people all the time to stay with us. I always kept anyone who came to visit in the community that didn't have anywhere to spend the night. I always took them in, even the kinfolks of neighbors. I remember when Roy Dan's uncle came down from New York. He and his wife stayed up here with me so they could have a room by themselves. I guess I was a lot like Papa.

Jettie

I always had a lot of help from Mrs. Click and Miss Minnie. They were so good to take care of Corrine and let me get out and work in the gardens and go places even long before Ben went into the army. It didn't matter if I was working on something for the church or school or just mission work around the community. They were always there to help, and that was especially needed after Corrine was born. Desmer helped a lot too while she lived up here and I could always call on one of the Pierce girls, if I needed to. They were an unusually nice family and all the girls were always so respectful to me. I just don't know what I would have done if it hadn't been for all of them when Ben was in the army. Of course, back then we walked everywhere. Mrs. Click and Miss Minnie would usually walk to church with me. One time Mrs. Click fell and broke her ribs, and it took much prodding to convince her to go to the doctor. It wasn't too long before she had to move out of the community to live where she could be taken better care of. Some of her children continued to live in the cabin here.

Every year there were always one or two students who needed special help and others in the community with very unusual situations that I would try to work with. If they really wanted help and were willing to learn and change by working hard, I would do whatever I could to help them.

Well, this one year, there were two girls with unique circumstances that I was especially trying to help. One was about sixteen and in the second grade. The other was a twelve-year-old who had never attended school. I had determined that I was just going to go all out and get those girls caught up with the other students their age. It didn't take to long to figure out that the sixteen-year-old just didn't seem to care if she learned or not. Sometimes she would show up for school and sometimes she would be out for days or weeks at a time. She didn't live all that far from the school; she could have gotten there if she wanted to. So I decided to put all of my attention on Jettie, the twelve-year-old.

Jettie was actually kin to us. Her daddy was Eddie, one of Ben's younger brothers. Zora, Jettie's mama, was barely in her teens when Jettie was born and Eddie was only about fourteen or maybe fifteen. They were both too young to get married, to each other anyway. It wasn't that it was all that uncommon around here for a girl to get married when she was twelve or thirteen years old, but it was almost always to a man who was much older than she was. A boy of Eddie's age would have a real hard time taking care of a wife and children, raising crops and animals. And, for sure, that was a lot more than Eddie wanted to take on. Zora wasn't real keen on responsibility either. She just stayed on with her family and not all that long after Jettie was born, Zora ran off and got married and just up and left Jettie there.

Jettie had a terrible home life. The folks down there where they lived were pretty wild and she had seen and experienced just about everything. There was a lot of drunkenness and violence—and a whole bunch of foolishness. In the family there had been a lot of incest and Jettie herself told me that her uncle had been the first one to do anything to her, but there were other family members who had molested her too.

Jettie wanted to come and live with me. She wanted to get away. She wanted to have a chance to go to school and learn. Nobody down where she lived went to school, and if they did, it wasn't for long. They'd either quit after a year or so, or because of their rowdiness they would not be allowed to come back. Her grandparents were not all that bad to her, but they never did protect her from the others. They were extremely poor and ignorant. Oh, they were nice enough people, all right, but very short on common sense.

Her grandparents had no objections to me taking Jettie so that she would be able to go to school, but they were a little hesitant. Even with the welfare money they received for Jettie, they hardly had enough to survive on. So I told them, "Just don't mention the welfare check to anyone. I can keep Jettie without a problem; you can go ahead and keep the money and use it just like you have been doing. Spend it for food and what you need. You don't have to worry about giving Jettie any money either. She won't need any. I'll buy her clothes and give her whatever money she needs when we go to town." I didn't want them to take her back just in order to get the welfare money.

For school I got both first and second grade books for Jettie. At school I had to start her in first grade. Because I had so many children in my school, I couldn't take special time with her there to help her get ahead. But I found a couple of the older girls to help her and then every night Miss Minnie and I would work with her. First, I helped her with her first grade work, and then Miss Minnie would help her with some of the second grade work. Sometimes Desmer would come and help her too.

Jettie had a speech problem when she was little that she never did outgrow. Her whole family talked the same way, so it may have been the way she learned to talk. It sounded like she was tongue-tied. She was rather short and a little chubby, but a real pretty girl with black, long hair. She kind of favored Eddie. Every morning I would plait Corrine and Jettie's hair. I guess Corrine was nearly eight years old then.

Jettie was rough talking and she drank coffee and used chewing tobacco. When Jettie first came to live with us, I told Corrine, "Now, she can do lots of things that you can't do. I've told you what's right and wrong and how to behave. There's been no one to tell Jettie those things and since she hasn't been told, she just doesn't know any better. And since she doesn't know better, it would be wrong for you or for anyone to make fun of her and not be her friend. I'll talk to her when the time is right. In the meantime, we're just going to love her and we're going to do our best to be sure she feels welcome."

From the time Jettie first moved in with us, she loved school and learning. She was excited about everything and eager to please. She had never in all her life received so much attention and she simply glowed with the glory of it. On Saturday night, after her first week at school, I had Corrine and Jettie bring in their tub water from the spring so I could heat it for their bath. When it was time for Jettie to get into the tub, I heard her in the kitchen. So I called for her. "Jettie, what are you doing?" She answered, "I'll be thar rat directly."

I went in the kitchen to check on her and there she stood at the table with the big ol' lunch box that Corrine, Jettie, and I shared. She had packed it full of biscuits, fried apples, sausage, and few other things. I said, "Jettie, what are you doing?"

"I'm a-fixin' our lunch. We're goin' to Sunday school in the morning and we'll be needin' a lunch." She thought Sunday school would last all day like regular school did.

On the way home from church the next morning, we were walking along towards home with Miss Minnie, Mrs. Click, and some of the children that lived along the way. Jettie was carrying my Bible for me. She was always wanting to help me with something. Well, all of a sudden she got mad. I don't know what about, but she angrily threw my Bible to the ground. It kind of worried me, her throwing the Bible like that. All the children thought it was awful too. But I told them, "She doesn't know any better. She's never been told about God and the Bible." She really didn't know anything at all about spiritual things or treating God's Word with respect.

Why, earlier that week, I had seen Jettie standing looking up at a picture of Jesus on the wall next to Corrine's bed. I had given that picture to Corrine for her birthday and I guess Jettie was trying to figure out just who in the world that man was. She saw me looking at her and she said, "Miss Opal, that man up thar, he might be rat good lookin' ifin he had a save an' a ha tut?" She meant "shave and a haircut," of course.

I didn't know whether to cry or to laugh. I didn't know what to say to the child, so I just said, "Yea, that's Corrine's picture that I got her for her birthday." That's all I knew to say. See, it had never been pointed out that it was a picture of Jesus. She'd had no way of knowing who He was, but by staying with us and going to church, I knew that she would soon know all about Him.

For the first few times she went to church, she was real quiet, never saying anything to anybody. Not one word. When the preacher started preaching, she would lay her head down in my lap and go to sleep, or maybe pretend to. She was as big as I was, but I let her lay there in my lap. I wouldn't say a word to her. I just left her alone. The preacher and everybody would shake hands with her and talk with her before and after the services and pretty soon she snapped out of it. I guess she could tell that she was loved and accepted and it made her feel comfortable enough to start talking to people and participating in the service.

I kept her dressed just as well as I did Corrine. If I got Corrine something new, I got Jettie something. She and Corrine got along real well. Corrine didn't think a thing about how she was when she first came. I was always real proud of Corrine and the way she treated Jettie.

The girls at school were all so kind to her too; they'd do anything in the world for her. I had told them the same thing I had told Corrine. When I told them about the tobacco, at first, they thought that was just awful. But after that I never heard them say a bad word about Jettie the whole time she was there. She didn't have a cross word with any of them.

Well, it wasn't long to until the boys felt just the same as the girls. They just loved her to death. Of course, she had to whip up on a few of them before that happened. Why, I'll tell you what! She could just whip the foolishness right out of them boys. I declare, if they bothered her, she'd just as soon whip them as look at them and she could wear any of them out.

Jettie stayed with me three years; that included the whole time Ben was gone away in the army plus a little time before and then a little after he came back. She was the best thing that ever was. When she was ready to start her fourth year of school, she was in the seventh grade. There was so much change in her. At the beginning, when Jettie first came to stay with us, of course I had no idea that she could accomplish all of that, you know. It wasn't me bragging. It wasn't nothing I had done; it was the Lord. I saw the need and thought I might be able to do something about it—so I took it on. Of course, Miss Minnie and everybody was so good to her. Everybody wanted to help her out.

By that time her grandparents wanted to have her back home. They had moved to a little ol' shack they had built off the highway up in the hollow above the grocery store so she would be close enough to catch the bus to school there in Del Rio. Her grandparents were getting older and she was big enough now to help them out and be of some benefit to them, besides the welfare check. I knew that they needed her worse than I did. She went ahead to the seventh and probably to the eighth grade. But

I don't think she finished the eighth before she got married. She would have been nearly eighteen years old then.

You would never know that she had been through anything like she had as a child. She became a Christian while she lived with me. She married this young man that came from a pretty good family—the Hux family. He was my Aunt Annie's sister's step-grandson. He was a Christian too and worked at the factory. They soon got a little dairy started and she milked cows and sold milk.

She worked like a mule and raised a house full of kids, twelve of them, but I think three of them died young. I believe she had about five girls and four boys and they all finished high school. Isn't that just something, now! She got every one of her children through school. Nearly every one of them got a job at Stokely and a couple of them still work up there. They all made the best kids that ever were; just turned out good, every one, and I reckon every one of them belonged to the church, too.

It was unusual and that's all there was to it. It wasn't anything I had done. She just got out and away from those influences long enough for it to make a difference. I always said if she hadn't gotten an education, there would have been twelve more uneducated children around these parts and maybe another generation of them after that.

About three years before Jettie died, she had a stroke. She couldn't talk a word, but she got so she could say single letters, like she'd call me O. She'd just smile and be the happiest go luckiest, sweetest thing that ever was. You would never know there was a thing wrong with her except when she tried to talk. She lived about two years that way.

That day when we walked down the road and she threw my Bible, I never knew she would turn out the way she did. She had seen everything. I mean, they had a lot of awful things going on down there and she had seen all of that. She had been right out there when some of them had been killed. Some had been railroaded and some had been shot. She had been through all that madness, but I do believe that the Lord intended from the very beginning for her to be somebody special and He saw to it that it happened.

That's one reason I always helped everyone that I could, didn't matter who they were. After all, you just never can tell when one of them might turn out to be like a Jettie.

Jettie's Father

Of course, Eddie was just tickled to death when I took Jettie in and he was so proud of the way she turned out. At the time Jettie came to live with me, I guess Eddie already had two more children: Eddie Jr. by his first wife Lucille, and Edna by his second wife Sarah. Altogether, including Jettie, Eddie had a total of twelve children. The last one was born in January of 1959.

Lucille—Eddie's First Wife

Eddie had met Lucille when he was working down in South Carolina. They got married and in no time had a baby boy. Little Eddie was about a year older than Corrine.

Lucille's mother had died when she was a baby and her daddy never remarried. With no mama and no sisters or other women around, she had never learned any of the things that she would need to know when she became someone's wife. Her daddy didn't pay her much attention either. They seldom even ate a meal together. He would buy crackers, white sliced loaf bread, and most everything else they ate came right out of cans. When Lucille got hungry, she would eat a slice of bread or open a can of something and heat it up. That's all she knew about cooking. She pretty much tended to herself as a child; she was a very sweet person, but she didn't know the first thing about cooking or taking care of a baby.

I don't quite know why Eddie and Lucille left South Carolina. It might have been that he lost his job or maybe they had problems with her daddy. For sure, bringing his wife back up here to his mama's was not the brightest thing for him to do. Lucille didn't have the first idea about country life. She didn't know a thing about our ways and she didn't know the first thing about real cooking.

Now, you take someone like that, someone from the city, and put them in the country with a very particular woman like Mrs. Myers and it's something sad to watch. I had always thought that Mrs. Myers was a nice person, real nice to be around. She was full of fun and quick to tell jokes and things like that. She had come from a big family and all of her sisters, every one of them that I knew, were all real nice too. But there just weren't many people who liked outsiders or would put up with much from them. They were not at all patient with the foreigners or willing to understand their ways or, for that matter, helpful in teaching them the ways up here. I guess they just didn't feel that it was their place to teach them the things that they should have grown up knowing. Mrs. Myers, from the time she was just a young girl herself, had cooked for twelve or thirteen, three meals a day, and taken care of the other children in her family. And then she had raised a big family of her own.

It was never a problem for me to fit into the Myers family. I was from the community and I had known Mrs. Myers from the time I was a little girl. I had helped her when she was sick and had even cooked for her and her family when I was only thirteen or fourteen years old. I didn't have to think about fitting in or worry because I knew how she did things. It was just as natural to me as breathing and didn't bother me a bit.

But it was very hard to fit in if you didn't grow up around here. Poor ol' Mrs. Myers and the rest of them just couldn't understand Lucille and the things she did, so they sort of forced her out. One thing about most people up here, even if they do try to accept you, if you do something against them or you don't keep your word, why, you're better off having never existed. There aren't many second chances. If you are an outsider and a person thinks you did them wrong, they'd just as soon spit on your grave as to even look at you.

Now, Lucille really meant well and it wasn't that she didn't try or wasn't willing to do her share. She just had absolutely no idea what to do or how to do it. I felt real sorry for the girl and would go over to the Myers as much as I could. I tried to be there so I could help her out. I even had her come down to my place so I could teach her and help her fit in.

One morning when I went over to the Myers, Lucille said that Mrs. Myers had told her to cook up some shab beans. Lucille was all upset, but hadn't dared to say a word to Mrs. Myers or to ask her how to fix the shab beans. When I got her calmed down a bit, she said, "She gave me these loops of beans and told me to start cooking them and we're not even going to eat them until tonight and they're going to be done in just a few minutes. They're already steaming and will be boiling any time now. I just don't understand why she had me start them so soon."

I knew she had been used to cooking things out of cans, so naturally she would probably just think that the beans needed to be heated up or boiled for a little while. Probably didn't even think of adding any seasoning to them either. She seemed to feel better when I said I would take a look at them. When I did, I had to laugh. That was the funniest thing ever. I lifted up a string of beans with the spoon and said, "I guess you thought we were rather strange eating strings with our beans."

I pulled the strings of beans out of the water and, while they cooled down a bit, I told her how we harvested the beans and sewed them together like that to dry them and store them until we were ready to use them. "When you're ready to cook them, first, you rinse the beans off and then take the strings out. Usually it's a little easier if you soak them a little or parboil them a bit. Then you add fat meat and cook them for hours until they are very soft and that usually means cooking them all day long." I told her how a few of the chapel women liked to eat their beans almost crunchy and everyone in the community thought that they were crazy.

By that time the beans had cooled, so she and I pulled out the threads, added the fat meat, and put them back on the stove. She felt a lot better and nobody ever knew she didn't even know how to cook beans. It doesn't take much to make a person feel like they fit in and to teach them how to do something.

Most of the older people were particular about one thing or another, usually about what they ate or drank or how they did certain things. The two things that Mrs. Myers was the most persnickety about were her clean rain water and keeping the flies off the food that was left out.

Of course, since the dogs and chickens would be right up by the house and there were no such things as screen doors, there were always a good many flies in the house. Biscuits, bread, and some other foods were left out all day long and they always had to be covered with a cloth. In the city, they didn't have that much of a problem with flies and I don't think they left their food out like we did either.

Like most people up here, the Myers only used water from the spring or fresh rain water for drinking and cooking. They called it the "good water." Since they lived a good way off from the closest spring, Mrs. Myers conserved her spring water and the rain water she caught around her house. They would use water out of the branch, never the good water, for washing clothes and taking baths. It always seemed a little strange to me that Mrs. Myers thought it was all right to wash some dishes in branch water, but would never let so much as a drop of water from the branch touch her milk pail or milk crock. To her that was just the most awful thing, but to Lucille water was water. She had no idea of the difference or why it was so important, and Mrs. Myers never took the time to explain those things to her. She just thought that everyone should know those things no matter where they came from.

My mama was very particular about water too. Our spring was close to our house and we had plenty of good water that we used for drinking, cooking, and washing dishes. Mama wouldn't let us put the hand washing pan up on the stove by where we were washing dishes. She wouldn't let us drink water out of that branch out there either and we couldn't use the drinking dipper to get water out of the bucket of branch water. We basically weren't allowed to let that branch water come close to the things we ate or drank out of. Of course, back then there were three or four families that lived upstream from us and there was no way to know if they emptied bathwater or something else into the branch. A lot of times when it was hot, the animals would stand or lay in the branch to cool off. And in the fall or early winter when we butchered the hogs, we would empty the contents of the intestines and rinse them out in the branch.

Lucille did know that Mrs. Myers could get fighting mad about the flies getting on the food. So one day, seeing how the flies were all over Little Eddie and his soiled diapers and not knowing any better, the poor girl dipped some of the clean rain water into Mrs. Myers big milk crock and rinsed out little Eddie's diapers in it. Mrs. Myers had the biggest fit over that. Of course, I wouldn't have liked it either, but I'd have just told her not to do it anymore.

Well, Mrs. Myers didn't explain any of that to Lucille. She just let her have it good, up one side and then down the other. As you could guess, Lucille didn't stay around but just a little while after that happened. If they had taken the time to teach her, she would have done just fine and made Eddie a real good wife.

Ben in the Army—February 14, 1944 to March 26, 1946

When Ben was an E5 in the army and stationed in Saipan, he would write to me and I could tell from his letters how homesick he was for everything. He would tell me how much he missed certain foods. Like one time he said, "I'd give anything if I could have a little cup of jelly from that fuget apple tree!"

Well, as soon as those apples were ready, the girls and I picked them. We had the best time making that jelly because we were making it for Ben and knew how surprised he would be to get it. I put some in an old tea cup with a handle because it wouldn't break like glass, you know, and sealed it with wax. But then I had no idea of how to package it for mailing. The postmaster told me, "There are a couple ways. It might sound a little strange, but you can pop some popcorn and use that for packing around the cup or you can put cotton around it—and be sure to write 'fragile' on the box." So Corrine, Jettie, and I made popcorn and securely packed it around the jelly. The girls added drawings and a letter saying how much fun they had helping make the jelly for him. Of course, they also enjoyed eating the popcorn.

The army wanted an American teacher to work with about a dozen of the army personnel's children in Saipan and offered me a job to go over there to teach for a year. Ben didn't think it was safe and didn't want me to bring Corrine over there. They would have paid me real good and paid all my travel and other expenses too. I had several other teaching opportunities during that time while Ben was gone. I was asked two or three times to teach at a boarding school. The army also wanted someone to teach nine army personnel children in Arizona. But then I wondered what would happen to my school children here while I was gone and what would become of Jettie.

Ben's job at the base in Saipan was to load and refuel B-29s. When he did this at night, he would have to drive the planes without lights to the area where they were refueled and then back to where they were loaded. One night someone sabotaged one of the B-29s he had loaded and before it got off the ground good it crashed. Ben knew the plane was going to explode and he screamed at his men, trying to get them to follow him. It was dark and, I guess, during all that commotion they just couldn't hear him. They were confused and ran in the wrong direction, to the side of the fence that didn't have a gate. They were climbing the fence trying to get over when the plane exploded. The explosion tore their bodies apart and left bones and flesh hanging from the fence and the fire burned everything else up.

Ben never did get over that. He had a medal and a citation that told about how brave he was to drive the planes through all kinds of terrain at night without any lights. But Ben never said anything about his citation and the good things he had done. He never talked about it and he was never the same person again after that explosion.

There's not much more to say about Ben. I was worried about him because of what he had been through and I looked forward to when he would be coming back to us. Finally, he wrote and told me that he thought he was coming home real soon. So I got all of his clothes out and hung them up just like they were before he left. You see, when he first left for the army, I had boxed up all his hanging clothes so they wouldn't get dirty and dusty. Well, I made sure that all his clothes looked good and I hung them up. I wanted everything to be and look exactly like it did the day he left. I wanted him to feel like he was back home, not someplace where everything had changed.

After a while, when I realized he wasn't coming home just yet, I took down all his clothes and folded them up and put them back in the boxes and pushed them down the hallway where they would be out of the way. Then I heard from him again that he was coming home and again I took all his clothes out and hung them up. And again he didn't come. It seemed like I did that over and over, but when he finally did come home I had everything ready for him. All his things were the same, everything looked the same, but that first night he was home I knew deep down inside that something was wrong with Ben and that our lives would never be the same.

We didn't have any window shades in the mission house, so when we went upstairs to bed, we would always get our nightclothes and blow out the light before we undressed. Well, that night I put the light over by Ben's side of the bed and went to get my gown. And he just up and said, "I'm not going to stay here!"

I thought I had heard him wrong and asked him to repeat it. "What did you say?"

"I'm going home!" he said, very agitated.

"This is home."

"It's not either."

"It is too. I bought it and I've got it all paid for except $200." I finally convinced him that I owned the mission and that we wouldn't have to move and pay rent somewhere else.

That seemed to satisfy him and he said, "Well, I'll finish paying for it," and he laid down and went to sleep. That was the last thing he said until morning. I knew then for sure that he was not right. I slept in another bed that night to keep from waking him up because he had me scared so. I wasn't sure what he would do.

I suspected that his mind was bad before he came home because of what he wrote in some of his letters. I thought he said some strange things, but I never brought it up. I didn't want to believe it. A time or two he wrote, "Yea, I know when I come home you won't let me stay long before you'll send me to Eastern State." Eastern State is a mental institution.

The next morning I got up and fixed breakfast. When it was ready, I sent Corrine and Jettie upstairs to tell him to come on down and eat.

After breakfast he wanted to go see his family. I told him I couldn't go with him because I had to teach. He told me to get someone to teach for me, so I got Anna Lee, one of the Pierce girls, to substitute for me and we went to see his family. The whole time I prayed that he'd be okay once he was home for a while, but the damage had been done.

18
1947–1959

The Last Mission Worker

The last interesting mission worker to stay up here was Miss Loggins. She was a teacher from over there at Midway, up next to Johnson City, who was interested in mission work and wanted to learn more about it. I don't know whether it was the Presbyterians or her own church in Midway that sent her down here to stay and work with me. I really didn't care who sent her, for I considered her a gift from God.

For years, I had tried to get someone like Miss Loggins to come and help in the community. I was teaching regular school during the day and then I had night school at the mission house for adults who wanted to learn how to read. On Sundays, I taught Sunday school and sometimes when the preacher didn't show up, I'd fill in for him. And then on top of all that, there was the regular mission work of helping those in the community needing assistance of some sort or another.

There hadn't been a real mission worker here to help since the mission had closed. Of course, Miss Loggins didn't know anything about mission work, but she was a fast learner, always eager to help anyone she had a chance to, and willing to do anything that needed to be done. She was friendly and had an excellent singing voice. I don't know if she had been crippled in the past or whether it was a birth defect, but she walked a little odd, almost hobbled. It didn't slow her down any though. She was a big help with the night school and was real good to watch out for Cary. She was pleasant to be around and a likeable young woman.

Somewhere There's an Eye Watching You

It was after Thanksgiving in 1949 when we had our hog killing. Cary, who was a little over two years old, had been out with his daddy and the other men all morning watching them butcher the hog and prepare the meat.

Miss Loggins had been up in the woods collecting pine and cedar branches to decorate the stair banister and around the windows in her room. Well, when she was coming back to the mission house, she went by where the men were working to check on Cary. Just as she had rounded the corner, she heard Clark just a-cussin' away, so she said, "Come on, Cary. Let's go upstairs and I'll show you my Christmas tree." She just had a little tree, maybe about two feet high. We had a big tree downstairs that went almost all the way to the ceiling.

Well, when Cary saw what a little tree she had, he put his hands on his hips, circled his way around it, and then he said, "I'll be GD," only he said the whole word. Miss Loggins didn't know what in the world to say. She thought that was the funniest thing that ever was and she came downstairs just a-laughin'.

"What in the world are you laughing about?" I asked, and she told me what Cary had said. And just about that time, I heard Clark outside yelling out those same words. "That's exactly where he got that!"

He had never heard talk like that before, you know. Even I had never heard that said in the house; I wouldn't stand for that kind of talk. And to think that he would pick it up that quick! But then again, he was a smart one and once he started talking he was real bad about picking up and repeating everything he heard.

His daddy might have said things like that when he was out and got angry or something, but not around the house. I never had heard Ben say anything like that. Of course, later, after he got sicker, that was another story. Then it was just one thing after another.

I had always told Ben, you have to be careful around even the tiny ones because you don't know how young they start to remember things. People say, "Oh you can't remember that young!" But you can. I remember a lot of things that happened when I was young. That's why I've always said, "It's very important that you watch what you do. You might think it doesn't matter what you do or say around a young child like that, but you never know when little eyes are watching or little ears are listening.

Miss Loggins on Being an Example

Miss Loggins was a good Sunday school teacher and everyone, especially the young people, seemed to like her even though she was considered an outsider or a "foreigner" by the older folks. That was one of the reasons I wanted to come back and work with my own people so bad—I knew the ideas they had about outsiders.

Having another teacher for the night school helped a lot too. The students liked the classes but didn't want to settle down for too long at a time or have reading lessons every night. So once a week, on Friday night, we would have special programs. Sometimes we would play games, but mostly it would be a music night, especially after Miss Loggins started leading the singing. The students would bring their guitars or we would sing along with records.

One Sunday after Sunday school, there was a crowd of young people down there at Theresa's. Most of them were sitting on the ground in front of the house watching these boys standing on the porch steps playing their guitars and singing country songs. Miss Loggins got up on the steps and broke into melody with them. When they started playing "If You Shut Up Your Mug, I'll Fill Up Your Jug with That Good Ol' Mountain Dew," she just rared back and sang that song right along with them. I don't remember all the other songs they had been singing, but when she sang the song about mountain dew, it riled up a few of the people something awful. That was it, as far as some of them were concerned, and after that they wouldn't have anything to do with her. They acted like she had committed the awfulest sin that ever had been. I don't know what happened—whether they said something to her or not, I just don't know—but anyway, she didn't stay long after that. She left without saying anything and she never did correspond with me either.

I thought, "Well, how silly now!" If they had let her stay, just think about what she could have been to this community. Who knows, she might still be here till yet, but Miss Loggins singing that one country song ended her mission work in this community. Of course, she wouldn't have done that for anything if she had known that the people would be offended and react so unfavorably. I felt right sorry for her. Later, her sister came over here once and stayed a short while, but it was no surprise when she was not accepted either.

So many people don't understand when they are doing mission work that others set a higher standard for them to live by. It's not always right and it's not always fair, but it is so. And for some people, it's easier to judge and gossip than it is to accept and forgive. Well, I guarantee there's not a perfect one among us yet! But I guess when they are so busy making a big thing out of someone else's shortcomings, they don't have time to look at their own faults.

That was one reason I did a lot of things different than other people, even the people up here, because I knew they expected me to be different, you know. Some people probably think I'm a little extreme about some things, like the preacher down at Del Rio who called me "that deep water Baptist." He teased me all the time about it, but I didn't care; I guarded my tongue and my actions because what I did and what I said and how I acted meant a whole lot to the people around here. I would sure rather be careful then be embarrassed by what I do or say.

Since people tend to imitate or become like those they look up to as their heroes or role models, it's important that you pick someone with strong values to follow and it is extremely important to watch very closely what kind of an example you are to others.

Papa's Death (3/4/1879 –7/20/50)

Even though Papa had what they called heart dropsy, he was still the jolliest person that I had ever known. Everyone loved being around my Papa. At seventy-one, he was still straight and tall. By looking him, he was strong all right, but because of his two hundred and sixty-eight pounds and ailing health, he couldn't go long without sitting down and taking a break. His feet would swell and during those spells he could hardly breathe. He had a tooth that kept bothering him too. At first it didn't slow him down much, but as it kept getting worse, I wondered if it was abscessed.

On Saturday the ninth of July in 1950, even though Papa wasn't feeling well, he decided that going fishing up at the swimming hole would be much better than sitting around the house moping. The people who lived up there not too far from the fishing hole said he complained of a toothache and was feeling kind of sick when he came by their place. They had him sit down and rest for a while. When he felt a little better, he got up and went on to the swimming hole.

Later that day, Papa came home feeling so bad he didn't even clean the fish he had caught. Instead, he got out a pair of pliers and pulled his tooth and then went to bed. I happened to be up there at the time, so I cleaned the fish for him. The next day he was dragging around, so on Monday I called and scheduled him a doctor's appointment. The doctor gave him some medicine, maybe for infection; I don't know for sure. The following Saturday Papa had a light stroke and he died on Thursday.

The doctor said he died from the fluid that had built up around his heart and from the stroke, but I always believed that his tooth had something to do with his death. I speculated that maybe the tooth broke off when he pulled it and the part that was left caused an infection. Or maybe his tooth had been abscessed and, when he pulled it, the infection got into his bloodstream and poisoned him and all that caused him to have the stroke. I don't know, of course, because I didn't go to medical school, but I just always believed that his tooth had something to do with him dying.

Mama lived another nine years before she died. She was almost seventy-seven. Mama's hair had never been a pretty gray, like some elderly women I know. It was sort of yellowish-gray. We really didn't know what to do to make gray hair pretty. The thought had never entered our minds to use special shampoos or rinses; besides, we just didn't have the money for a bunch of fancy treatments and such, so we always used the cheapest of shampoos. When we saw her in her casket at the funeral home, it surprised us because her hair was as white as snow.

Buying Land

After Mrs. Click died in 1951, the Click Place was owned by her son James. He lived in the cabin and took care of John, his epileptic brother, until he died in 1958. James also let his sister live there with her son and daughter. After James fell in love and married, he decided to sell the Click Place and move his sister and her children to a house closer to where he and his wife lived.

James came to me and told me, "I'll let you have this place for one thousand dollars. You can pay me two hundred dollars a year until you pay it off." I made the last payment on the Click Place in December of 1964.

A few years before James offered to sell me his place, just after Cary Alvin was born in May of 1947, the man who owned that little dirt floor cabin in the woods up there on the hill just below the pond told me he was ready to sell. He wanted three hundred dollars for three acres and I thought he was holding me up. "Why, I never! One hundred dollars an acre!" There was no way that I was going to buy it at that price.

He and his boys drank a lot and sometimes they caused problems. One night there was this awful commotion going on outside down at the Old McMahan Place that I had bought from my brother-in-law. There his boys were just a-hoopin' 'n a-hollerin' trying to turn my outhouse over. My dogs had taken off down there and were barking and growling, fighting with their dogs. Why, those boys were as drunk as skunks. It's a wonder that they didn't slip and fall in all that mess and drown when they toppled my toilet. Then they would have smelled like they acted. After that, I said I'd give anything to have them out of here. So I went ahead and bought them out. It was well worth the three hundred dollars.

Consolidated Schools—1955

When the county first started talking about consolidating the schools, they talked about how much better it would be for the children. At the public school in Del Rio, there would be separate classes for each grade and each class would have their own certified teacher who would spend the entire school day teaching them instead of having to share one teacher with eight different grades. With these changes, the children would learn more. There would also be teachers who taught special classes like art, music, and physical education, and all the students' textbooks would be furnished by the county. The school would provide a cafeteria where the children would have hot lunches, an equipped playground, and a library with books the students could check out. There would be special education classes for those students who were not as bright as their classmates.

All of that was good, but they were trying to do it too fast and there were too many things that they did not take into consideration. A lot of families up here still did not know much about life outside of their community. They were different than the people who lived in town, even a town as little as Del Rio and only seven miles away. The people were poor but did not realize just how poor they were. They couldn't buy clothes for their children like the town people did. Many of them had never used an indoor bathroom or seen running water or drank out of a water fountain before.

It was not that I was totally against consolidation. I thought it could be a good thing, but it was happening too quickly for our country roots. The people back here were not ready for it. There were many children that I knew for sure would not stay in school long if they were forced to consolidate. We had put too much work into getting these children to where many of them could actually go on to high school. There were others who did not support consolidation, but they didn't say or do much about it. But I, for one, fought against it right up to the very last day. I had nearly begged the officials to wait another year, maybe two, so we could better prepare the children for what it would be like to go to school outside the community. Or, better yet, if they would just let us keep the one-room school, we could teach the children who could not adjust or refused to attend school in Del Rio.

The school district simply could not understand my reasoning. Why wouldn't a child not want to attend a nice new school? Well, they finally told us that we could continue in our one-room school, but only if we met every single one of their conditions, which were: maintain a school library of at least five hundred books; build and maintain a playground that consisted of swings, a slide, and play areas, and have playground equipment like balls, bats, jump ropes, and other things for the children to play with; and we were to have a minimum of twenty students attending classes on any given day. I had always had way more than twenty children, so I didn't suspect that to be a problem at all.

We worked hard to raise the money needed for the playground equipment. I contacted everyone I could think of and asked them to send library books. By the time school started, we had everything the school district required. I don't believe we would have had a problem with attendance either if I had been able to teach, but I was pregnant with L. Conn, who was born that year in November. In my place, the school district assigned an older type lady that the children did not know or particularly care for.

The children didn't understand what consolidation meant and were determined they wanted to go to school in Del Rio. They thought they wouldn't have to get up as early because they would be riding the bus instead of walking miles to school. They didn't think about having to get up before daylight and walking in all kinds of weather to where the bus picked them up. All they thought about was, "We get to ride a bus to school!" But they didn't know how long that bus ride would be by the time they rode all over picking up all the other children.

They had been told that the consolidated school would offer a tasty hot lunch just like we fixed for them here. They didn't count on having to pay for their lunch or that the food would be different than what they ate at home. Most of the families couldn't afford to pay for lunches, so if the children were to eat at all, they would have to bring a lunch from home. The other children made fun of them because of what they ate and their lack of manners. They didn't think about having to pay for all of their school supplies or not having clothes as nice as the other children and being made fun of.

They didn't think at all about any of that. So on the day that the consolidated school started, the children could not resist the temptation of seeing that bus go by and not jumping on it. That day there were only two students who came to school. I don't know what I would have done if the teacher the county assigned there hadn't needed her job so badly. Neither of us wanted the school to close and we knew then that unless we came up with a solution soon, we would lose the school for sure. I knew that several of the students would not stay in the consolidated school very long without quitting, and I was determined to have a school that they could come back to. So, I told her that I would take care of it.

I got some of my last year's students who were starting the ninth grade to say that they would come to our school and pretend to be in the seventh and eighth grades. Then I had them each go and find two other younger looking ones from the high school who were willing to be our students for a few days. The next morning we had fifteen from the high school, the first and second graders from the day before, and two students who didn't want to go back to Del Rio. That made nineteen. We hoped the officials didn't check that day and that more students would come on Wednesday. That next day we had five more children who didn't like Del Rio, so I told one of the older ones they could go back to the high school. Every day I let a few more older ones go back to their school, always keeping one more than we needed. That way if something happened to one of the young'uns, if they got sick or something, we would still have twenty. We got all the way through the first week with no problem. But the next Monday, the school official was already at the school when the students arrived.

Seeing him made me nervous, and I started worrying, *Do they know that I've been using high school students? Will I have enough students here today?* I still had seven students who should have been going to the high school. I was counting on the fourteen students we had on Friday to be back. That would make twenty-one children and maybe there would be one or two more who didn't want to go to Del Rio. However, that morning we didn't have any new students; in fact, one of the students we had gained decided to go back to Del Rio. But we would still have our twenty and we should still be safe. When it was time for school to start, there was still one empty desk. It was a real nice day and, as it turned out, JL had decided to play out in the woods for a while before coming to school.

We told the person inspecting us that we had twenty students but he counted and said, "I've only counted nineteen students. Where's the other one?"

"I guess he's late or maybe he's sick today."

"You know you have to have no less than twenty children every day in order to keep this school." As it turned out, they had already suspected that the missing high school students were coming to the school up here. He told all the students, "Pack up your things and in the morning everybody get on the bus and go to Del Rio, and the rest of you who should be going to the high school, we expect you to be back in your classroom!"

That was the end of the one-room schools up here. I had no way of getting the books and other things from the school for a while and, by the time I could, people had taken or destroyed everything that we had worked so hard to collect and buy. You could see books scattered all up and down the road and in the creek. I had left all the dishes that I had collected for cooking, and every bit of those was destroyed or taken off too.

After the consolidation, I had to leave our house with Cary and Seldon and walk by lantern light all the way down to the Old Fifteenth where the bus would pick them up. One morning it was raining so hard and the wind was blowing something fierce. We didn't have an umbrella, but we were all wrapped up as best as we could be and in our overshoes. Why, there I was trying to carry that lantern in one hand and holding onto my walking stick with the other one and those two little boys hanging onto me trying to walk down that road. When the bus driver arrived, he said that the storm was getting worse. "It's comin' up like a regular tornado. Gon'na be a real dangerous storm. It's too dangerous for ya to go back up the road to your house. Trees are liable to fall an' kill ya. I know I sure wouldn't be goin' back thata way."

"I don't know what to do now. I guess I could ride with you down yonder to the church and stand out on the steps there. At least I'd be under a roof." When I got off the bus down by the church, the lady who lived across the road saw me and I stayed with her until the storm was over.

Del Rio

I was right about the children not liking the consolidated school and it wasn't long before a lot of them were skipping school. They hated it there. If I hadn't been pregnant, I would have gone to Del Rio with them and helped out just so they could adjust and have someone who understood them. Later, after L. Conn was born, I did start teaching there. I was able to help a lot of the children, not just the ones from our community but from other communities that were a part of the consolidation too. There were many of them that had great difficulty fitting in and adjusting. Some of the children were scared to death to go to the bathroom. They had never used anything other than an outhouse before and that flushing noise frightened them. This routine went on for years, because the consolidation of schools did nothing to help the back mountain families change, so every year I would have some that needed special help adjusting to school. I remembered what it felt like to be away from home in a school where everything was different and strange. And I thought about Mrs. Henderson's letter to me and just how wise she had been.

"Think about all the things you are learning, and even though it is difficult, it will help you to understand how hard it is for people to accept change. Understand the fear of change. When you come back here to become a teacher, you will have to help your children accept change. By going through this time, you will be able to better help them."

Even four and five years later, I still had children like that. There was this one little girl that would wet in her clothes every time she got upset and that seemed to be just about all the time. At first I didn't have panties or other clothes for little girls. L. Conn was, I guess, five or six, so I would take two or three of his little underpants that he had outgrown to school and hide them so the other children couldn't find them. Some of the teachers fussed about the little open place in the pants, so I got out my sewing machine and sewed them all up. Then I had something for that little girl to wear and I would take her wet things home and wash them.

One day a man brought his boy to the school and wanted to talk to me. "Miss Opal, our boy here has trouble learning things. They told me you've taught older children how to read and write."

"I did when I taught in the one-room schools. I don't teach the special education children here. I have a regular class, but they do have classes like that."

"No, Jimmy's the age of your students and I want him to go to your room and be taught by you." I knew the father was afraid of how his boy might be treated. I told him the special education teacher was real nice, but he wouldn't hear of it. So, I agreed to take Jimmy if it was all right with the principle.

"There's another problem with Jimmy—he hasn't learned to use the bathroom in time."

"That won't be any problem. My lands, if that's all that's wrong with Jimmy, I can teach him that. You just send Jimmy some extra clothes."

Well, Jimmy never did have to use those extra clothes. I told all the boys, "Anytime you have to go to the bathroom, take Jimmy; he'd be glad enough to go with you. Just say, 'Let's go, Jimmy,' and take him along."

Jimmy did real fine. Why, he wasn't a bit of trouble and, even though he was a slow learner, he learned a lot. When Jimmy got older, he was able to learn how to drive a car and took care of his grandmother.

Teaching at Del Rio

At Del Rio, instead of buying or making my own supplies, they were all furnished by the school. I had big rolls of wide white paper to use—all that I wanted or needed. It was easier decorating the classroom too, because there was more wall space. We had good lighting so we didn't have to depend on the windows for our main light source.

All the way across one side of the classroom there were shelves, wide ones like cabinets to put books and supplies in. Above the shelves there was a bulletin board. I'd cut off long pieces of the white paper from the roll and tack it up on that wall. Then I'd draw pictures of mountain scenes like Mrs. Henderson had taught us to draw at the mission school. We left that background up all year, decorating it for every season and holiday by drawing and cutting things out and sticking them up there. We had paper chickens for Easter and for Christmas we'd cut out red and green decorations. We had freedom to do whatever we wanted with our classroom and the children loved decorating it. They were so proud of how pretty it was and bragged to everyone about it. One year when I was working with the Head Start Program for our final project on animals, we made a huge cow, bigger than life, out of great big heavy cardboard pieces that we glued together, and then the students painted it. They all thought that was so special because they did something that no other class had done. That was for sure the biggest cow anyone had ever seen. I guess that making things to decorate our classroom and field trips were the things they looked forward to most.

One of the first assignments I gave my students at Del Rio was to collect as many different kinds of leaves as they could find from the trees around their houses. When the children came with all their leaves, I planned to teach them how to identify them. We would put all of the same kind of leaves together up on the board and then label each group with the name of the tree they came from. Well, after I gave the instructions for their assignment, some of the little girls said, "Don't know whar to get us no leaves."

"Can't you go out in your yard and get some?"

"Thar ain't no trees 'round our house."

I thought everybody had trees, ya' know, but I found out, sure enough, they didn't. A lot of them lived in little tenant shacks that a landowner had built out in the middle of a field for some of his workers. That made me so mad. How was it possible that people could live in the country and not have trees or even wildflowers? I could not imagine children not having at least one tree to climb or wildflowers to pick. I thought that was awful.

So I started bringing my classes up here to the mission land on field trips and let the children explore the forest surrounding it. Of course, I still took the kids up to Hall Top once a year too, usually at the end of the year. After all, children born in the country should know their leaves.

The children were always excited about field trips. We would leave the school around eight thirty and come up on a school bus. We would get off close to the spring and walk up here and cover this whole area. I would talk to them about the different types of trees and teach them how to identify them by their leaves and bark and sometimes their shapes. I'd teach them about periwinkle and ferns and other plants. Then while I fixed them a hot lunch, usually hot dogs and a side dish, they would wade in the branch and catch spring minnows and crawfish while running and playing like children should.

When it was time to head back, they'd have to name ten trees before they could start walking back down towards the Old Fifteenth. I'd let them think if they couldn't name ten trees, they'd have to walk down by themselves. Naturally, they all wanted to go together. I'd get down there next to the road in front of the barn where there was no way to sneak around me. They'd show me their leaves and name the trees and I'd send them on down to wait at the end of the lane at the church until I got there. It was always a good teaching trip and the children had the best time.

Things were a lot different at Del Rio, but I liked it a lot. It was nice to have other teachers who I could hold as dear friends. Consolidation was different and a big adjustment for me too. Sometimes, it was really funny.

Teaching eight grades in one room was a much bigger job than teaching one grade, but I never had one bit of a problem getting a substitute teacher for my one-room schools up here. I knew my substitutes too—

what kind of people they were and how they handled the children. At Del Rio I never knew who the substitute would be.

One time when L. Conn was in the hospital a new teacher came to substitute. At the schools up here I used to make our ball bats out of a piece of wood. They didn't look like regular baseball bats; they were flat on the end where you hit the ball. They looked kind of like a small oar. I brought my bat to Del Rio so the children could play with it. During class time, I would stand my bat up behind my chair in the classroom so nobody would get it. Well, I guess the substitute thought that was my paddle for spanking the children. So when the children started acting up, like they often did with substitutes, she walked over there and picked up my bat and hit it across the table and said, "You move one more time and I'll use it on you!" Why, that just nearly scared those children senseless thinking that she would hit them with a baseball bat. The children didn't move during class, but when it was time for a break they decided to all go outside by climbing out the windows. Anything to be funny, you know. I guess children have always thought they could get away with things when they had a substitute teacher. Well, I never did have any problems with my students at Del Rio that I couldn't handle—and I never used a paddle or a baseball bat on any of them. I'm sure your family raised you right, Lori, and as you get older and wiser, someday you'll pass those values to your own children.

19
1959–1969

Catherine Marshall

Catherine Marshall first contacted me in 1959. "I'm doing research on a book that I am writing about my mother, Leonora Whitaker, and her experiences as a teacher at Ebenezer Mission back around 1910. My father, Reverend John Ambrose Wood, was the preacher there at that time."

She told me how her mother was just a young girl, not yet out of her teens, when she came to work at the mission. It was there that her parents had met and fallen in love. She said that the other characters in the book that was to be called *Christy* would be fictional or based on the lives of some of the children who attended the mission school and their families.

Catherine asked me if I had any old pictures of the chapel house and the school building, or any information about Ebenezer Mission. Well, of course, I had both. She asked if it would be all right for them to come for a visit; her parents were getting old and she wanted them to be able to see the mission site while they were still able to get around.

Mama and Papa and us children didn't live up here when Catherine's mother worked at the mission. I had never heard of her either, but I had heard about Reverend Wood being very strict and outspoken about what he felt the people should or shouldn't be doing.

If they weren't in church, he would say, "What were you doing?" or "Why didn't you come to church?" The people thought that he was trying to boss them around. I don't remember too much more that the people here said, but I think a lot of them thought he was going to try to stop them from making whiskey and growing tobacco. Some of the people did say that he was the type of preacher who was determined to make everyone become a Christian. But I doubt that Reverend Wood thought he could do that. Everybody knows that you can't make people believe or change if they don't want to. People are going to do what they want, regardless of your intentions to change them. I'm sure that Reverend Wood must have cared about the people and wanted the best for them. A lot of folks up here were just stubborn and set in their ways. They didn't want to think about changing, and a lot of the men thought that religion was only for women and young children.

I'm sure my grandmother and My Aunt Flora had to know Leonora. I just never heard them mention anything about her.

Writing a book is not at all that easy; it took Catherine Marshall nine years to research and write *Christy*. She started off by interviewing her mother and father around the table at their house. They told her all they could remember about the mission children and their families. During the summer of 1959, she and her parents came up here to see the mission house for themselves. Leonora and Reverend Wood couldn't believe their eyes; things had changed so much since they had been here as young mission workers. So many of the people had moved out and many of their little cabins had fallen down or were covered with kudzu and other vines. The church that she had seen her husband build had been moved to a different location. And even the mission house itself was not the same. It was about sixty-five years old by then and had aged a lot in the forty-five, almost fifty years since she had lived there.

They both enjoyed coming back to the mission, and at times it was incredibly emotional for them. To be sure, just being here in the place where they had met, worked together, and fallen in love had to bring back a lot of memories. Having them here meant a lot to me too and made me remember how things were when I was younger. It was people like them who gave the people up here hope. I am who I am today because of the mission workers—people who allowed God to use them even though it meant sacrifice and hardship and many times rejection. Most of my life, from the time we moved down there by my grandma and grandpa Corn, and especially after I started school, the mission and mission workers were the most important part of my life. Even after all of them had gone and the mission closed, the work of the mission was my life. I knew how important this little cove must be to the Woods. They were both wonderful people and I was glad that I had the chance to meet them.

Catherine came back and visited with me several more times to get information about the school and the area, and while she was up here, she used the phone book to pick out some of the names for the characters in the book. Another person who helped her with pictures and information about the area was Mary Ruble, the county historian.

I also became friends with Catherine's sister, Emma Lynn Hoskins, who lived in North Carolina not far from Asheville. Catherine always called her "Little Em," so that's what I've always called her. We started exchanging cards and letters during the time Catherine was doing her research up here. The funniest thing is that her husband helped in the forestry service and sometimes actually came to this area. After we had been writing for a while, she came out here with her husband so she could meet me in person. I was so surprised! I said, "You can't be Little Em!" And she said, "I am." I knew she was a good bit younger than Catherine, but she looked even younger than I had thought she would. She promised to return for a second visit someday. Little Em's husband has to come to Hot Springs this spring, so maybe she'll come out here with him.

Ever since Ben got back from the army, he experienced sick spells. Sometimes he would be afraid and distant, almost like he wasn't there or that he didn't care what was going on around him. He acted as though he didn't know what he was doing or who was around him. He would withdraw into himself, in his own internal world. Something was going on in that mind of his, but I never could figure out what exactly.

There were times that I was sure that he didn't know me from anybody else. Even when he first came home, he'd sometimes forget who I was. He didn't know his own wife. He didn't say anything, but I could just tell. Sometimes he was nice to me and affectionate and sometimes he wasn't. And then, at other times, he would be normal, just as good as before he went into the service. As the months passed by, I could tell he wasn't happy. In fact, if he had a happy moment during the rest of his life, you couldn't tell it. He was like a different person. It was like a distant relative moving into your home and you just got used to them being there—you just got used to it. It is really sad…and very lonely. But I knew if I wallowed in the situation, I would have shriveled up inside and died.

It concerned me about having Catherine and her parents in the house. I had no idea how he would be, how he would act, or what he would say to them. As it turned out, he remained quiet and somewhat withdrawn, but otherwise, he did just fine.

Ben had some pretty bad times and caused me a lot of hurt, but there were a lot of good things he did, too. I always liked to cook, but I just never found the time. Corrine didn't care much about cooking either, and she never did stay around home much. Ben helped me out most days by fixing all the meals, but if he was in one of his bad times and didn't have supper cooking when I got home from school, I'd have to rush to make biscuits, peel potatoes, and cook up a quick meal. Some Sunday afternoons we would bake pies all afternoon so we would have something sweet to eat during the next week, and many times he would handle that all by himself. When the boys were small, they always wanted to be around him when he was cooking and baking. They'd watch and sometimes he would let them help him. That's how the boys all learned to cook like they do. That's where they got that from, from their daddy.

Ben always believed in everyone working and doing their share. And even though he wasn't ever able to work a regular job, he certainly wasn't lazy. He was good with the children; I didn't have trouble getting away to do things because Ben would take care of the boys and I knew I didn't have to worry about them. I didn't have to get after them to get ready for anything because he was always there and they knew they had to mind him.

At first very few people knew he was sick, but I could tell that his health was getting worse. I guess some people just thought that he was too lazy to work. A lot of the teachers in Del Rio thought I had such a bad life, having to put up with the things that he did and earn all the money for us to live on. One time I finally came out and told some of them, "Well, I thank the Lord that I do have a husband even though he is sick!"

They said I was crazy, but I told them, "No I'm not. He may not be able to hold down a paying job, but you know it means a lot to me having him there to help me with the children and chores." That was true, too. Think about it—I had to get up at four in the morning to get ready for school. It took a long time to get to the school in Del Rio because the roads were so bad. Why, up here on this end our road was no more than a bad trail, and the rest of the way to the Old Fifteenth the road was nothing more than ruts and washouts. Old Fifteenth wasn't much better, but the county did scrape it on occasion. Ben would get the boys up after I left and help them get ready for school. He saw to it that they were fed and had their hair combed and, when they were small, he would walk them down to catch the bus.

The teachers at Del Rio realized just how sick he was really when I started missing a lot work to take Ben to the doctors. They were genuinely concerned about me with all the extra work I had to do to keep up with things. Before too long, just about everyone figured out that Ben was getting sicker, especially when they found out he had been in the hospital.

Ebenezer Burned

It was on Saturday, January 20, 1962, when, I would guess, a fire in the stovepipe chimney caused the mission to burn down. I started grabbing things, but the house was burning too fast for me to salvage much. All I was able to save was an old ragged teddy bear, my school bag, and a box of pictures.

I don't know why I grabbed the teddy bear. I guess because that morning I had gone to the attic to get it and it was just laying there. I was going to make it a new outfit and give it to L. Conn. He was a just six years old then.

Of course, those pictures are worth more than anything now. A lot of those pictures were the ones I had taken of the mission and people around here when I was a young girl, an aspiring writer compiling my first book. After I first started teaching school, I took a lot more pictures. I still had that same little camera.

The only reason those pictures were saved was because I had loaned them to Catherine Marshall. She had sent them back to me, but I hadn't yet put them away. Later I loaned those same pictures to the movie people who were thinking about making a movie of *Christy*. They made some enlargements for me that I kept in nice picture albums. Those books have traveled everywhere. I still have hundreds of pictures, scattered all over, that I need to put in albums.

Everything else was lost in the fire—all of our furniture, clothes, just everything. The books and records of the mission were destroyed. Letters and important things that I had saved for years, as far back as my days at Highland, were all gone. I didn't look at them a lot anymore, but every once in a while I would dig them out and read those old letters from Mama and Papa, and especially the one that Mrs. Henderson had written to me when I was so homesick. I had also written notes in journals from the time I was quite young. I guess I started doing that about the time I did the pictorial history of the area. They were notes about different things that had happened up here, ideas for stories that someday I might write. If I ever had written a book, it probably would have been a fiction based on the real-life story that happened before

I went away to Highland about an educated young woman from a wealthy family in Newport who fell in love with a back mountain young man. I always thought it would make an interesting story. I even had a title picked out: *The Thirty-Minute Marriage.*

The young woman was a teacher in the one-room school not far from where Lawton Turner was living in the dirt floor cabin that I ended up buying in 1947 from that rowdy family who overturned my outhouse. Lawton's family lived up from him just over the ridge on Rocky Top Mountain Road. Well, the teacher and Lawton, who was three or four years older than me, fell in love and got married at his cabin. After the wedding, as most everybody was leaving, she told Lawton, "Go back up to your mother's and get my comfortable shoes so we can walk up to our favorite spot when everyone's gone. I'll stay here and say goodbye to the rest of our wedding guests."

After Lawton had been gone for just a little while, her uncle and the sheriff and somebody else appeared. She talked with them for a minute and then, without any explanation to the other people, she rushed down the hill with them towards the sheriff's car that they had parked down at Papa's.

When Lawton got back, they told him what happened and he took off after them down the hill to catch them but, of course, they had too much of a head start. Lawton was halfway down the hill when he saw them getting into the car and start driving down the road. The roads were not good, so they couldn't drive fast, but they were fast enough that as hard as he tried, Lawton could not catch up with them. When he got up to Roy Dan's, he saw the car going up the hill and he gave out and came back.

In about a week, Lawton got a letter from her saying, "I'm sorry, but I'm not going to be your wife anymore." Just like they were little children playing house. "When my uncle and the sheriff came, they told me that somehow my mother had heard we were getting married. It was such a shock to her that they had feared she might have had a heart attack and didn't know if she would survive. I will have to stay here and take care of my mother. I will not be teaching at the school anymore and I will not have time to see you again."

Nobody around here ever knew if her mother truly had that heart attack or not.

A good bit after that, she was seen getting on a train with her grandmother. She had a market basket on her arm covered with a towel. Of course, rumors got started from that and spread all over the place.

A married man could sleep with other women and even have children with them and no one thought much about it. But when Lawton's wife left him and wouldn't come back, everyone in the community faulted him like he had done something awful. They had never lived together or anything, but he was stamped as a married man and people held that against him. People back here were very peculiar. I never could see where Lawton had done anything wrong and neither could the rest of our family. But my sisters and I weren't very nice to him either. One time he tried to go somewhere with us, and I was actually kind of hateful. "Mama said we couldn't go with you because you was an old married man." Lawton had always been a friend of ours and, of course, that hurt his feelings. It would hurt anyone, but we didn't think about that at the time.

Lawton didn't hear tell of her again until World War II when he was in Germany. That's when he got a letter saying that she had divorced him and he was free to marry again if he wanted to. It was so strange that she waited all those years to get a divorce, especially after only being married for thirty minutes.

Lawton married twice after that. Sometime after his next wife died, he married his nephew's widow. She was a real sweet woman, but after her husband was killed in a wreck, she just sort of stayed to herself and didn't go out much. She told me once, "After my husband died, I felt so lost and I was so lonely. It seemed that I would never be happy again. Lawton was real nice to me—always making sure that I was taken care of. That's just the way he's always been with everyone. He's a good man. But he was lonely too and one day we realized that we liked being around each other—and when we were, we weren't lonely. That's when we decided to get married."

Old Storehouse in Slabtown

At first, after the mission burned, I had planned on moving over to the Old McMahan Place. After all, I owned the place and it just seemed to me like the sensible thing to do. But that idea really upset everybody something awful, especially the friends I taught with in Del Rio. They went wild because of all I had to do in nursing Ben, plus all the regular work that had to be done around the place. One of the teachers actually came right out and said, "It would be better if you found a place out of the cove. That way we'll be close enough to help you get Ben to the doctor or help with some of the chores or whatever you need us to do."

Of course, she was right. They all were. I had so much to do and I was just plain wearing down. Every night when I got home, I had to fix supper, get the kindling and wood for the next day, and then finish whatever other chores needed to be done. Of course, the boys all helped as much as they could, but there was more than enough work to go around.

Sometimes I wouldn't get but a few hours of sleep a night, and even in those precious hours it seemed like I slept half awake. I was always listening for any unusual sound that Ben might make, and then I would get up to check on him. Sometimes, during one of his bad spells, it was easier for me to sleep in a chair by his bed. There were stretches of time that might last for days or several weeks when he would sleep soundly. But even then I had to get up at two o'clock every morning and build a fire in my wood burning cook stove so I could heat water to make hot compresses to put on Ben's shoulders. While I waited for the water to heat, I would prepare his food for that day and lay out the things he needed.

Ben's sickness was the only reason why I would have ever lived outside of the community—that and people insisting that I move. It's during times like those that you realize how may people there are who really care about you. It turned out that my friends had given me good advice, even though they had to get pretty firm with me before I listened to them. My teacher friends, every one of them, gave to a fund so we could get a house and have enough money to pay the first month's rent. I don't know what I would have done or how we would have made it if we'd had stayed up here during that time.

We found a place to rent. It wasn't much, just an old storehouse in Slabtown, but we thought it would be a good place to settle in for a while. My friends from school helped me in so many ways. They did everything, like helping with meals and other things.

Soon Ben was doing a little better. He was getting out some, but he did not want to go to church. He would take us, but he wouldn't venture inside the church building or have anything to do with it. And that snake-handling business at the other church upset him so. Of course, that upset a lot of others also.

Late in August of 1962, we had our buckets in hand and were fixin' to go pick blackberries when one of our neighbors knocked on the door. "Come in," I told her. And before I could say another word, she blurted out, "You can move now. We bought this place and we want it now!" She said it just like that, and we had no choice in the matter. Our rent was paid through the end of the month, so that only gave us a couple days to find another place.

We didn't know what we were going to do. We set our buckets down and Ben said, "Instead of pickin' berries, guess we'll just have to go lookin' for a new home. We at least need to find a place to sleep."

So that's what we did. We left and drove around all day looking for our next home.

Spice Wood Flats Road on Lafayette Moore's Place

We found the nicest little place way back in the woods in an area we had never heard of before. It was off the highway out past the school, headed away from Del Rio. The house was completely surrounded by trees and it reminded me a lot of our land, except it was kind of swampy there. Of all the places I have ever lived outside of the cove, I liked this one best.

I didn't talk to anyone about Ben's health or how he was doing unless they asked, and even then I didn't tell them any more than was necessary to satisfy them. It was so much easier going to school if the teachers didn't say anything about Ben or ask questions all the time— so much easier when I didn't have to talk about any of that. A couple of the teachers had said something to me a few times about me letting him drive the car all over the place. They'd say, "If I were you, I'd stop him. He wouldn't run my gas all out!" Well, they weren't me and they had no idea what it was like to live with someone who had been sick for so long.

If Ben slept during the day, he would stay up during the night wandering around the house, and then I'd be wide awake wondering if he was all right. I had to get up early to teach school and needed my sleep at night. I would find things for him to do so he would move around during the day or at least for a while in the late afternoon or evening. Sometimes I'd find things for the boys to do with him, or I would give Ben a dollar and ask him to go down to the store and get a loaf of bread or something. He would stay gone then for a good while. I guess he would find someone to talk to or just ride around. Then, if nothing bothered him, he would sleep good that night. I hadn't slept in the same bed with him for some time because every time I turned over or moved, it would bother him. We didn't have any room in the house for another bed. We did have a couch that I could sleep on, but I didn't want to be that far away from him, so I would sleep in a chair by his bed.

After a while, Ben got so bad that I was afraid for him to drive to town, so one of us or one of the neighbors would offer to drive him. Ben wasn't much of a talker. Once in a while he might tell a joke, but he talked very little. He might have talked with the men in town, I don't really know, but he probably just listened to the others talk about all of their problems. That's what they usually talked about, all the problems they had. Of course, I had problems too, but as far as I could tell, they didn't get any better sitting around talking about them. It was a problem having to teach school and to do all the other things that had to be done. But as far as Ben being a problem like a lot of sick people are, he never really was like that. He wasn't demanding at all. The only thing he didn't like was for us to leave him alone.

Around the house, he didn't talk much either. He would sleep or get up and turn on the radio. If it hadn't been for teaching school and my children, I would have been pretty lonely around him. I never thought much about that, though, and I have never been one to worry about being lonely. I've always been able to find more than enough to do.

One night Ben wanted to go to church with me, but once we got inside, he just laid down on the bench and slept the whole time. I just let him sleep until it was time to go home.

Ben's daddy and the rest of his family never came around much. His daddy and them would call once in a while, but none of them ever bothered to come see him. I guess they didn't realize how sick he was until the very last. Then they came and brought food and did everything that they could possibly do. I would take Ben to see them every time he wanted to visit. The last time, it was at night when we started up to his daddy's. We got about halfway there and he said, "We had better go back home." He just didn't feel like going and that was the last time he ever mentioned anything about going to his daddy's.

Then one day, Ben took a real turn for the worst, so I rushed him to see his doctor in Newport. Well, his doctor wouldn't even see us. Here Ben was, sicker than he had ever been, and his doctor acted like he didn't want to be bothered, so we went and talked with another doctor. That doctor delivered the news. "Your husband has some very serious lung problems and we have nothing here in Newport that will help him. We'll have to send him someplace else. Eastern State's the only place that's close by that can handle all of his problems, or you could send him to Asheville."

I said, "Let's send him to Asheville." That was in November of 1964. They admitted him in the hospital there in North Carolina and kept him there. On Christmas Day, the doctor's office called and told me to come on up to the hospital as soon as I could get there; the doctor had something he wanted to tell me. We rushed around to get ready to leave, but then when we got there, they told us we would have to wait because it was Christmas and the doctor was out sledding with his little boy. That made me so mad! I just blurted out, "Well, why didn't he know that it was Christmas when he had you call and tell me to hurry over? Why would he even have us come on Christmas?"

We had to sit around there and wait, and wait, and wait until after dinner for the doctor to finally get there. Ben already knew he was real sick. "Exactly what is the matter with me?" When the doctors told him, he just looked up at the doctor and the first thing he said was, "Can I just go home?"

"Yes, but you'll have to come back. We have a new treatment for your lungs that we haven't used at this hospital before and we want to try using it with you. We need you to come back on Monday or Tuesday."

Ben didn't want any more treatments. "I don't want you experimenting on me. I want to go home and stay there. My family can look after me as good as the people around here can." So we got his things together and they told us what to do for him. We put him in the back of the car and brought him home.

One of the things they told me was that Ben had to have a piece of beef liver every day. So I'd have to get up every morning early and cook it. Then I would make gravy to put over it so it would be soft. I put a biscuit with it on the plate and put it in the stove so he would help himself to it when he got up.

By April of 1965, I knew he probably wouldn't last much longer. The last few days he got so bad that he couldn't get in and out of bed by himself. I wasn't strong enough to lift him or support his weight leaning on me either, so I couldn't help him. I had two neighbors, one below me and one above me, who took turns helping me. The Hendersons were especially good to help. Word got out and people from everywhere brought by food so I wouldn't have to be worried about cooking. In fact, we had so much food there that one of my neighbors said, "Mercy! You've got a mess of food here. Why don't you package some of it up and use my deep freezer there and freeze a heap of it?"

On Saturday the 24th, I knew for sure that Ben wouldn't last much longer. L. Conn wasn't home right then, and just to get the other two away, I sent Seldon to the neighbors with some food to put in their freezer and I sent Cary up to the Henderson's to call Ben's folks.

There was another soldier, a friend of Ben's, who had died a few days earlier and was buried that afternoon. When the people left the funeral, a lot of them decided to come by our house. The first visitors were with Ben, and I had just stepped out to invite some of the other people to come in for a minute when I heard Ben start screaming. He was looking right at the people there with him and screaming at them, "If you don't come on you'll get burned up! You're gonna burn up, you're gonna burn up!" and then he died. I guess they all thought he was seeing the fires of hell or something. They looked like they had seen a ghost and the blood appeared to drain from their faces. It seemed to help somewhat when I told them about the explosion at the airfield when he was in the service. Isn't that just something, after all that time, he was screaming for those men to come on and go with him? It had been twenty years that he carried that memory with him. I can't imagine that kind of torture.

Well, everyone who had heard the screaming came rushing in. Of course, they saw right quick that Ben was gone. They took everything off the bed and put a clean quilt back on there and placed Ben on it. That's the first thing people always did up here when someone died. It was called "laying them out."

I don't know how I managed to handle all this, but somehow I did. It just had to be the Lord who gave me the strength; that's all that it could have been. When he came back from the army, we just had Corrine and then we had our three little boys. There were never any times that I wished I hadn't had the children. There were many hard times, but I was always glad that I had my young'uns.

Ben's death was really hard on the boys. Cary was a freshman in high school and Seldon was in the 7th grade. L. Conn was only nine years old. I couldn't do much with them; they just couldn't understand it. They had always done things for him when he didn't feel well. They knew he was sick, but they hadn't thought about Ben being that bad off, not sick enough to die. When people saw the way they took on over his death, they would say, "Your Ben must have been a good daddy to them boys." Ben was good to them, but he wasn't good to anyone when he took those spells. When he was normal, he was good.

The Hendersons were just great. The night Ben died they wouldn't let us stay at our house. "You don't need to be cooking tonight or worrying about making breakfast in the morning. You and the boys get a few things together and come down and stay the night with us. It'll be easier on the boys, too. We'll take care of everything. You just take care of them boys." In the morning, she got some of the neighbor women and they went down to our place and cleaned up the house, cleaned up everything.

Even with Ben gone, I still could not move back to my old community where I owned land. The land was just too far away and the roads were not good. I wanted to be there for the boys, just as close to home as I could be and spend my time with them.

Seldon had rheumatism or something like that, and the dampness of the place we rented bothered his leg, so I started looking for another place to rent. About a year after Ben died, we moved to Ground Squirrel on the Claude Nicholas Place. It was another pretty nice house for the same amount of rent, only twenty dollars a month. Somehow we always made do.

The Book
Life didn't end for me or the community after Ben's passing, of course. Only a couple years later, when Catherine Marshall's book *Christy* was finally done and published by McGraw Hill Company in 1967, it quickly became a national bestseller. In fact, it was one of the top ten novels of 1968. Why, you can just imagine what a commotion

it caused up here in these parts! There were people who loved the book and the attention it brought to the area. Others acted like they were insulted and resented the way Catherine described them as impoverished and shoeless, even though that was referring to the condition of this area some fifty years earlier. But most of the people were excited and proud to have a book written about our community and, for sure, absolutely everyone was trying to figure out who in their family could be this character or that character. Everybody was carrying on something fierce! There were even fights over the characters. You could hear the ramblings everywhere: "Who was Fairlight?" "Who was Bird's-Eye?" "Dr. MacNeill? Why, there weren't never no doctor living up here!" You would hear them saying that a certain character was their grandfather or mother while others would say, "Well, that couldn't have been my mother because my mother knew how to read!"

Christy was not meant to be a factual book; rather, it was intended as a fiction novel. In fact, Catherine told me that the book was only about sixty-five percent based on the life of her mother and the rest was just fiction put in to make the story more interesting and to add conflict; compressing several years into one gave it more action. I guess it included stories that happened up here from about 1909 to 1913.

She said some of the characters were real and some were made up by combining two or three real people, while other characters were just totally fiction. For example, I believe that the character Fairlight was a combination of my Grandma Corn and a young girl named Carrie Teague, who lived up here in the hollow in the house above the Click House.

Carrie was always traipsing around and playing with the children. She was probably creative and physically more like Fairlight, too. Carrie was only eleven when she married, and she had her first child before she was a teenager. Her husband was much older. He was very proud that he had a young wife to wait on him and he enjoyed spoiling her. He didn't make her go out and work in the fields like other married women had to do. Now you just know that no young girl wants to sit in the house by herself all day, so she would take her children out in the woods with another girl who had also married young and her little children. They would spend all day out in the woods or at the creek where they would fish and play in the water. They weren't all that much older than their children.

My grandma was older, probably in her fifties. She had a lot of the personality and character qualities of Fairlight. The family unit would have been more like my grandma's. Grandma liked to sew, and possibly the shadows could have been referring to her. She used to tell the time by where the shadows were on the knotholes on the porch.

She'd say, "Look at this knothole. When the sun gets to here, go tell Florie to come and put on the bread," and "When the sun gets to this knothole, go look in the mailbox." She actually kept track of time by those knots on the porch.

She would sit there on her porch late in the evening as the shadows crept down from that hill over there, or she would sit by the window and sew until the light was gone. She wasn't afraid of the shadows like in the book, but it would aggravate her sometimes when in the early evening the shadows would block out the sunlight and she would have to stop sewing or whatever she was doing. She wasn't afraid of death either, like Fairlight was; she was ready for it. The shadows in the book probably represented the superstitions of the back mountain people because many were afraid like that.

Of course, we all knew who Ruby Mae was and the family who had the epileptic son. Some of the characters didn't turn out the way Catherine had first thought they would when she got started on the book. Fairlight started out as a minor character, just a face in the community, but ended up being one of the main characters. And she had planned for Birds-Eye Taylor to be one of the main characters, but he ended up being a minor one. She wouldn't tell me any more than that, so I was right in there with everyone else wondering who people were. But I did have an advantage in my guessing because I had told Catherine about all the people here and the stories of the community.

When a book has that much fiction in it, things don't have to be told exactly like they really were and there certainly were several differences between the book *Christy* and how things actually were at the mission. For one thing, the mission school had already been going for several years and went through the eighth grade. Until the chapel was built, all the classes, which were only for boys, were taught in the front room of the mission house. In addition to the basic subjects, Latin and algebra classes were also available for the few brighter and more advanced students. There were also more workers than just John (David Grantland) and Leonora (Christy). They had a housekeeper, Bible teacher, and a Sunday school teacher, and many times a nurse who not only served the school but also the surrounding community. I can remember the nurse who was there during the influenza epidemic of 1918. One of the chapel women was typically in charge of everything along with as many as four or five workers. The two bedrooms on the second floor each had double beds where the women workers stayed. John slept in the bunkhouse across the road.

Guess it was sometime in 1910 or there abouts that John and Leonora were married. They continued working at the mission as a team for several more years until Leonora got pregnant with her first child, Catherine, and then they moved to Greeneville, Tennessee, in order for Leonora to get medical attention. There just wasn't any way of getting a doctor back in here quickly when one was needed. There was not even a way to get a car back in here until several years later.

It didn't matter to me that it was fiction. I was proud to have helped Catherine with the stories and pictures of this area and to be able to show her the actual records from the mission school. But when a person writes a great book like *Christy* about the place where you grew up, you just naturally have strong and good feelings about them. And that's why I loved *Christy* so much, because it was a story about the mission I had loved since I was just a young girl. I read it over and over and made notes in my copy of *Christy*.

MGM Studios

After *Christy* became so popular, I think it was in late 1968 or very early 1969, Metro-Goldwyn-Mayer studios bought the movie rights. Catherine told me they were considering Katherine Hepburn for the part of Alice Henderson. If they did get her, because she was such a big name, they might just go out and find someone who was not known at all for the part of Christy. They had done that with *Gone With the Wind* and it turned out pretty good. She told me, all excited like, that Isobel Leonnert was going to write the script for the movie. I had never heard of her, but Catherine said she was the very best. She had written the script for *Funny Girl*, but I had never heard tell of that either. That Isobel woman sent a crew of cameramen to take pictures and film some girl walking through the snow, like Christy did to get to the mission, to see what it might look like. All of that fell through and there was never a movie with Katherine Hepburn.

Another time MGM sent publicity people to Ebenezer to photograph the area and scout locations. It was a big thrill to have MGM people talking to me about *Christy*. Howard Horton and his wife came and spent the day. He looked at all my pictures and then went around and took shots of the mission foundation, the area cabins, and landscapes with his camera that gave dimensions. Every once in a while we would hear talk about some studio wanting to make *Christy* into a movie, but they fell through every time. I did get several nice pictures from some of the photographers, though. They made enlargements of some of my pictures and gave them to me along with some of the ones they took of me and Barry and Benja. Catherine wrote to me and told me that a producer friend of hers named Ken Wales was interested in making the story. Catherine wanted more than anything to see *Christy* made into a movie, but she died in 1983 before that could happen. In 1984, there was more talk about a company buying the rights for the *Christy* movie and the movie location manager came to visit me to discuss things about the story. They came back again a little later to look around more. I believe that they will make the movie this time, but I wonder if I will live to see that happen.

In 1968, Sam Myers Died

When Sam Myers died, Blanche, Ben's younger sister, was real nervous about making all the arrangements. She was all fidgety and wanted me to go to the funeral home with her—it was, for sure, a good thing that I did go.

When we got down there she didn't know the answers to most of the questions they asked her. Like, "What were the names of your daddy's father and mother?"

Well, she just squirmed all around and finally said, "I don't know who his father was. We just never talked about it, but his mother's name was Fronie."

I thought I'd better help her out. "Columbus Washington was his father and his mother was Saphronia Burrell, but they called her Fronie."

On the way home she asked, "How'd you know all that about my family?"

"I just like keeping up with things like that. I've always written down what I've learned about our family's genealogy and other interesting things in my Bible or in a notebook. I found out about your grandparents when Cary was born. See, when I told your folks that I had named him Cary Alvin, your daddy said, 'How come ya named 'im that? How'd ya know that was a family name?' I said, 'Well, I didn't know it. He's named after a girlfriend of mine.' Then Sam told me that your family was not really and truly Myers. His great-great-grandparents left Germany by ship to come to America with their two little twin boys, Alvin and Calvin. On the way over, there was a young man who was taken up with them. You know how you get taken up with cute little children about eighteen months old."

I proceeded to tell her the rest of the story. Somewhere off the coast of America they were shipwrecked. I don't know if they were in a storm or what. Both the parents were killed, but the young man found the babies and tied them to pieces of boards and latched them together with himself. He saved them both.

All that was known about the babies was that they were eighteen-month-old twins from Germany. The twins wore little lockets around their necks with their first names engraved on them. When they were rescued, the young man took them to a lawyer in some town on the coast of the Carolinas to find out what to do with them.

It turned out that the judge in that town took up with those kids and adopted them. He was Judge Myers and that's where the Myers come from. That's as far back as we know about the Myers side of the family.

"A couple other interesting things about your family," I told Blanche, "is that Ben's Uncle Charlie married my first cousin Annie Pack, and Aunt Ollie and Aunt Della were sisters whose husbands were cousins."

The Church Is Sold

In the mid '40s, a few years after the church was moved down to the new location, we lost our preacher. The Presbyterian Church said they would send preachers to fill in until they could find us one on a more regular schedule and for some time they did just that.

We had a few members from the church in Newport that would come and try to help out, but there just weren't many who were willing to come this far and travel these roads. One time a woman came to put on a special Christmas program and several times they sent preachers whose entire sermon would be on tithing. The Presbyterians thought that the people up here should pay towards the preacher, but they were already giving all that they could. All that preaching made them feel bad, like they had done something wrong. Well, the people here for sure didn't like someone hammering them about something they weren't able to do.

Of course, it's always right to teach people what the Bible says—that they should tithe and give to the Lord, but you have to know your congregation and where they are in their understanding. You teach them to give what they have. Teach them that the widow just had two mites and she gave it all. There are a lot of people sitting in big churches in the cities who give what would seem like a large amount of money to the people up here, but compared to what they have, that fifty or hundred dollar bill is not much at all.

Seemed to me at the time that God wanted to meet the needs of the people, but the officials were looking at the color of the ink in the bottom line to see if it was worth it.

Our church people were givers. They just didn't always have money to give, but they were always real good about helping each other when there was a need. Some others in the community wouldn't help anyone who wasn't blood kin.

I don't know exactly when it was that we got our next regular preacher, maybe a year or so before Papa died in 1950. Not long after Papa's funeral, the preacher and his family were in a wreck. His little boy was killed and his wife badly crippled. They decided to leave the area and go back to Georgia so her folks could help take care of her.

Then, after that happened, the officials just seemed to lose interest in us and never sent anyone else. I called the church in town a couple times to ask the pastor if they had some young people who would come and read stories to the little ones on Sunday afternoon and help with the Sunday school classes. He would never talk to me, so I left messages. One of those times someone did call me back and said, "We do have a couple of people who might come if we can find a volunteer with an old jeep or old truck to bring them. The people here just don't want to drive their new cars over those rough roads. Otherwise, if we don't find someone, we won't be sending anyone else up there to preach or help out."

As you can imagine, that made me furious. A lot of the people up here had pretty good cars. They weren't new. They were A-models and T-models and models like that, but they were nice. Nobody needed a jeep to get up here, especially if they were going no farther than where the church was.

The people at the church never did know that the Presbyterians had pulled out and weren't helping us any more, not until 1969. I just couldn't tell them, so I pretended all those years like the officials were still running things. I would find preachers every once in a while, usually not Presbyterians, who would come and speak or we would just sing and I would have one of the men of the church read Scripture. They would read and then the people would read. There was one young man from the Presbyterian church who came as often as he could to help out during that time.

We kept on having Sunday school, just like always, as if a regular preacher were there. If there wasn't anyone to teach, I would just tell someone to go read a Bible story to the children. We had vacation Bible school and Christmas and Easter programs.

Of course, after the Presbyterians left, I never did pass the collection plate. I just didn't think it right for me to take the people's money; besides, there wasn't anybody in the community working an outside job and getting paid. What was the need of embarrassing people? I paid the light bill and took care of all the bills that the Presbyterians would have paid. I saved my own tithe and bought the things we needed for the church, and if we needed something more we would make up things and sell them. At Christmas and other special times, I would save back extra money so we could have treats and a program. Sometimes it was hard for me to keep up my tithes to the church. After paying the church bills and my bills, I wouldn't have much left and all I could afford was a quarter a week. Every Sunday I'd put a quarter or whatever I could in a jar. I had twenty-two dollars saved up when the house burned down. I never did find it. Somebody else might have found it, but it probably just melted in the fire.

In 1969, Cary's father-in-law was coming up here and preaching for us. After one of the services, Mitchell told the preacher that he wanted to be baptized. Well, Preacher Webb didn't know what to do so he came to me. "I'm not Presbyterian and I don't know a thing about your rules and regulations for baptism."

So I told him, "I don't know that we've ever had a baptism before and I don't know what our regulations are either, but I'll ask the authorities and find out." Well, I didn't know who to ask. Up until then, when something came up, I would always tell them, "I'll ask the authorities," or "I'll see what the officials have to say about that," or "I'll talk to the higher-ups," and then I would go home and pray about it. That way I never did have to lie. I just did whatever I felt the Lord wanted me to do. Sometimes if I had trouble in the church or if the boys would cut up, I'd say, "Don't do that 'cause you know I'd have to report you to the authorities." That's all I'd say and that went on for years.

I didn't know what I was going to do about a baptism. I prayed about it, but I still didn't feel like I had the answer. In fact, the more I prayed the more it seemed like I should talk to someone from the Presbyterian church to learn just what the Presbyterians did. So I got somebody to take me to see this retired pastor I knew. I told him, "I got in a jam and I don't know if you can tell me what I need to know or not, but this boy wants to join the church and be baptized and I don't know a thing about that."

He answered, "I can tell you that and something else about the Presbyterians that you need to know. They're planning to sell your church building. I think the people who want to buy it plan to have it moved down to the highway and use it as a bar or clubhouse or something like that. They're planning to make an offer real soon."

"Selling it out?!?"

"Yeah, they're going to sell it out and put the money in this new church in town."

"They can't do that. That's just not right. We wouldn't be able to have funeral services or nothing. Weren't they even going to tell us? What can we do?"

"I'll tell you what you can do, but you had better do it fast. My son is their lawyer. You need to go on down and meet with him. Tell him you want to buy it."

His son told me that the other people had made an offer that morning for a thousand dollars. Well, I thought for sure we could come up with five hundred dollars and they would let us have the church. The lawyer said, "No, your offer has to be more than theirs. If you can get one thousand and one dollars, we'll sell the building to you."

"We can and we're going to get it." So, I talked to Mitchell and we worked it all out. That Friday morning, Mitchell, Mitchell's daddy, the preacher, and I marched into the lawyer's office and signed the papers to buy the church building. We didn't say anything to anybody about it. I didn't tell the congregation. They didn't have the first idea of what was going on.

It was the funniest thing when the next week the Presbyterian preacher came down to the school to talk to me. "I want to let you know that we have sold your church."

"Yes, I know all about that. We found out what you were doing. Why, we would never have even imagined it! One church selling another church to be used as a bar! Why, I never! So, we just went ahead and bought the church ourselves last week."

He couldn't quite believe what he was hearing. "Who did you buy it from?"

I told him the lawyer's name and he said, "Well, he is the lawyer for the church. If he sold it to you, then it's all yours."

There were a whole bunch of Presbyterians real upset about it too—just like taking a stick to a hornet nest—when word got out about the officials trying to sell the outpost church to sinners in order to get more money to build a new church in town. That caused a split in their church and I heard that the young man who had been such a big help to us a while back withdrew from the Presbyterian Church. Someone told me that, but I don't know if it's true. They said he wouldn't even go to church for a long time because he resented the way they treated us.

Our New Church

After we got everything settled about buying the church, we started arguing about what we should call it. I said, "It's going to be called Ebenezer!" And it's still called Ebenezer to this very day.

A little later, when we were planning to build some Sunday school rooms onto the church, we were told we would have to go to some office in town and get papers filled out so we could have a tax exemption. So,

Mitchell went into town to do that for us. They asked what the name of the church was and he told them Ebenezer.

"What denomination is that?'

He told them, "Independent. It's Ebenezer Independent."

"Independent what?"

"Just independent."

"You can't be just independent. There has to be a denomination listed there."

Mitchell didn't know what else to say, so he came back to ask me, "What should I say? What denomination are we going to be?"

"[14]Not Presbyterian!! That's for sure! We'll be Baptist." So he went back and told them we were Baptist.

"What kind of Baptist?"

"Well, I don't know what kind. Miss Opal just said Baptist. What kinds of Baptist are there?"

"Well there's Freewill, there's Missionary." And they told him some others too.

So he had to come back and ask me again and I said, "Missionary. Tell them we are Missionary."

When he went back and told them Missionary they said, "Where's your covenant?"

"Covenant?!? What else do you need to know and what else do we have to have?"

"You have to have a covenant. If you don't have one, we can do one here for you for two dollars."

Mitchell had never heard tell of a covenant, so he came to ask me. At this point we had moved past annoyance and aggravation to just plain ridiculous. I said, "Don't ask me. I don't know. That's the reason I have you looking after all of this." We got so tickled after that. All we could do was laugh about this lengthy legal process we were going through.

---

14   Opal's anger was only directed towards the local Presbyterians. Even though she felt abandoned and then betrayed by them, she still had strong ties with numerous Presbyterian friends, pastors, and mission workers for the remainder of her life. She was deeply grateful for all the Presbyterian mission and Highland Institute did for her.

So Mitchell went back again with two dollars in hand and told them we wanted a covenant. When we got that covenant, Mitchell and I went over to the church and stuck it up on the wall. We both said at the same time, "That thing ain't never comin' down." And then we just laughed. The date of the church's reorganization was July 20, 1969.

After the reorganization of the church, we had several different preachers come up here to preach for a spell at a time. One of the preachers said, "We're going to have to change our classes around. I don't believe women ought to teach adults. Mrs. Myers can teach the children if she wants a class, but I don't think she should teach this one." So we just made a joke out of it and I went ahead and took a little class and did everything else I was allowed to do. I would tease and say, "Well, I don't care if I have a class or not, and I don't care if my name is on the role or not. Neither of those has a thing to do with my place in this church or going to heaven. But, I'll tell you right here and now, what's really important and what really matters is that nobody else sits in my seat and that I get to ring the bell. I've been sitting here on this bench and ringing this bell as long as any of you, and as long as the Lord lets me do it, I'll be right here. This will be my seat and I'll ring the bell." I was only joking, of course, but maybe everyone took me seriously because no one ever sat in my seat and everyone waits on me to ring the bell. Funny, isn't it?

Vacation Bible School

I had a friend in Newport who loved attending Bible conferences. And, for sure, she did go to a lot of them and met people from all over the country. Well, at one of those conferences she met some people from a Baptist church in Detroit, and in talking with them discovered that they sent teams out on mission trips to conduct Vacation Bible Schools all around the country.

She told that group about us and our little church and they decided to come up here, a whole bus load of them and then some. My friend took care of all the details from this end of things, including making arrangements with a company in Knoxville to bring out and set up a trailer or a food wagon, I think they called it, for cooking. I took care of getting the word out about the Bible school and getting the church ready. Of course, I had a lot of help from the church people. We fixed up the church and cleaned up the churchyard so there would be a place for them to pitch their tents.

We didn't have any wells in the community, so all the water they used would either have to be carried up from the creek down below the church or brought over from the big spring on the other side of the creek. That was the only way any of us up here could get fresh water—out of the springs. They could use creek water for washing themselves and the dishes or for cleaning up the tables and such, but they would only use the spring water for drinking and cooking. With all the people coming, that meant there would have to be a lot of water totin! I went down to the spring and cleaned it out real good, then stacked rocks on both sides of where the water came out. That kept leaves and other stuff from blowing in and covering the spring.

The group from Detroit was supposed to be there by ten in the morning and the food wagon was to be delivered around two o'clock. Well, I thought everything was ready and going pretty smoothly until that afternoon, when someone from the church called and said, "The men from Knoxville are here with the food wagon, but they won't leave it without the hundred dollar deposit. The Detroit people are supposed to pay, but they ain't here yet. They're a-runnin' real late. What we s'posed ta do?"

Well, I had no idea at all about what to do, so I just prayed. In the midst of my prayin', wouldn't you believe that I recollected a lady in Newport who belonged to the Presbyterian church there. When we first bought the church, she gave us the first hundred dollars to pay towards it. So I called her and told her about our situation and she was glad to help. I assured her that the people from Detroit would pay her when they got here, but she said not to worry about it. It didn't matter if they paid her back or not. The company left the food wagon and went to her house to pick up the check.

It wasn't until that evening that the Detroit people actually got up to the church. They seemed to have one delay after another. The last one was because of the weight limit on that little bridge down yonder just after you turn off the highway, you know, where the road crosses over the stream there. The bridge was a narrow one, mainly for people to walk across and for cars; it wasn't safe for anything heavier. Trucks usually went around the bridge right through the creek bed. Of course, the bus driver didn't want to do that. When he saw that bridge and the weight limit, he told them he couldn't take them any farther and ended the trip right there with them sitting in their seats wondering what to do next. There were four or five cars loaded with luggage and supplies that had followed the bus all the way from Detroit and, of course, the bridge was fine for them. The driver and some of the men unloaded the rest of their suitcases and supplies from the storage area under the bus and stacked them on the side of the road. "Maybe one or two of you can stay here with this stuff and you others can walk the rest of the way and carry some of the lighter things." They thought that maybe they could start doing that and their people driving the cars could go unload and come back and get some of the heavier things. But I guess that it was just the Lord's will that they ride up to the church because right at that same time a big ol' logging truck came along headed towards the church. He started driving through the creek, but when he realized what was happening, he said he would take them. There were forty-five people who came down from Detroit with all their belongings, so it still took a couple trips.

We had people sleeping everywhere. We moved all the church benches against the walls and a bunch of them slept there on the floor inside the church. The others slept in tents—there were tents all over the yard.

During the morning, they had Bible school for all ages including the adults. While that was going on, some of the workers would be cooking lunch. Then there would be more classes or crafts in the afternoon. I can still remember the singing and laughter. I mean to tell you, I do believe there were more people on that hill than there were ants in it.

In the evening, we would have big campfires where we roasted hotdogs and marshmallows and then there would be an evening service with more singing and preaching. The entire community had the best time ever. This was truly one time that all the "outsiders" were welcomed and appreciated. Many of the community people even joined in and helped clean up the dishes so the church people could take a break. The last day of their stay we sent them off with a big picnic of fried hamburgers and everything else you could imagine.

I still hear from that Detroit group. Every Christmas they send us a little donation. This year they sent twenty-five dollars and we're going to use it towards building a partition between our Sunday school rooms.

Fixing Up the Church

We always have a project that we're working on for the church. We've kept up with our pledges for projects for five years now, all except for building the partition between the Sunday school rooms. This is the first time we've gone over our deadline for getting a project done. But there's been so much sickness and such since winter started. I haven't been feeling good for a while now either, so I haven't been able to be there to preach and keep the project going. We've got nearly enough to pay for it though, with the donation from Detroit and then the money two of Catherine Marshall's friends from Florida sent us to use as a memorial to Catherine. As soon as I get feeling better, we'll get that done. It won't take us long once we have enough money to buy the materials. The men folk up here can build it in no time at all and then we will be able to have one side of the classroom for a nursery and the older children will have a place of their own on the other side.

I guess we've really had projects like that from the very beginning, since we first decided to move the mission church to its present location. The old church had to be taken apart very carefully to prevent the dried out old wood from splitting. Board by board, piece by piece, and nail by nail, everything was saved so we could use the same building material to build the new church, since there was no money for additional supplies.

That first winter after the church was rebuilt there by the cemetery, we realized that the boards in the walls had not been placed close enough together or overlapped. The cracks between the boards were wide enough to let the cold wind blow through the church, biting our fingers and toes until we nearly froze. Back then women didn't wear pants to church, but for sure we wore our heaviest, long stockings under our dresses or skirts and big ol' heavy boots. The men weren't any warmer than we were, and those poor little young'uns were so bundled up they looked more like fat ticks on a dog—too big and round to barely move.

Even though the winters were so cold, we couldn't come up with money for more boards to cover the inside walls or even enough money for insulation, which we certainly could have used. Every week I would go down to the church early enough to gather downed wood and kindling from that property right there by the cemetery and start the fires so it would at least be a little warmer by the time the people got there. This one winter, I guess because it was such an especially cold winter and everyone was burning more wood, the man who owned that property told me not to use anymore of his wood. Well, I didn't know quite what to do. I couldn't carry that much wood from my place, so it only seemed natural to have everybody pick up a piece or two of kindling wood from their own places and bring that along with one larger piece of wood with them to church. Then during the week, with the help of some of the others, I worked at getting a stack of kindling and some good sized pieces of wood to the church—enough to start a decent fire. The next Sunday when the people came with their wood, the church was already warming up and pretty comfortable, if you left your coat on. We stacked up the wood they brought outside the door to be ready for the next week. During the week, when some of the men cut firewood for themselves, they would drop off a piece or two so we were able to keep a nice little stack of wood outside the church all winter long. That, along with what the people brought, would usually be enough. That's how we all stayed warm, well, as warm as one can be with a cold draft coming in.

One winter I guess Lawton Turner got tired of being cold from that fierce wind whipping through the church like it did. "I'll put a hundred dollars up if you panel this church!" Well, that started something amongst the congregation, and soon inspired everyone to give. We saved and worked all through the next summer. If people didn't have any money, they would make something and sell it. A little later another man and two or three children dug the pit out there behind the church and built our first toilet.

When Mr. and Mrs. Divens built that nice big modern log home down below the road on Old Fifteenth and moved up here, they did a lot to help the church. They're both just naturally business-minded and know what needs to be done and how to do it. Mr. Divens is a big shot, but he never acted like one. He would get down on his hands and knees and do a lot of the dirty work himself. He had Benja help him put the insulation under the church because Benja was so little and skinny that he could easily move around under there. Then Mr. Divens put up all the underpinning. As long as Lawton was able to, he would help too. In fact, he and Mr. Divens did most of the work that had to be done. Sometimes Mr. Divens would hire someone else to do a special job. He would always make sure that the church got a really fair price and then he would pay for it and let us pay him back in installments. That way we didn't have to pay any interest. We're still paying on our air conditioner. Every fourth Sunday, whatever we collect in the offering is given to Mr. Divens.

Mr. Divens taught the adult class most of the time too. He's well-read and knows a lot, and is a good teacher even though he did get a little above their heads. He reads all these Bible dictionaries and Bible helps and things like that, so you can imagine how much he knows. In these parts, we need more Mr. Divens; he is really good for the people. Most of our community can read and write, but this is just an average country crowd.

The first Sunday I was back at church since I'd been sick, there wasn't a soul to teach the class but me. Mr. Divens was out sick, so they asked me, "Miss Opal, since Mr. Divens isn't here, would you teach the class?"

"Why, I haven't been here for so long, I don't know where you are or what Mr. Divens has been teaching you and I don't know nearly as much as he does."

"Go ahead. You know the Bible better than any of us do. If we put a chair up there for you to sit in, could you just teach us a little?"

"I don't need a chair; I'll be fine standing up. This pulpit is just the right height and makes a fine place to lean on; besides, it's hard for me to get up and down."

I've held the adult class several times since I've been sick. Mitchell teaches most of the time now, but when he's been gone, I'd take it. Of course, I don't really consider what I do teaching. Most of the time, we just read the Bible and enjoy the Scripture stories. And it's still mere tradition that I sit there on that same seat every time I'm at church. It's funny, but nobody will sit in that seat if I'm there and they always ask me if I want someone to ring the bell for me because I have trouble getting up and down. I guess after all of these years I really do have my place and position in my church. My place or seat is a bit back from the front on left side of the church, and my position or job is "bell ringer." Of course, outside the church, I had a lot more positions that didn't have a fancy title like that.

Helping Others

One of those jobs was being a helper. At one time, when we lived in the mission house, we had a big long cupboard full of things that people could borrow. If someone got sick, there were clean nightgowns and linens. Or, when there was a death in a family, we would loan out clean sheets and pillowcases, towels and things like that for family members who came in from out of town and spent a night or two.

When someone in the community died, the body was always brought back to their home for a viewing. That meant that the person's house had to be cleaned up, linens and curtains washed. Food needed to be cooked and brought in for the family and for the viewing. I did all of those things or got a group of people together to get things done faster.

At the viewing or at the funeral, there were always people who liked to go and see how the dead person looked after the funeral home fixed them all up. It sounded kind of morbid to me. I didn't care a thing about comparing the living with the dead, but others would talk about how good this one looked or how this one didn't look anything like he did in real life. I thought, *How foolish!* It was a very strange curiosity indeed, and a senseless thing to be talking about. There was too much else that needed to be done to help out rather than talking about a dead person's appearance. The families didn't need to be hearing such talk and they shouldn't have to think about all the things that needed to be taken care of. It seemed that there were always children or babies to help out with, so that's what I did. After I had started teaching up in Del Rio, a lot of the teachers there kindly helped out with sheets and food or whatever I might need. Whenever there was a need for food, we would share whatever we might have in our own cupboards.

I was really excited when I found this man who had a hospital bed that he would let me have for forty dollars. We decided to sell candy to raise the money to pay for it, and several of the children took that on as a project. The candy came in boxes of twenty-four bars and for every box we sold we made eighty cents. Fifty boxes or twelve hundred bars of candy was a whole lot of candy to sell, but it really didn't take us long to raise that forty dollars. We'd get fifteen or twenty boxes every week or two and give them to the young'uns and they would sell them on the school bus and to their neighbors.

It was funny how people responded to our latest purchase! When we first got our hospital bed, no one wanted to borrow it because they were just sure somebody had died in it. "Well, I do imagine that several *somebodies* have done just that!" I would tell them. "But you can rest assured that we took all the bodies out and cleaned it up real good." When Frank Turner got sick and borrowed that bed, people changed their thinking. You see, everybody saddled up to Frank as one of the big shots in the community because he had really made something of himself. He was just about the only one around here with any money to speak of. So, after he borrowed it and slept in it without dying, they didn't seem to have a problem about it anymore and several of them ended up using it too.

Everyone around here looked up to Frank as someone special. He was born with less than nothing, but worked hard to make something of himself, and the community people respected him for that. Frank was older when he started school and worked around the mission, helping however he could, to earn his tuition money. The chapel women managed to get him a scholarship and helped to send him off to high school. I've heard Frank tell several times that when he graduated and came back here, he had an education but not much of anything else, not even a good pair of shoes. He actually had to borrow the shoes he wore when he went out to get his first job. Later Frank went to work in the coal mines in West Virginia, where he worked his way up to head electrician. He lived on as little as he could manage and saved all the rest of the money he made. A lot of the people up here considered him well-to-do.

Mrs. Etta Nichols[15], most everybody called her Granny, was another person who I would say did the work of a missionary too. She was fourteen years older than me and had been a midwife since her early thirties. She helped birth babies all over the county around the Del Rio area. Well, in 1967 both Etta's mother and mother-in-law became very sick and moved in with her. With the responsibility of caring for two sick women, she didn't know what she was going to do or how she was going to get out to deliver babies and, at the same time, take care of the sick in her own house. I gave her that hospital bed and told her to use it there in her birthing room. I would come and look after her mother and mother-in-law when I wasn't teaching so

---

15   There was a book written about Mrs. Nichols, *Etta "Granny" Nichols: Last of the Old-Timey Midwives* by Sharon Smith-Ledford, in which Opal is mentioned (pg. 139). However, there is a misstatement. When Opal was eleven years old in 1922, it was Mrs. Marston rather than Leonora Whitaker who influenced Opal. Leonora and her husband left Ebenezer Mission in March 1912.

she could take care of her cases. You see, we worked together like that, similar to how the chapel women helped people.

So that became the floating hospital bed. It was a real nice one with a tray that would pull over in front of the patient so they could eat on it or write notes. It had little steps that pulled out to make it easy to get in and out of bed. That bed's been all around the community. I don't know where it is now, but I don't believe the Lord would let anybody destroy it. I like thinking it's still out in the community somewhere with somebody using it.

Decorations Day Project (Memorial Day)

Every year just before Decorations Day, I always took up a collection so we could pay somebody to clean up the cemetery. Last year we collected one hundred and twenty-seven dollars, but the money disappeared. We don't know who the money was turned over to or where it went. We still have no idea of what happened to it and, because of that, we couldn't hire anyone to do the job.

So not long before Decorations Day, some of the church people came to me and asked, "What are you going to do? There ain't nobody cleaned up that cemetery yet?"

"Why, my lands! Why don't you'uns get out there and hunt somebody?"

"We wouldn't know what to say or do. People wouldn't pay us no mind."

"Are you saying that you want me to take care of it?"

"Ya."

"Okay, you tell everybody to be at the cemetery on May fourteenth and we'll clean it up. Then we'll decide what to do from there on."

There were only three people that showed up. One of them showed up out of frustration from the dogs digging holes all around the cemetery and doin' their business right there on her mother's grave. The dogs that were doing that actually belonged to her uncle and she was furious about it! "We have got to get a fence put around this place!"

Well, we marked off the cemetery boundary and talked to the land owner about wanting to put a fence up, but he claimed that where we wanted to put the fence would be on his property. He said he would move the line to where it should be and then we could put up our fence. Well, he moved the line way over where it would actually put some of the graves on his side of the fence. The people got really upset, just fightin' mad. "We can't let him take land off the cemetery! What are we gonna do about him?"

"We won't do anything. Never! We don't have to. The Lord will take care of him. Just forget about it."

I really didn't think there was much to worry about anyway. If he took a strip off that side of the property, it would take his parents out of the cemetery. So, I didn't see any need of making a big deal out of it. The Lord could change his heart without a word from us and that's exactly what happened. Every time something came up like that, the Lord would take care of it and we never did have to worry about it.

That year we started getting volunteers to clean the cemetery and used the Decoration Day offering for the fence. We decided to do that every year, and with donations and raising money, we planned to have the fence paid for in three years. We're working on that now. We've got one side wired and we've got enough money to make up another side, and then we've only got two sides to go. Ben's brother gave me a hundred dollars to put towards it when he was up here the last time. You see, many community people who live away from here don't have a way of taking care of their family's graves and they're glad to give money to get that fence up.

The projects over the years never seemed to dwindle. It might take a while, but we've always been able to get the money. If people know what you're trying to do and think it's a worthy cause, they will help out. So all I ever had to do was talk to everyone about this project or that one and then they would talk to someone else about it. Eventually the right people heard about it and wanted to contribute to the effort. We would also sell candy, homemade lye soap, and other things like that at Del Rio Days to raise money for different projects. Now with taxes and such, there's not much profit in selling candy like we used to, and they don't let the kids sell candy around the school anymore.

There was a special secret project that I started helping someone with back in the '50s that we're still doing. To this day, no one knows who I work with on this so I still can't tell their name. Anyway, this friend of mine would give me money to help one child every year. Sometimes it would be the same child for several years or it could be a different one every year. It just depends on the need. My friend started off with five dollars and now she's up to one hundred dollars a semester. The money goes towards buying their lunch, books, and other things for school. The last time I decided to choose one special family that we could help for several years. I've already helped three of them through high school and now I'm working on the fourth. I've helped several like that and they really appreciate it. It wasn't all that much money—just enough to help them to continue with their education. I've always kept it a secret because so many people would feel bad because I didn't help them. Most of the time the children we were helping didn't even know because I would give the money to their mother and she would use it for the child. I had to be real careful not to offend people, though. But helping others is why God gives us blessings, so we should use what we have to better the world in some small way. That's always how I felt about it, anyway.

20
1970–1986

Barry and Benja Moved In

Seldon ended up joining the army and Cary married Cathy Webb and had two boys, Barry Alvin, who was born in July of 1968, and Benjamin Anthony "Benja," who was born on October 23, 1969. Cary and Cathy divorced and the boys came to live with me on December 15, 1970. Barry wasn't quite two and a half years old and Benja, even though he was just a little over a year old, still couldn't sit up alone or help himself.

As soon as my landlord found out about Barry and Benja, she came and exclaimed, "You can't take in those kids."

"Why, I can too!" Well, we went back and forth like that and I ended it by saying, "Yes, I can have my grandchildren here. I can get a babysitter for them while I'm teaching and it will all work out just fine." That was the end of that—at least for awhile.

I got the babysitter and their daddy paid for her. But when I was there with Barry and Benja, they certainly kept me busy, kept me hoppin', for sure. They weren't mean children; they didn't get into stuff and destroy things. They were just very active.

Not too long after they moved in with me, about the time Benja could finally crawl and get into things, Barry came up next to me in the kitchen, and I kept hearing a strange sound of something following after him. About that time, Barry turned around and said, "Come on. Come on, now!" and there came Benja just a-crawlin' away, trying to catch up with him. How Barry ever got him out of his bed and put him on the floor, I'll never know! Just a pure wonder that he didn't drop him on his head.

Barry and Benja went with me to church right from the start. I always believed that you should get children started in church when they were little.

When Corrine was still a tiny baby, we took an orange crate, put a blanket in it, and had it sitting on the stage there at the church to lay her down in. She just stayed there and Miss Minnie would keep an eye on her.

Miss Minnie helped me too when my boys were little. She carried Cary to church on her back and I carried Seldon. That's the way we carried them all the time until they were big enough to walk long distances. Miss Minnie would have them sitting by her or hold them during church and they never moved from their seats. I never had to tell them to sit down and I never had to take them outside for a scolding. They knew exactly what they were supposed to do. Of course, Miss Minnie and Mrs. Click helped me a lot. I never would have been able to teach and do the things I did all those years without them.

So, when I started taking Barry and Benja to church, I did the same thing—I would take Barry and put him down on the seat next to Miss Minnie and she would hold Benja. They always stayed right where I put them: I never had a bit of trouble. Even later right up through when they were teenagers, Barry and Benja sat with me in church.

Where we lived, I would have to go across the road to get the mail. I always took both of them with me because I was afraid they would follow me out in the road and get run over. But when it was raining, I didn't want them walking through the field of mud so I would dress them up in their coats and caps and they thought they were going with me. I would sit them down on the porch and put their coat tails under the heavy trunk sitting near the door so they couldn't get up to follow me. You talk about screaming! Those kids would scream, but I just went on. As long as they were crying, I knew where they were. We had a little dog that got killed right there in the road one day and that made me scareder than ever. If people couldn't see a dog, you know they probably wouldn't see a little child either.

Children are easier to handle when they're little than when they are big. People would say, "Won't you be glad when they grow up?"

"No, I won't be glad when they grow up because these young'uns are just too much fun little." They were something else. But you know, I enjoyed them at every age.

My landlord hadn't said any more about Barry and Benja living with me for some time. Then one day she came and told me, "You're not supposed to have two families living in this house."

"I've not got two families. These boys are my family."

But she insisted, "When you took Barry and Benja in, they are another family, the family of your son." I knew then what she meant. She was saying that I shouldn't have taken them in and I should have consulted her. I guess that's true, but when you get desperate like that you just don't think. I told her as soon as I could find another place we would move.

September 1972 to October 1972 —*Marjorie Reeves*

By the 1st of September, this was in 1972, I had found another place and paid my first month's rent. But, since my garden wasn't all harvested yet, I had asked my old landlord if we could stay there for two more weeks until I could get all my crops in. Part of what I had left to harvest was the corn I used to feed my hogs. That would save me from having to buy more feed. Everything worked out fine, and at the end of the two weeks I had everything from the house and barn moved. Then I got someone to help me bring my hogs over. We had one off the truck and in the pen and the other one was coming down the ramp when this man came running up saying, "Wait a minute!

Wait a minute! Marjorie said to tell you not to let your hogs put one foot on her ground. She doesn't allow hogs on her place."

Well, that was just a little more than I could handle. "What do you mean she doesn't allow hogs on her place? I never heard tell of anyone in the country not having hogs. I didn't know anything about this when I paid her my rent money. She didn't say a word to me or ask me what kind of animals I had or if I had hogs. You go back and tell her that there are already four hog feet on her ground and there'll be four more just as soon as we can get them there. I've got my rent paid until the end of this month and I'm going to put whatever I please on this place for the rest of this month. Then we'll be out of here, hogs and all."

October 6, 1972, to May 22, 1976 —*Fords by the Bridge*

So there I was, hunting down a place to rent—again! It was becoming a tradition for us. The more moves we made, the harder it got; I was so tired of moving around. You see, I had all this fine land up here with houses and barns and everything, but if I was going to teach I had to be closer to the school. I couldn't live way back up in here. But my heart lived here; it always had and it always will.

This time all I could find was a little ol' shack that had a wire fence all the way around it. It was way back in the woods over there by the creek right before you get to that last bridge as you leave Old Fifteenth. Now there's a nice brick home there.

It was so small and I knew I wouldn't be able to put five or six rooms of furniture in that little thing, but that was the only house I could find. I would just have to pack up a lot of my things and store them around in different places. The Newmans had told me that they had an empty basement that they never used and that I could store anything I wanted to and leave it there as long as I needed to. On the day I moved, I had five or six people helping me and I mostly stood there directing people where to take each item. "Take this to the barn. Take that to Mr. Newman's. Take this to the Ford House. Take that to the hen house. Take this to the barn. Take that to the..." just over and over and over and they still got everything all mixed up. They were trying to unload it in the right places, but when it was all over, none of them could remember any better than I could where things went.

Barry and Benja

One time when Barry and Benja were still fairly little, they got some tools and took all the nuts off the tires on L. Conn's car. How they got them loose I'll never know! I don't even think that I would have been able to do that. Then they just laid the wrenches down and went on to something else, leaving the car there with the tires looking like they were fine. Well, it might have looked like nothing was wrong with the car, but about the time L. Conn got down to the mailbox the tires fell off. He came a-hoppin' back to the house looking real strange and I asked him, "What in the world is the matter?" Barry and Benja were standing there just as innocent as could be. They were only about four and five years old.

"All the tires just fell off my car. All the nuts are missing!"

Well, Barry and Benja took him right out there and showed him where the tools and nuts were. They knew exactly where they had left them. L. Conn didn't get mad; he laughed it off. It was funny, too. To me it sounded exactly like something I would have done when I was little. They tease about Benja doing so many mischievous things, but I guess he got it honest, because I was always into trouble just like that.

They were all the time doing something funny—Benja still does. Benja would go around singing crazy things, not a song or nothing, just making up words. One time he was in a play and had to sing with another boy. They were supposed to sway back and forth in time to the music as they sang. Well, the longer they swayed the more they exaggerated their sway until they got so carried away with it that they were doing more swaying and rhythm-keeping than singing. They were really cutting up. The more the audience reacted, the more they performed until everyone was so tickled and laughing so hard they had tears in their eyes.

Barry and Benja always thought a lot of me, Barry especially. People said he acted like he worshiped me, but they always accused me of petting Benja and I guess I did. I always felt so sorry for him because his parents didn't call him and talk to him like they did Barry and I thought he wasn't treated fair. I guess they couldn't stand his mischievous ways, but I liked his ways. They reminded me of my younger days.

I'm glad I had those boys. They added so much to my life, even though it was a lot of work! Washing for them took the most time. They were both in diapers when I took them in. After I changed them, I would rinse their diapers out and soak them in a pail of water. Then every night I would wring them out and wash them and hang them outside. In bad weather, I had to fix up something around the stove for them to dry on. I didn't have to worry about having enough kindling saved up or think about building a fire every morning because we used coal. Every night before going to bed, I would put some coal in the stove and it would still be hot in the morning. That's the reason L. Conn doesn't know anything about getting wood and building a wood fire now, because he never had to do it.

When Benja got a little older, maybe eight or ten, he made little go-carts out of just this and that—all kinds of scraps and parts and things. One of his favorite things to do was to take his go-cart up to the top of that steep hill behind the Old McMahan Place where we lived then and fly down towards the house as fast as he could. At the last minute he would swerve off to the side of the house. He knew exactly what he was doing, but he scared everyone else near to death.

Barry and a Messner boy decided one time that they were going to build a go-cart. They put a motor on a piece of wood and put wheels on it. They rode that thing all around here, having the best time with it. Then Barry decided he was going to build an airplane. When he finished putting it together, he took it up on that high bank where that swinging tree is and jumped off with it. He thought it was really going to fly, but he found out different.

I miss the boys since they've grown up. I miss Benja worst of all, and people can't seem to understand that. One reason I do, Benja was always there for me. If something happened to my sewing machine, if a light bulb went out, Benja was right there to fix it. Barry didn't think too much about fooling with that kind of thing. Same thing was so with L. Conn and the rest them. They just don't care. Oh, they'll fix it all right, but they really don't care.

Retirement

In 1973, the school district announced that teachers with a four-year degree and a minimum of thirty years of teaching could retire and get one hundred and fifty dollars a month plus a cost of living raise every year. And, of course, teachers with forty years of experience would get much more.

I had already taught for forty years, but some of those didn't count towards retirement because I was teaching for the government and not through my school district. I had a total of thirty-seven years towards retiring, but I was still working on my degree. I wasn't quite sure how many more credits I needed before receiving it, but I thought it would be only one or two courses. So I figured if I taught three more years I could easily finish everything I needed to get my full retirement.

In order to start teaching in any of the one-room schools, I had only needed to complete one full year and I had done that at Milligan College right after getting out of Highland. From there I had just taken two or three courses here and a term or two there, like Carson Newman extension courses, whenever they had been available in Newport; courses at Johnson City and a correspondence course from Chilhowie in Virginia. I had been doing that for at least thirty years— taking courses that I was interested in or felt that I needed in order to be a better teacher.

Since I was getting closer to retirement, I thought it would probably be a good idea to get all of my records together and take them into Newport and have someone there look at them. So, I took them into the administration office of the school district. "Here are all of my records. Now, tell me what more is required to finish my degree."

"Degree!?!" she said, "You've not even started on a degree!"

I began stacking my credits and certificates in little stacks on the counter as I told her, "Well, I've had a year at Milligan College and I've had all these courses at Johnson City and these from Carson Newman. These are my correspondence courses from Chilhowie. I should only be a few courses short. Just look at my records," and I shoved them towards her.

"I have looked at them. Nearly everything you have here is in religion. This is from a Baptist institution and this one is from the Church of Christ."

"What's the difference? I didn't know that denomination or religion made any difference."

"Well, it certainly does! We just can't count all these religion courses towards a teaching degree."

So there I was with my thirty-seven years of teaching for the school district but not nearly enough credits to get me even close to a degree. They ended up offering me a retirement equal to the thirty-year plan. Of course, in those thirty-seven years I was never paid as much as my friends who were degreed teachers. I was averaging three hundred and fifty dollars a month and here they were offering me a hundred and fifty dollars to stay at home.

After I got to thinking about it, it really was pretty funny. I was one of the very few who could honestly say that I had too much religion. Yes, sir, being paid half of what I made as a teacher to stay home sounded like a good deal to me. I really wanted to be home with Barry and Benja. I wanted to be sure they went to school, be able to help them with their homework, and teach them when they came home.

Ethel Louise, Desmer's youngest daughter, is a teacher here at Bridgeport. At least one of us in the family is keeping the school teaching tradition up. She has her masters in education and I'm just so proud of her. We all are. Maybe one day you'll be a schoolteacher too,

Lori. But no matter what, I want you to know you are loved. I have faith in you and I just know you'll make all of us very proud!

When I first started teaching in 1933, I made fifty dollars a month. Then in 1949, I got a raise to sixty-nine dollars a month and I had to pay my insurance, teacher's dues, and taxes out of that. I had just gotten up to three hundred and fifty dollars before I took early retirement.

Moved Back to the Log Cabin in 1976

We had been at the Ford House for over three-and-a-half years before we had to move again. Barry was just two months away from being eight years old and Benja was almost six-and-a-half. Moving was wearing me out and I missed being on my own land in my own community. I loved it up here more than any place I had ever been or could ever go. Since I wasn't teaching any longer, it seemed like I even missed this cove more than ever. While I was thinking about that, getting even more homesick for my land, it just hit me! There was absolutely no reason left why I couldn't move back home! I heard myself saying, "That's it! We're going home and I'm not ever moving again!" It was May 22, 1976, when I moved back to the Old McMahan Place—my very own little log cabin in the cove that I loved.

With my belongings scattered nearly all around the county, moving this time was going to be different. I had no idea where some of the boxes I had packed ended up, and my old trunk was missing too. I could remember one of the ladies helping me pack all of my good sheets and pillowcases along with my bedspreads in that trunk. It was supposed to have been brought up here and stored in the barn. It was only a few years ago that I finally remembered that I had stored things in the Newman's basement. That's where I found my linens. It was amazing, after all that time in the basement, they had not mildewed or anything. I've still got all those sheets 'til yet. Of course, now they're just about falling apart.

Otto and the Bean Story

I have never been more happy anywhere than I have been here on my land. Since the book *Christy* became so well known, I've had hundreds of people from all over the country come here to find the place where the mission once was. I love telling them about the area and the mission and how things used to be. We still live somewhat backwards from how most people in other places live, and I practice many of the old country ways with my food. It's funny how people react.

One day I had ten gallons of beans that I had sorted and snapped off the ends spread out on top of this big table. I was sitting there stringing those beans with a needle and thread just like I had done from the time I was a young girl helping Mama.

Otto, a Hungarian, was there waiting on L. Conn to get ready. He just kept watching me with this questioning look on his face while I worked away sticking that needle through a bean and then pushing it down the string. I was getting so tickled because I knew he was wondering what in the world I was doing with all those beans. I didn't say anything about the beans; I just kept working away and watching his reactions out of the corner of my eye. We were talking about, you know, just this and that, but he kept walking around the table glancing from me to the beans. Then he'd walk around again. "What are you doing with those beans?" he finally blurted out.

"Oh, I'm just sewing them together."

"What are you sewing those beans together for?"

I just couldn't resist it. "So none of them will get lost, of course!"

Well, he just stopped dead in his tracks and looked at me real strange like.

I had to laugh. "We sew them together into loops like this and then dry them."

"Dry them—I've never heard of dried beans!"

"They're real good. People around these parts like them a whole lot."

I guess there aren't many people who know about stringing beans anymore. I'm sure it would seem real strange to them to see someone sewing their vegetables.

Visitors, Guests, and Boarders

Throughout the years I've had a lot of different people living up here in the houses on my property or sleeping in my barn. When we were living in the mission, I had several families at different times living in the house that I bought from my brother-in-law's brother—the Old McMahan Place. One family moved in there and stayed until they got their house built. Several others lived in it for a few months or maybe a year or so. We've had several people who stayed in the Click House too. Doug was one of those. While he was staying there, he was going to fix up that dirt floored cabin up below the pond, the one I bought from the family who turned over my outhouse. He actually started working on that. If he had stayed here, I had intended to give that place to him, but he found a place that he could buy.

You could always hear talk up here from someone or another about the types of people I took in to help. Usually they would refer to them as "those hippie types," but not all of them were—Doug wasn't. It just worried them something awful that I would let some strange-looking people stay up at the Click House or in my barn. Most of them thought I would let someone stay who would hurt me in some way. My boys never thought much about the ones I took in and I would just tell the others, "I don't care how they look. If someone comes to me for help, they're gonna get help! You can't tell what people are going to turn out to be by judging their outsides. Just look at what happened to Scott and some of the others! To me it's just been like watching butterflies come out of their cocoons."

Besides that, I always kind of figured that God had a lot to do with the people showing up here. I knew He loved them and He had a plan for their lives and I just reckoned that if He sent them here, then I was a part of His plan for them too. It didn't matter that the mission house burned down and wasn't here anymore. I was His mission house—

His temple like the Bible says we all are. When I was young, we called where the mission workers lived the dwelling house and we thought it a pure wonderment the work that God accomplished through that place. Years later I discovered that God calls those who belong to Him His dwelling place and, if we really let the Holy Spirit dwell in us and lead us, then it is indeed amazing what He can accomplish through us. When you just think about it, probably if we each did what He wanted us to do when He wanted us to do it—really acted like we were His dwelling place—there would be much less need for missions and ministries.

Scott came here from Newport during the time of hippies and he was a sight for sure with his long dirty hair and mustache. Scott had heard from Granny Nichols about me taking in people. He and his wife thought they might rent one of my houses and stay around here for a while. But instead of one of my houses, they ended up sleeping in the barn when it was nothing but two-by-fours and boards inside. I never did try to make anybody pay rent. I'd usually have them do chores for me and if I did get rent money from them, I would save it up and give it to them as a surprise when they left. Rent or no rent, those who weren't willing to work didn't stay around here all that long. Scott changed a lot while he was here. He and his wife became Christians and he later taught in a Christian school and now he's a preacher. He just turned out real good and made a fine man. A lot of them turned out real good, like Jackie and Danny. They ended up going back to Florida. Jimmy was another one who became a preacher.

Another one of the people I helped decided to stay around this area and has been so good to me since I've been sick. He brings me candy and things like that. At Christmas, he gave me some bedroom shoes and a housecoat. The other day he brought me some Twinkies, you know, those little packaged cakes. When I was in the hospital, they put me in a semi-private room. The private rooms cost twenty-five dollars more a day and besides that, they were all full. Well, don't you just know that as soon as one of those special private rooms became available, he had me moved into it. He paid for it and everything. He even gave me some money to help out with the doctor bills. See now, he was one who appreciated what I had done for him too.

When the Indians, Bob and Donna, came to me for help, it was snowing and blowing so hard that I just couldn't tell them to leave. Donna's Indian name was Bear, and that's what everyone called her. Bob really wasn't an Indian, even though he considered himself one. He was actually more like a mountain man and he made all his stuff from nature. He painted pictures; painted one on that saw up yonder on the wall, just like that, in no time at all.

Bob and Bear had a pretty messed up life when they came up here. They had a young boy named Dakota, but they had never gotten married. Bear begged me to take her little son and raise him. "I can't take in your son. He's just a tiny young'un and he needs his mama and daddy. I'll help you in every way I can, but you and Bob need to get your lives together, accept responsibility, and raise your own child. Little Dakota deserves at least that much." While they lived here, a lot of things changed in them and they decided to get married. Bob actually made the dress that Bear wore the day of their wedding. A little while after they married, Bear's stepmother found them a little house on the reservation, so they went back to New Mexico. Her real mama had died when Bear was just a young'un.

Then there was a boy named Sherby that stayed in the Click House for a while. He was another one of them with real long hair, but you couldn't tell it none because he wore his braided up around his head. He was the son of a Presbyterian preacher in Richmond, Virginia. His father and mother were real strict with him, and must have been rather snooty because they would never let him play with any of the other children where he grew up. He always had to stay in the house and study and things like that. I reckon he had just gotten fed up with it, 'cause he told me that after his daddy died, he decided to leave home and just took off walking down the road one day. He met up with a bunch of these hippie types, he called them Rainbows, and they took him to Michigan.

In Michigan, he met Shirley, one of the Rainbow people from up there. Shirley's friend Charity and her two little children had heard about me and planned to come down here to live for a while. She told Shirley and Sherby that she would bring them down with her and that they could all get a house and live together. That would give her someone to help drive and watch her kids on the way down here.

They got down here early one evening in October. Sherby cleaned out the Click House so they could move in what little stuff they had. I said something to him about my apple tree needing pruning. "Well, I told my mother I'd be back for Christmas. I have from now until then to help you with whatever you want done." I said that would be fine.

Shirley went into the house like she was going to stay, you know, but she was acting rather strange. She'd pace around, go to the window and look out just staring out at nothing in particular, and then she'd pace some more. Directly, Charity said to Shirley, "Me and the kids need to go over there to town before dark and get some things. You want to go with us?" Shirley went with her and they didn't come back.

Sherby stayed on by himself in the Click House for a while. One night he decided he was going to leave, and he started off over the mountain towards Bridgeport. I'm not sure where he had planned to go, but my dog Stevie just kept following him and wouldn't leave him. Sherby tried just everything to make him go back home, but nothing worked. It was late when they finally got over to Bridgeport, so they took cover and slept in somebody's wood shed. That dog stayed right there with him all night long, so the next morning he had no choice but to bring Stevie back.

We talked about his leaving, and I told him that if he went across to Del Rio instead of going to Bridgeport, he would come out nearer to the highway where he could get a ride. Guess it wasn't God's time for him to leave these parts just yet, because on the way down to Del Rio he ran into Auldin. They talked and Auldin asked him if he would stay with him for a while and help him with something or other— don't know exactly what it was. After he moved in with Auldin and got settled, he came up here to spend the night with me a few times. One time he brought me a set of new sheets and pillow cases. "You look kind of puny," he said when he saw me. "How about I help you out with your chores and things for a while?" He didn't know I was sick and I didn't know that I would end up in the hospital that very day. When I was in the hospital, he sent me a box of candy and did other special things like that. He had a good heart.

Commitment and Dreams

When I was young and just starting school, I knew about God. I knew that He was special and that He loved me. But I didn't think a lot about Him, except maybe when I went to church or when the mission workers talked about Him. The most important thing to me at that time was my family, sitting down by my mama's knees or sitting in Papa's lap. I guess I never thought about God taking care of me or watching out for me. That's what my parents had always done and I just didn't think about God that way. It never occurred to me that He had a plan for my life.

As I grew older, He became everything to me. I learned to respect God and depend on Him. I learned that He would give my life a purpose to live for and would help me if I did my part. I guess, in a way, I had always wanted to know God, but it wasn't until I stayed with Mrs. Henderson and Mrs. Robinson and the other mission workers that I really and truly came to know Him as my Savior and Lord. That's when He became my all, and I realized that I was even more important to Him than I was to Mama and Papa.

I had always been taught by Mama and Papa that commitments and promises are very important and are meant to be kept. It didn't make any difference if you made them thoughtlessly or even as a joke. If you made a promise, you kept your word. That's all there was to it! There were times when I made promises without thinking much about it—without thinking things through. But even after I made a promise like that, I took it seriously whether I meant it or not. I don't guess I would have ever married Ben if I hadn't promised him that I would, but I'm glad I did. Life was not easy after he came back from the war. He did some things that really hurt me and at times I felt so alone. But I wouldn't give anything for my children and grandchildren. If I hadn't married Ben, I wouldn't have them and Ben wouldn't have had someone to take care of him all those years.

When I made the commitment and promised God that I would come back here and teach and be the mission to my community, that's all there was to it. For a while, that was a difficult promise to keep. I wanted something else for my life, but I couldn't have it and keep my promise. Plus, I didn't know of anyone else who would do the work of the mission. I didn't know of anyone who was that interested or that committed to help the people up here like the mission workers had. So I guess that was another one of the reasons I was so determined to come back. But being determined didn't make it any easier. My thoughts spent a good bit of time battling around in my head. That's when I'd remember what my parents had taught me and I could almost hear Papa saying, "If you said you were gonna do something, you'd better be a-doin' it!"

The mission people believed that way too. "Before you make a promise, be sure you have the commitment to carry it out."

My papa was like that. If he made anybody a promise about anything, that was it; he was for sure going to carry it out. If my parents said something, they always did it, and we could always count on it.

If they told us we couldn't go somewhere, it didn't do us any good to go back and keep whining and begging. We learned early on that acting like that only made things worse. Sometimes we would ask Mama, "Can we go up to Aunt Susie's?" or "Can we go out to see Aunt Bess?" They were both old people in the community.

"Ask your Papa," she'd always say.

If we hadn't done our chores, he would tell us what we had left undone and we knew that we could forget about that little visit we had planned. It wasn't going to happen even when we finished our work. We knew we weren't even supposed to ask to do something if we didn't have our chores done. We never had to wonder about what was right and what was wrong or what was important to our parents. Oh, for sure, we tested them a few times, but it didn't take us too long to figure out that what they said was what they meant and our responsibilities, like work and study, came before playtime and adventure.

I remember one time we were scared stiff. Mama and Papa had let us go to Uncle Doc Turner's to spend the afternoon, but we were supposed to be back by five o'clock. After we had been there for a while, Maggie, Burl, Ben, and Ethel decided they wanted to go visit someone in West Myers on the river. We knew we weren't supposed to do that— you know, go someplace without Mama and Papa knowing. When we went to the Turner's, we never had to think about the time because the Turners would tell us when it was time to go home, but trollopsing around the mountains and down by the river, we had no idea what time it was getting to be. I doubt that we even thought about the time until it was too late.

There were only had a few people who lived there around the West Myers train stop. There wasn't much more than a house or two. At one time they had a school over there with preaching services in it, but it didn't last long. Later around the time of World War II, there were bauxite mines there. The bauxite was used in the manufacturing of aluminum.

Well, we stayed there for a while and then started heading back. When we rounded the pond, we decided to go into this big ol' house that was supposed to be haunted. We had no idea what time it was, but we did know that Mama hadn't given us permission to be there.

Of course, we were late getting home and we had to admit to being where we weren't supposed to be. That was the last time we went to West Myers and it was some time before we could go back to the Turner's.

Mission To Be Rebuilt

If I could do one more big thing in my life—one more project—I would rebuild the mission. I would still like to have my life make a difference to somebody else, some other child. I had always dreamed of the mission being restored. Maybe it wouldn't be like the mission had once been, but it would be used to help underprivileged or troubled children and families. I felt this so strongly that I considered it a calling from God.

In the early 1970s, I thought that my dream for sure was going to come true. Reverend Willis Clawser of the Ambassadors for Christ from somewhere around Hershey, Pennsylvania, read the book *Christy* and decided to come here to see where the mission had been. Reverend and Mrs. Clawser were somewhat familiar with places around here since they had been working with an orphanage over in the Rogersville area for the past eighteen years.

I was still living outside the community, but somehow Reverend Clawser tracked me down and told me of his desire to rebuild the mission. In November of 1971, we made arrangements to take a trip into the cove. Along with Reverend and Mrs. Clawser were four people from New Jersey, and Freda Bretschneider, a feature writer with *The Newport Plain Talk*. At that time there was no way to get a car up to where the mission's foundation still stood. It was invaded by weeds and tall grasses so that you could not tell where the road once was. Even if we could have seen the road, it would have been unusable— nothing more than deep ruts. We rode in the Clawser's truck as far as we could go and then we walked in the rest of the way. I showed Reverend Clawser and the others the foundation of where the mission had been. Then we walked farther into the cove up to my house there at the Old McMahan Place. He thought that hill out across from my house would be the perfect place to build the mission.

"You can rebuild the mission on my land and use my land for that purpose as long as you want to, under two conditions. The first is that when the land is no longer used for that purpose, it will revert back to the Myers' heirs. The second is that there is to be no talk of denominations or politics. This mission is not going to have anything to do with either one. I want you to get that right now!" He agreed to my conditions and we decided to call the new mission Christy Land. A little later we talked about calling it The New Ebenezer Mission in Christy-Land.

Nothing seemed to happen for some time. We finally did begin to build, but things didn't go well and we were never able to rebuild the mission. It only ended in arguments, fights, and bad feelings. It was all very disappointing.

Regrets

Earlier this year, within the same week, I lost two of my sisters, both younger than me. Velma died March 30, 1986, and Beatrice died on April 4th.

Since then I've been thinking a lot more about getting old, especially because I've been sick for a while now and may not live much longer. It makes you realize just how short life on this earth is—how quickly it's over.

You know, it seems like only a short time ago, I was running barefoot through these parts playing poison or playing house with my brother and sisters and our friends—or when I was listening to Miss Marston talk about Windsor Castle and English flowerbeds. It seems like only yesterday I was sitting in that ol' school desk next to Ernest playing "horsie." So fast, it all goes by just so quickly.

My life has been filled with blessings: my family, my children, my grandchildren, my church, and the people that I love there, my school children. I could go on and on with so many other blessings that the good Lord has allowed in my life. I am thankful for a long life and that I still have a good mind. I don't really have any regrets—except maybe that I was never able to rebuild the mission.

Some people up here could never understand why rebuilding the mission was so important to me. Even to this day a lot of them ask, "Well, just what exactly is a mission?"

To me I think that's such a silly thing to ask. Many of them have heard of the mission and mission work all their lives, and yet they have not been involved enough to know what a mission is. Some of the others who have asked have actually worked with me on project after project and they don't realize that they are the mission just like I am the mission. All it really means is giving of your own self by doing whatever work you can do to help others. It's the ideas you have, the encouragement you can give, and inspiration you can pass on to help others do the same. To say it very simply, it's being a servant. It's being like Jesus was. So many people don't see it that way.

I guess it was kind of confusing to them—me always talking about wanting to rebuild the mission. To me, the mission was everything for so much of my life. I feel that everyone or at least every Christian has a responsibility or has a mission in life. Maybe the Lord will give me a few more years to serve Him. I would like that. I hope you find your mission in life too, Lori.

Much love,
Opal Corn Myers

Epilogue

February 14, 2007

Commonplace[16]

"A commonplace life! We say and we sigh,
But why should we sigh, as we say,
The commonplace sun, in the commonplace sky
Makes up the commonplace day.

The moon and the stars are commonplace things,
And the flower that blooms, and the birds that sing,
But dark were the world, and sad our lot,
If the flowers failed, and the sun shone not;
And God who studies each separate soul
Out of commonplace lives, makes His beautiful whole."

Susan Coolidge

---

16   Susan Coolidge, *A Few More Verses* (Boston: Roberts Brothers, 1889)

Just like Opal and the mission workers at Ebenezer, we are all common, ordinary people. What makes an ordinary person extraordinary? Maybe it's the choice to commit ourselves to something or Someone greater than ourselves—to look outward instead of always inward—to think of others more than we are concerned for our own lives. When we realize that there is a larger plan than just "me and mine," then we have the opportunity of becoming a part of God's "beautiful whole" and we start to see the world changing all around us.

Opal was not a perfect person. *Letters to Lori* allows you to see some of those imperfect parts and you can speculate about others. Neither were any of the mission workers perfect—and neither are you or I. It is not God's plan that any of us allow ourselves to be put on pedestals to be idolized or for our lives to be romanticized. That always has the danger of drawing attention to ourselves instead of pointing others to Christ. The danger of becoming "ivory-tower followers" who, like Miss Alice quoted in *Christy*, crumble and fall apart when things get tough—and believe me, things will get tough!

"I (God) can't use ivory-tower followers. They're plaster of Paris, they crumble and fall apart in life's press. So you've got to see life the way it really is before you can do anything about evil. You cannot vanquish it. I can. But in My world the battle against evil has to be a joint endeavor. You and Me. I, God, in you, can have victory every time!"[17]

Originally, I thought it would be a fun adventure looking for the cove that Catherine Marshall wrote of—but I found more—much, much more. At first it was the mountains of eastern Tennessee that drew me back year after year. Then it was the people. It was Opal, her grown children and grandchildren as I got to know them. It was Roy Dan, Mitchell, Ruby, and other people at the Ebenezer church. There was something about them that I loved.

With Opal, though, there was a special connection and, I do believe, I was drawn to her from the very first time I met her. She

---

17 *Christy*, chapter 7

was very much an ordinary person but, by her life and commitment, somehow she challenged me to be more than I ever dreamed I could be. I am not alone. I am one of the hundreds whom she attracted and challenged, and by telling her story, maybe her life will go on to challenge thousands more. I hope so.

The lives of committed people like Opal, Christy, Miss Marston, and the other mission workers are to inspire, encourage, and arouse us to be more like Christ, who was willing to give His life so that we all might have freedom and purpose. And then as we join together with God in the battle against the enemy of our soul, we can hold the victory—every time!

If you have been inspired by the life of Opal and Christy, then I challenge you to also look beyond yourself, beyond your circumstances, and make a difference in someone's life today. God bless you, always.

Memories

"How could I ever explain the feelings that I have for this industrious mountain woman? These feelings cannot be explained and I cannot place my finger on any particular attribute. She is simply the type of person with the qualities others admire and the world seems to be missing in our day and time. Maybe it is because she is that link with the past when diligence, honesty, kindness, accepting the stranger into your home, and being a good neighbor were the model—a time when the "Golden Rule" was the standard to live by instead of our selfish, greedy way of life. That is, I guess, what makes her loved and adored by so many. She has given unselfishly of herself and her limited possessions. She has planted a garden of love, generosity, dedication, and goodwill and it is harvest time." (from my journal 8-21-89)

It's now been a while since we've been back—but my heart is still there along with both my memories and the reflections of Opal as well. Some of my favorite ones personally are centered around Homecoming, always the second Sunday in August, and Decorations Day in May. On those occasions, for years, our family would travel to Opal's, arriving early enough to help with the preparations. Manly would help Larry

(L. Conn) mow the grass around the houses and picnic areas and then weed-eat both sides of the road all the way down to the Old Fifteenth. I would help with the cooking and we would catch up on all the latest happenings. Of course, Heather could always be counted on to help make the mud pudding. Before Decorations Day, Manly and I, along with our kids, would help mow and clean the cemetery. It made us feel like we were a part of the family and the community.

Larry was especially good to us and a joy to be around. He has a heart like Opal's and also loves being around people the way Opal did. Manly will never forget the time when we were leaving after a Homecoming when he ran the tire of our car into a sharp rock, rendering our tire flat. We had no spare tire with us but, without any hesitation whatsoever, Larry gave us his. The next time we came back, we brought a brand new tire with us. He could not believe that we would replace his old tire with a new one, and he just went on and on about it.

Another time I was at Opal's, her sons took Jonathan, Heather, and me for a ride in the Scout over Round Mountain. Oh, my! White knuckle time for sure! But the kids loved it.

On May 8, 1991, I got a call that Opal wouldn't last much longer. The call was not a surprise, since she had been seriously ill for some time, but I had hoped to see her just once more. Quickly, I threw some things together and left within minutes. Manly was going to pack up the kids and the things that I forgot to pack and follow me. Just after I left, Manly got a call saying that Opal had passed. Knowing that I was going to stop for gas, he jumped into his car and took off after me, hoping to catch me before I left the gas station. I decided to go on to be with the family and Manly went back home to pack.

The viewing and funeral was something that I will never forget. We arrived at the funeral home in Newport and sat with the family. Manly was one of the pallbearers. Before long, every seat was filled and people were lined up outside the funeral home door all the way around the corner. They came in the door at the front of the room we were in, walked by the casket, and then down the isle to the door at the other end of the room. Some people wept openly, others talked about the memories they had of Opal as their teacher, and others mourned in silence.

When the procession left the funeral home, we were probably about the fourth or fifth car back from the hearse as we began the twenty-mile journey to Ebenezer, the church she had loved since her childhood. Somewhere on the highway between Newport and Del Rio, I looked out the back window to observe an unending trail of cars—literally as far as I could see. It was amazing the number of lives that Opal had touched. Not long after we turned onto the Old Fifteenth, the hearse overheated. As we waited in our cars for what felt a long time, I thought that many of the people, tired of waiting, might turn back. But when we got to the church, there were more people than that little church could hold. It was so packed that many had to stand outside. The only vacant seat was Opal's. As I sat there waiting for the service to begin, I could vividly imagine Opal ringing all the bells in heaven.

The weather that week had been rainy and the ground around the gate into the cemetery was nothing but mud. Too muddy for the pallbearers to walk through safely carrying the casket. They had to lift it over the fence at a drier spot.

Because of Opal, my life is richer and fuller. And now, after all this time of repeatedly hearing and reading Miss Marston's words as I continued to work on this book, I, too, truly believe that even I can do and become anything I want to be—if I am willing to work at it—and never give up on my dreams. After all—"I can do all things through Christ who strengthens me."

A Dream Come True

Opal never gave up hope that *Christy* would one day be made into a movie. It was her biggest dream and most of the letters I received from her mentioned something about *Christy*, especially during those times when someone from Hollywood came to visit her. She loved talking about Ebenezer Mission and *Christy*.

After Opal left us and passed on to be with the saints, she probably talked with everyone in heaven about Ebenezer just like she had talked to everyone on earth. Can't you just imagine Opal, Catherine, Leonora, Miss Marston, Mrs. Henderson, and the other mission workers getting together, drawing everyone into their conversation about *Christy* becoming a movie until finally all the occupants of heaven were pleading with God, "All right! Enough, already! Please, dear Lord, let someone make the movie so we can change the subject!"

Opal would have been so thrilled to see the *Christy* TV series and I'm sure she would be totally pleased with what Executive Producer Ken Wales, also a person with a purpose and commitment, accomplished with the *Christy* series. It was the answer to the prayers of many—on earth and, who knows, maybe in heaven too.

The Writing of *Letters to Lori*

Writing this book has taken a LONG time. My children, who were young at the beginning of this task, are now all grown and married. Matt is a lieutenant colonel serving in Baghdad, Iraq. He's married to Shannon and has two wonderful children—Ashley (17) and Josh (12). Jonathan is the adolescent services director and clinical supervisor at Clermont Recovery Center and also has a private practice in the Cincinnati, Ohio, area. He is married to Stephanie. We're still hoping for some grandchildren there, but at the present their Boston terrier Rudy is the baby. Heather is married to Jared Lanza and lives in Maryland. They have the sweetest little girl named Autumn (5) and their son Lincoln was born September 2006.

Like a few other things, if I had known what would be involved and how much time and effort would be required, I don't know if I would have taken it on. But I truly believe that it was a project the Lord wanted me to complete. I can only hope that Opal's life will encourage others to be the Lord's dwelling place and that they, too, will serve Him with their whole being.

I have in my possession an article[18] written about Catherine Marshall that says she was "often discouraged during the writing of *Christy*" and "many times I tossed aside the manuscript, just knowing I would never complete it." I will never be any where close to a Catherine Marshall, but that much we have in common. During those times of almost wanting to give up, it seemed that God always sent someone at just the right time to encourage me. Some of those were John Bartlet, manager of a Family Bookstore in Cincinnati and now with Answers in Genesis; Kenneth Wright and Betty Lindner, friends from our days at Teen Challenge Cincinnati; Joyce Smoak, Manly's aunt; and my daughter Heather. I also had the privilege of meeting a very gracious man, Ken Wales, Executive Producer of the *Christy* series at the ChristyFest™ in 2000. He also encouraged me to complete my book. My greatest and constant encourager has always been my husband Manly, at all times believing in the project and in me. He loved Opal as deeply as I did.

A couple of comparisons between Catherine Marshall and *Christy*, and me and *Letters to Lori*: it took Catherine nine years to produce her masterpiece *Christy*. It's only taken me eighteen years—I've worked twice as long but still, as a writer, I'm not half as good. *Christy* started out to be about Catherine's mother, but it evolved into much more and she published it as a novel[19] that she claims is about 65 percent factual, the rest fiction.[20] With *Letters to Lori*, I have tried to stay 100 percent true to what Opal told me and her stories have been changed very little. Some dialog was added to make them a little more readable, and I also added description to tie segments together or to make the reading more comprehensible. The grammar was also greatly improved, but not made perfect, in order to make *Letters to Lori* more understandable. There are a few places where I had to interpret some information as best I could. But I'm sure there is one thing both Catherine and I shared while enduring these projects: we will forever be changed by the lives of those we wrote about.

18 *Florida Accent*, Sunday, April 6, 1969
19 *Florida Accent*, Sunday, April 6, 1969
20 *The Miami Herald*, Sunday, November 12, 1972

Appendix A

The Characters

Christy Rudd Huddleston	Leonora Whitaker, married John Wood
Alice Henderson	Not real person
David Grantland	John Wood
Ida Grantland	Leonora's sister
Dr. Neil MacNeill	Not real person
Jeb Spencer	Toliver (T.J.) Corn (7/9/1854 – 11/6/30)
Fairlight Spencer	Suzanne Corn (3/1/1855 – 5/10/28) and Carrie Teague
Uncle Bogg McHone	Bogg Click
Tom McHone	Tom Click
The Nathan O'Teale family	Click family
Ozias Holt	D. F. Turner
Bird's-Eye Taylor	Tom Pack, 2 people in 1 [couldn't read second name]
Lundy Taylor	Wiley
Duggin Morrison	John Fish
Ruby Mae	Miss Minnie Fish—Minnie Fish slept at my house for 12 years, going home each day for a while. Minnie never married but she had many 'fellows.' Her lover was killed in WWI. His name was Carl Robinson.
The Beck Family	The Hux family
Aunt Polly Teague	Marg Humphreys
Granny Barclay	Cassie Ball
Mrs. Tatum	Beulah Burnette
Ben Pentland	Belt or Jim Griffin, they both carried the mail. Belt was Miss Minnie's uncle.
Dr. Ferrand	Dr. Guerrant—His son was the head of Highland when I attended there.

APPENDIX B

Important Dates in Ebenezer Mission's History

December 6, 1899—Katherine Plantz leaves her home in Hartford, Wisconsin, and travels to Read Hill, Tennessee, seven miles southwest of Del Rio. She begins teaching at Fairview School and doing independent, faith-based mission work.

Spring-Summer, 1900—Katherine teaches at Wales Industrial School for Girls in Barnard, North Carolina. She begins planning a similar school for homeless boys at Read Hill.

October 1900—After a trip home, Katherine returns to Read Hill with a second teacher, Hattie Meyer of Watertown, Wisconsin. They teach at either Fairview School or Mt. Zion Baptist Church.

January 1901—At Katherine's invitation, William Nowack, also from Watertown, joins her in Tennessee.

April 6, 1901—James N. Click sells two acres of property to Katherine for $30.00 on which a three-story mission house is constructed.

November 7, 1901—William and Katherine marry in Madison County, North Carolina.

January 21, 1902—The Nowacks open Ebenezer Training School for Boys.

May 18, 1905—The Nowacks sell Ebenezer to the Society of Soul Winners, founded by Dr. Edward O. Guerrant, and leave Tennessee to begin a faith-based mission in China.

September 1909—John A. Wood of Johnson City, Tennessee, begins work at Ebenezer, finishing construction of the church/schoolhouse.

November 1909—Ebenezer Mission begins holding classes in its new church/schoolhouse.

December 1909—Leonora H. Whitaker of Dillingham, North Carolina, begins work at Ebenezer.

May 10, 1910—John and Leonora marry in Asheville, North Carolina.

May 15, 1910—The church/schoolhouse is formally dedicated during a three-day celebration.

1911—Due to Dr. Guerrant's age and health, the Presbyterian Church, U. S., through its Executive Committee of Home Missions, assumes control of the Society of Soul Winners.

March 1912—John and Leonora Wood leave Ebenezer Mission and move to Greeneville, Tennessee, where John becomes pastor of Meadow Creek Presbyterian Church.

September 27, 1914—John and Leonora's first child, Sarah Catherine Wood, is born in Johnson City, Tennessee.

September 1923—Ebenezer Presbyterian Church is formally organized with twenty members.

1927—The Nowack's Tennessee Ebenezer Mission records are burned during the Chinese Revolution.

1928—Ebenezer Mission closes after the Presbyterian Church, U. S., withdraws its support.

1940—The church/schoolhouse is disassembled, moved one mile from the mission site next to Mt. Zion Cemetery, reconstructed, and dedicated on Easter Sunday.

1944—Ben and Opal Myers purchase the former McMahan property and Ebenezer Mission.

1958—Author Catherine (Wood) Marshall decides to write a biographical novel based upon her parents' experiences at Ebenezer Mission during 1909-1912.

1959—The Woods and Catherine visit Opal to research Catherine's planned novel, *Christy*.

January 20, 1962—The mission house catches fire and burns to the ground.

1967—*Christy* is published and becomes a best seller.

1969—To avoid having its church building purchased and moved, Ebenezer Presbyterian Church severs its ties to that denomination and decides to affiliate with the Independent Missionary Baptist denomination.

1992—A reconstructed barn, home of Larry Myers, Ben and Opal's youngest son, burns.

September 27, 2002—The old McMahan cabin, home of Larry and Karen Myers, burns. The Click (O'Teale) cabin is the last home standing at the mission site.

2003—Larry Myers begins rebuilding a new cabin on the barn's concrete foundation.

2005—Larry and Karen move into their new home.

On September 27, 2002, I learned via the Internet that Larry's cabin had burned to the ground, cause unknown. Neither he nor his wife, Karen, was home that morning. A hunter discovered the blaze. He spent precious time trying to find a neighbor willing to let him use their telephone to notify the fire department. By the time firefighters arrived, Larry's cabin was a total loss. As is common in the mountains, Larry carried no fire insurance, due to its expense.

Opal's annotated copy of *Christy* and other precious historical artifacts, not destroyed in the mission property fires of 1962 or 1992, were reduced to a smoldering pile of ashes. I mourned Larry's loss and wondered if he would rebuild or leave.

In early 2003, I started thinking that someone should write a history of Ebenezer Mission. The articles I'd read were confusing and differed greatly on such crucial facts as when the mission began and how its founder's surname was spelled. I thought it necessary to supplement oral tradition with facts from whatever written sources existed. These facts would refute, support, or amplify oral tradition, forming a comprehensive history of the partnership between the missionaries who served Ebenezer, and those parents who entrusted their children to its ministry.

After several years of attending ChristyFest™, the annual celebration of Catherine Marshall's novel held in Townsend, Tennessee, I was asked in 2003 if I'd lead a book discussion—one which would correlate the history of Ebenezer Mission with *Christy*. As I wrote my presentation, I started thinking that the "someone" to write Ebenezer's history was me.

I revisited the mission site in June 2003 as a planned activity of ChristyFest™. Still grieving his loss, Larry wept as he thanked our group for their prayers and support. He was rebuilding a log cabin on the concrete foundation not destroyed in the 1992 fire. Rather than move off mission property, his family was living in two small camping trailers. I drew upon his determination, and knew that by sifting through the ashes of Ebenezer Mission's four fires—three in Tennessee, one in China—I could collect, collate, write, and share its history.

It's now August 2007 and I am nearly finished with the research phase of my book. I've traveled to nine states; my Rolodex file contains about two hundred addresses. I've met people who have generously assisted in what has become my personal quest and a labor of love.

I thank Barbara for this opportunity to inform you of my upcoming book, tentatively titled: *Sifting through the Ashes: The History of Ebenezer Mission.*

You'll learn about Katherine Plantz, who at age twenty-three, left Wisconsin with no more than a suitcase and a dream, trusting that God would help her plant a mission "far back in the mountains." You'll read the untold stories of Leonora Whitaker and John Wood, Ebenezer's most famous missionaries, whose lives were immortalized in print as Christy Huddleston and David Grantland.

You'll be inspired by stories of Appalachian parents and their children, who, according to worldly values, were "raised up poor," but by means of opportunity and education, "turned out rich." You'll be challenged to consider God's plan for your life, as were the Ebenezer missionaries, who, when told of fields "white already to harvest," answered God's call to service.

My book will draw upon letters, articles, and interviews gathered from all over the United States. Of special interest are previously unpublished photographs of Ebenezer and its staff beginning in 1899. Purchase information will be available at www.christyfest.org.

I was privileged and honored to proofread Barbara's manuscript. Her book, *Letters to Lori,* is a marvelous story of Opal Myers' love, courage, and dedication. May we all draw inspiration from it!

Marilyn Dean Mitchem

Heather, Barbara and Opal fixin' shab beans on the front porch (summer of 1990)

Ken Wales, Executive Director of Christy TV Series, with Barbara & Manly

Stewart Finlay-McLennan (Dr. MacNeill), Barbara, Randall Batinkoff (David Grantland)

Barbara and Emma

"The story of Opal is wonderful. It needs to be told!" Emma Wood Hoskins, Catherine Marshall's sister

Barbara and Mike Hickman (Bird's-Eye Taylor) CBS Christy Series and PAX movies

Barbara and Tom Blomquest, Supervising Producer/Writer for CBS Christy Series, Executive Producer/Writer for the PAX Movies

ABOUT THE AUTHOR

Barbara League is a seminar trainer, workshop leader, and consultant in the field of addiction recovery and other life-controlling problems. She has worked with numerous churches and ministries, served as founding director of a women's residential recovery program, and was the director of community outreach at a men's long-term treatment facility.

Prior to writing *Letters to Lori,* she has written articles for newsletters and an article about Opal Myers, the main character in *Letters to Lori,* published in *Cocke County Tennessee and Its People.* Barbara has been instrumental in the development of several faith-based programs and ministries in the Greater Cincinnati area, including her role in designing information and instruction material for these programs.

Barbara was born and reared in Iowa, where she lived for fifteen years before moving with family to South Carolina. She now resides in northern Kentucky with her husband and labradoodle, Ivan. She is the mother of three married children and grandmother to four lovely grandkids, ages one to seventeen years.

Dear Reader:

Thank you for purchasing *Letters to Lori*.
It is my prayer that its message will challenge you to
become all that God created you to be.
Let me hear from you!

If you would like to order additional copies of *Letters to Lori*

Send Your

Name, address, city, state and zip code
Phone number and email address

To:

Barbara League
3779 Harvest Way
Elsmere, KY 45018

Include

$17.95 per book
$4.95 shipping and handling for each book
Allow 4 – 6 weeks for delivery.

If you would like more information on scheduling Barbara as a
speaker for your group or would like more information about
seminars, workshops, and trainings

Call (859) 727-2228
www.LMCinc.org
LettersToLori@fuse.net
LMCI@fuse.net